W9-ADY-120

FAST TRACK MARKETING

FAST TRACK MARKETING

Implementing Innovative Tactics in the Global Marketplace

John Hathaway-Bates

VNR VAN NOSTRAND REINHOLD
New York

Library of Congress Catalog Card Number 93-17993
ISBN 0-442-01512-7

I(T)P Van Nostrand Reinhold is a division of International Thomson Publishing. ITP logo is a trademark under license.

Printed in the United States of America

Van Nostrand Reinhold
115 Fifth Avenue
New York, New York 10003

International Thomson Publishing
Berkshire House
168-173 High Holborn
London, WC1V 7AA, England

Thomas Nelson Australia
102 Dodds Street
South Melbourne 3205
Victoria, Australia

Nelson Canada
1120 Birchmount Road
Scarborough, Ontario
M1K 5G4, Canada

16 15 14 13 12 11 10 9 8 7 6 5 4 3 2 1

Library of Congress Cataloging-in-Publication Data

Hathaway-Bates, John.
[Tactics]
Fast track marketing : implementing innovative tactics in the global marketplace / John Hathaway-Bates.
p. cm.
Originally published : Tactics. Long Beach, Calif. : Nerthus Publications, 1987.
ISBN 0-442-01512-7
1. Marketing—Planning. 2. Marketing—Management. I. Title.
HF5415.13.H367 1993
658.8'02—dc20 93-17993
CIP

To my daughters Sarah-Jane and Christina
for the love they have given me, and the
dreams they have provided me with

Managing a business is a rewarding and important occupation that contributes to the good of everyone; you are creating the base for civilizaton, and the health, wealth and happiness of all mankind. When things get tough, it is the manager who is expected to step forward and supply the solution, even if he has to change Society and destroy a few myths of "how things work." If my book helps you in any way in this endeavor, then the work it took to put it together was worthwhile and you have given meaning to it.

John Hathway-Bates

CONTENTS

FORMS

The forms in this book are the result of many years development and adaptation, and as far as forms are able to be general in application, they can be used to perform the management tasks of almost any marketing investigation. The need for careful analysis is essential in the development and monitoring of any marketing program, and using the examples described and illustrated as models, will enable you to create more precise forms and analysis programs to meet your own particular needs in any given situation.

FAST TRACK MARKETING

CHAPTER ONE

THE DIFFERENCE BETWEEN SALES AND MARKETING

The Concept of Tactical Marketing and Management

"TACTICAL MARKETING" differs from traditional marketing methods in that it deals directly with an existing situation, whether it is the implementation of a new concept or an adjustment to an existing program that is required to take effect immediately. **Strategic Marketing,** on the other hand, is used to project possibilities that are totally dependent upon optimum developments predicted to happen in the future on a broad scale. **Tactical Marketing** can therefore be integrated into an overall **Strategic Marketing** Program, as it deals with individual needs, programs and changes that will normally need to be fast-track in implementation and able to provide immediate results.

Tactical Marketing is 'market directed' and is a science rather than an art, in that it makes the future change one piece at a time to achieve an immediate result, or establish a path towards an overall marketing or management goal. As **Strategic Marketing** deals in prediction of what the future 'may' become, it needs to be general in nature; and that is a very difficult formula to deal with in the normal day-to-day operation of a new or expanding business.

A **Commercial Tactician** is someone who uses the tools of analysis to evaluate facts and trends, and then compares them with each other and market forces. Put more simply—*A Commercial Tactician searches for negative factors and then devises plans and systems to either get rid of them or take advantage of them.*

That is the description of **Tactical Marketing and Management** I have been giving for many years now. Understand that this is not an academic conclusion, it is based on successes and failures that I have personally been involved in. It is my opinion, and as such is subject to change as events change and alter the situation and circumstances from which it is drawn.

Take the facts, analyze them, compare them with each other, and making a decision about what to do next is already done for you. There is nothing difficult about it! The *Truth,* the *Facts,* projected against *Probability* will give you the right answer every time, even if it is not the one you really hoped it would be.

Tactical Marketing and Management is also dependent upon 'knowing' the facts. If there is anything difficult about the operation, it is getting the real truth and getting people to give it to you without it being embellished with justification and interpretation. It took me a while to understand that getting this 'truth,' these 'facts,' is not difficult if it is worked into a process of gathering a lot of 'little' facts and numbers, from a variety of sources, and then bringing them together to collate into a total overview of the situation.

The systems you are going to read about, interspersed with my opinions and experiences, do just that, they make 'fact gathering' a relatively unseen process which produces unbelievable results. If you do not like the actual task of sorting, comparing and collating, hire someone to do it for you. I have always done this, and believe that a good marketing administrator is worth two top salespeople to any organization.

"MARKETING" is a word few business people do not hear, read or say at least once every day of their working lives. Yet it is a word only a very few really understand. To most people the words **Marketing** and **Sales** are interchangeable, but in fact there is a real and important difference between **Sales** and **Marketing** that is essential to understand if you are considering implementing a marketing program. For many years now I have explained this difference in a simple sentence:

SALES *exploits* existing markets, whereas **MARKETING** *creates* new markets and methods to increase business activity.

Perhaps this oversimplification is a little contrived, but it does illustrate that while **Sales** is in most cases reliant upon the individual ability, mood or knowledge of the person employed "to sell"; **Marketing** is a management, research and promotional discipline, or if you wish, a science, used to gain access to business opportunities and acceptance by potential clients.

Unless the need is for a one-time-only sale, never to be repeated, then it must be accepted that in fact a *service* is being marketed. Anyone offering a service should accept at the outset that they are selling something which is ongoing and must be viewed on a long-term basis. In fact, everyone's real *product* is time, talent, reputation and capability to supply whatever they are in business to supply. Therefore, when management or ownership dictates a policy which makes *success* dependent upon immediate or *now* results, they must (sometimes at least) expect that those engaged in the actual selling may employ exaggeration or make promises to clients that are beyond the firm's capability. This may result in a large number of immediate *sales,* but such orders are almost certain to run into trouble and be counterproductive to the firm's activities in the long run. Therefore, the aim of anyone involved in marketing must be:

1. To encourage potential clients to **want** to buy.
2. To help clients **understand** what is being offered, and how they can employ it to their advantage.

3. To build the client's **trust** in the capability of what is being offered.
4. To assist the client to **identify** their needs realistically.
5. To build a **marketing** system which will gain, monitor, control and generate quality business as an ongoing activity.

Most professional marketers (individuals and organizations) sell *concepts* and *ideas* rather than tangible products, and no one will buy a concept of any kind unless they feel they can trust and believe in not just the ability of those involved, but also the professional service and care they will need to complete whatever has been promised initially. Perhaps this is why, in today's fast-moving society, the emphasis on success in almost all fields has changed in the last decade from *talent, expertise and experience* to **Marketing.** The reason being that unless you can market what you have to offer in the first place, you will be unable to use those talents and skills, or even begin to prove your ability, and thereby could be refused the opportunity to build a reputation of any sort.

Marketing a *service,* as opposed to marketing a *product,* can cause many people a problem when they try to isolate the difference between the two. Essentially, what some marketing people find easiest to do is to try to *create* a product of their services. This is understandable as it is, without a doubt, the easiest method to follow, but once this system is accepted and takes over as a marketing philosophy, are they not threatening the very reason for their existence and abdicating, to some extent, their professional responsibility?

As stated before, to be successful as a professional in any field, one must be able to *sell* ideas. For if the potential client can be helped to understand the philosophy of the trade, craft or profession involved, above and before all other considerations (or because of them), then success is not only possible, it is inevitable. Perhaps the greatest problem anyone can have is that sometimes a competitor will come up with better solutions and more relevant proposals. The usual (and very human) reaction is to defend one's own conclusions and hours (if not months) of endeavor by blaming the *sales techniques* of the winner. There is no way that even the most gifted marketer can be successful if the product or service is not at the very least adequate to the needs of the market. Very few people can be "fooled" into buying on a long-term basis something which fails in its most basic application.

So many people ask what has become known as the *free lunch* question—*What are the best sales techniques?* The answer is that there are no ready-made, foolproof techniques. There are no tricks to selling, unless you would accept *be in the right place at the right time, with the right commodity, talking to someone who wants it, needs it, will profit by it, and can afford it* as an answer. The real function of selling is demonstrating or showing something someone needs, and asking a price for it. Then unless that person does not like the color of your eyes, you have only to prove your case and the sale is guaranteed. All one has to do is get to the right person, at the right time, with what they both want and need, and that, in essence, is what Marketing is all about. There are two little sayings which illustrate this exactly:

> *If you want to sell a glass of water, set up shop in a desert, not in the middle of a monsoon.*
>
> *I dislike dentists so much I make a point of not even talking to them—until I have a toothache.*

In other words, you can only sell something, be it glasses of water or dentistry, to most people when they know they have a need for it. Therefore, **Marketing** must also be:

1. Finding the right people, at the right time, with the need, desire and ability to buy.
2. Developing a method to interest them enough to make them *want* to listen to your argument.
3. Creating the safest and most convincing way of gaining their agreement that they need what is being offered.

To sum up: **Marketing** is a vehicle, a way to transport someone to an interview or a way to get people to want to see something; it is a bridge between producer or supplier and a potential buyer. If you have a perfect product, idea or service, and you are unable to successfully reach your potential clients, then it is probable that you could lose everything.

Possibly one of the greatest causes for concern in today's world is the "departmentalization" of business in general, to the point where a form of bureaucracy has taken over in awarding positions of responsibility. The "generalists" who created the momentum of the Industrial Revolution have been replaced in business acceptance by "technocrats" and "specialists." While this can be justified for most professions and trades, even championed for some, experience would suggest that **Marketing** is still the domain of the "generalist." In fact, to be able to really develop the full potential of any service or product, the broader the range of experience, the more chance of success. However, "being adaptable" does not mean "being erratic," and therefore a plan of action must be developed and its implementation must be carefully monitored and controlled.

Organized **Marketing** *will* get you many more business opportunities, open the right doors, and give you information about who is in the market to buy and, in many cases, can tell you what the market needs at any given time.

CHAPTER TWO

THE REASON TACTICAL MARKETING IS NEEDED TODAY

Before the Industrial Revolution, those engaged in business operated in a far different manner than they do today. For example: It was not so long ago that the way to earn a good living as an architect or a doctor was to find a patron, and the same went for everyone down the line. The world today, however, is changing so fast that many people and firms would readily accept that they still operate with methods of gaining new clients which are several decades out-of-date. Today there are few who are able to do business in the way their predecessors did only 50, or even 20, years ago.

The clients of most firms these days are different also, for there are few Royal or Merchant Princes left to delegate complete responsibility to individuals at their whim; today the majority of clients are in fact committees without total power, other than at the discretion of either the shareholders or elected bodies who control them. Strangely enough, although there is much talk of *trust* and *image,* there are few clients today who are able to give their total support, whatever their personal convictions, the way clients of a hundred years ago could have done. Perhaps, therefore, one now needs to have public acceptance in addition to the individual's confidence to have any real chance of success in the modern world we live in.

Using architecture as an example again, it can be readily accepted that, in living memory, most buildings were *commissioned* to an architect to design, whereas today it is more common for a series of architectural firms to submit designs and proposals prior to winning a commission. Obviously, one can quote a hundred exceptions to this rule, but there can be no argument that today the majority of business is "sold" rather than "commissioned."

The pace of change is such that many of the customs and rules which we have all been taught to rely upon, are also in reality obsolete from the business viewpoint. The Industrial Revolution and mass production have changed the values and conceptions of all of us, and yet there are few who can be tempted to realize or accept it within their own working lives. Technology threatens at this moment the capability to commit to instant recall many of the tasks which take human beings years to assimilate and learn.

Argue as we may, aesthetics, professional responsibility, talent, ability, product value and the much quoted codes of practice, the most common judgment today is financial success, in the eyes of those who provide the finance. Even the professions have become, or are fast becoming, *pure business* with all the aims and success judgments of any other business. The listings for *Top* anything these days would seem to be graded in the profession's own journals, not on *Prizes Won,* or *Quality of Innovation,* or *Service Provided,* as much as they once were, but upon *Annual Sales Volume* and *Gross Annual Fees,* or *Number of Offices,* etc. The reports and articles we read these days have also started to bow to monetary size, and no longer quote *schools* or *innovation,* or even quality as they did 50 or 20 years ago, when almost each of the professions were often compared to a philosophy. Today, the most respected and accepted journals and magazines (those the professionals themselves read) talk of dollars far more often than any other consideration, unless they assist the prose of the writing itself, or are facts necessary to create the story.

Not so long ago it was accepted that: *professionalism is pursued to earn self-respect and an honorable reputation for achievement, whereas trade is confined to the one ambition—making money.* In that viewpoint, it would appear that even the professions are fast moving towards becoming *Trade* and away from being a *Profession* in the eyes of practitioners, their clients and the general public. It is a fact that in these days of taxes, regulations, and inflationary economics, everyone in business must consider the ability for financial success as being the most important talent they can possess.

Mass production and the capability to duplicate almost anything have destroyed many of the values and crafts we now mourn. For the cost of a mould or a litho plate, the works of Rodin and Michelangelo can now be produced in almost any material and be almost indistinguishable from the original. A woodcarver need produce only one door, and then a machine can produce several hundred in the same amount of time using the original as a "master" to create a computer program. Economically, the process has gone almost too far to reverse, if in fact we would truly wish to reverse it. We are living in a cooperative and interdependent society. Once, a single person could design an aircraft from concept to completion and then fly it. There can be few who would argue that designing an aircraft of today needs a team of specialists numbering hundreds. It would seem, therefore, that we are now at the point where the same holds true with just about everything, unless you wish to spend your life working on very simple tasks a thousand miles from civilization. There will, of course, be arguments to this viewpoint for many years to come, which is understandable, as no generation puts down the tools of power to another generation without defending the real benefits of traditions. Rather, there is a slow changeover from one to the other and, of course, those who have put in the most years with traditional concepts are normally those who hold the seat of authority, due to their time served and experience.

There is also the very real problem of teachers and lecturers in the schools and colleges, where it is hard to tell bright-eyed young hopefuls that by the time they reach maturity, the majority of them may only be production workers rather than *creators* or *leaders.* There are many misconceptions regarding teachers in colleges and schools, such as: Those who fail in the *real world retreat to teaching,* and, *Most teachers are years out-of-date because they stopped practicing their profession to teach it.* I hold these statements to be untrue, knowing the dedication needed to teach day after day, and most of the teachers I know spend many hours working to keep up-to-date. In reality, the greatest problem in the schools is the fact that so little time is available to spend teaching *business promotion* to students who, because of their specialized talents and now popular *individualism,* probably need this attribute the most. Teaching someone how to do something, but not how to promote the product of his or her commitment is wrong, but there is just not enough time to teach everyone everything.

The argument on whether advertising is detrimental to professionalism still rages amongst architects, doctors and lawyers, etc., as a sign of the inability of some to recognize change. Giving the situation we face today an analogy, consider if the Olympic swimmer would refuse a life belt when fighting for life in a raging sea just because it had never been needed in an indoor pool. True professionalism, image and self-respect are the choice of the individual person or firm, and have little to do with the fact that there is nothing which can be done to turn the clock back. Nor can outdated methods be relied upon to continue providing new business to allow the building of these attributes. Computers are already able to be programmed to do a great deal of what most people do daily, and some would find it hard to exist without the wonders of technology to help them. It is possible that soon the competence of a firm may be reliant on being able to pay the price of a computer software program, whereas once only personnel could affect its ability to succeed.

The marketer (or for that matter anyone involved in selling) must therefore learn to *read between the lines* the public relations pumped out via the mass media. The majority of advertising is designed to remind rather than convince, and it can only be employed this way if there is mass production, mass demand and mass buying. To the individual marketer or salesperson wishing to rise above a *representative* station in life, there is a need to remember that *professional marketing* can successfully defeat *mass selling* only if you are prepared to sell the profit the buyer receives, because *mass selling* can only *sell* to those who have already decided to buy.

The person who can understand that the Technological Revolution we are now in is going to be just as important as the Industrial Revolution of the 19th century will benefit just as those who recognized the Industrial Revolution for what it was.

The problems facing business in the next few decades will be the speed of innovation and market change. New products, new technology, and new demands and requirements put forward by users will dominate every meeting of business people from one side of our world to the other. The internationalization of every marketplace will present opportunities and competition. Science Fiction and Fantasy of only 30 years ago is here already, the challenges ahead of us in the next few years will be no less exciting and effective.

There is no doubt that we are now in an age of international competition, technological breakthroughs and economic controls, and it is these things which make **Marketing** important. Without professional marketing the very survival of many businesses (come to that, even national economics) could prove difficult, for as the old saying goes ''a house is only as safe as its foundation'' and marketing is the foundation of all business activity in the final analysis.

Please refer to Checklist Number 1 on page 304.

CHAPTER THREE

SPECIALIZATION—A BENEFIT OR A PROBLEM?

Many established firms specialize to the extent that they:

1. supply clients who are all engaged in the same field of business.
2. are retained for projects of similar type.
3. work within a particular size or financial range of projects.
4. actually promote "speciality" in one "field."

Why firms specialize, however, is often the result of chance rather than intent and, although a reputation for specialization can be a positive marketing advantage, it can also reduce growth potential. By trapping the firm in a restricted field, success can become dependent entirely upon the fortunes of the particular business or sector it serves. Surprising as it may be, most *specialists* become such in the first place by finding that one job follows another, until *suddenly* (after several years) they find that they have gained a reputation for being specialists. It sometimes comes as a surprise to hear from a prospective client that they *thought you only handled—whatever,* especially when you considered yourself a generalist and able to supply any need in your field.

Another reason is the *hire staff when you are busy— lay them off when you are not* business most firms have to run. A firm which gains a string of similar projects tends to hire staff for their experience in that field. The sales development, in natural progression, then promotes this *in-house experience* (and the latest projects these staff were hired to work on) and soon specialization is dictated by lack of activity in other fields. This trend has become more important in the last few years with the pace of legislation and codes of practice, along with the flood of new products being introduced. The organization or firm of the latter part of the 20th century may have to specialize, simply because there will not be time to keep up-to-date with innovations and regulations in more than one field.

Another factor which points to an increase in the need to specialize is that the clients themselves are becoming more specialized (and educated) in matters of evaluation. Any negotiator is in danger of being judged incompetent if he or she falls behind in the state-of-the-art in the client's particular sector. It is possible, therefore, that before this century is out, not only **will** firms specialize, but they will create bureaucracies and regulations of their own aimed to restrict competition in individual fields.

If the time is taken to consider history for a moment, in the light of the possibilities shown, it becomes apparent that any marketing program being established today needs to consider the advantages and disadvantages of promoting specialization more than ever before. For many centuries it was accepted that the client was his own architect and hired craftsmen and laborers to erect the structure. In time, a specialist in the form of a *builder* appeared, who offered his experience to manage the operation. Soon, some of these *manager-builders,* or what we might call *general contractors,* were recognized as above average, and that their experience allowed them to advise in the actual design stages. In time they became known as *master builders.* We all know the development of the architectural and engineering professions since then, but how many business people today recognize the changes, and reduced time interval between them, that we are now seeing taking place all around us in almost every field of endeavor?

It was the same for manufacturers before international trade and the modern transportation services became everyday factors of business. Once a blacksmith could make anything his local market wanted manufactured in metal, but as technology developed the options, specialization became necessary and competition stronger. Today, the farmer in Kansas knows his product may end up in Russia, China, Argentina or India, and does not question the fact. However, if he knew the *foreign* products he owned he might be surprised. Imagine if at midnight tonight every item in the world changed color to indicate its origin: English products going red, American products red and white stripes, and Japanese products turning gold, and so on. We might all be a little more shocked than we would expect. The number of *customers* increase every minute with the population, and the world is your market, so as you have such a huge demand, why should you not specialize in the product or service you are best at supplying, and make the most profit?

At present, the public, in most cases, still makes its choice between one firm or product and another, on its overall and general reputation, but as business becomes more international, and complex, this system begins to break down; for every *failure to perform* helps discredit this method of selection and promotes the hiring of *specialist expertise* or buying *new products.*

Many professions and trades which were once singular are now splitting into separate directions, as standards and laws have made specialization easier, and these subdivisions have formed their own associations and institutes. It is possible that in time this fragmentation of the professions and trades could become widespread as members polarize into specialist groups, or types of specialization, and create professional bodies to administrate and facilitate development of each of these *new* fields of endeavor. If this is allowed to happen without proper assistance and acceptance by the establishment, everyone concerned could suffer from the fragmentation, rather than benefit from any reorganization attempts to develop specialization.

These observations do in fact have an important meaning to the planning of any long-term marketing program (and these five years can be long term!), when one considers the following possibilities:

1. What would happen to your business if an association membership could affect the acceptance of your product or services as *relevant* to a particular client?
2. What if the activities of an association to which you did not belong brought about a public trust in only those firms or individuals which did?
3. Could your staff fall behind the *state-of-the-art* if they are excluded from the ongoing programs of one association or another?

In any business or profession the need for association with one's peers, ongoing educational and regulatory procedures is of paramount importance, and these needs increase in direct proportion to the scope of change and development within the trade or profession at the time. From the point of view of running a successful business, being part of the established commercial community is also important, in that interaction with those who shape the market must be beneficial. Therefore, it must be logical that restricting association to being only with one's peers (and, therefore, competitors in most cases) cannot be as productive as belonging to other *business* organizations. The need to keep abreast of one's own trade or profession's development, and the need to be part of the total business community at the same time means that membership of associations, institutes, or any other organization is probably a more important decision today than ever before.

Please refer to Checklist Number 2 on page 306.

There are, of course, many other considerations to evaluate during the development of a marketing program which apply to deciding whether your firm does, will or even wants to specialize. So it is wise to consider everything on both a short- and long-term basis, and then to make your choice carefully, and review it at regular intervals.

It is not probable that the larger multi-discipline firms will willingly discourage large-fee projects outside of their recent experience; nor is it likely that the smaller firms could financially compete with the giants in certain areas. The possibility of large firms *commissioning* small specialist firms to take a particular part of a project, more often than they now do, is however a definite bonus for everyone to look forward to. In many ways it is already happening, but the future seems set to make it the rule rather than the exception.

Economically, it is also probable that many firms in the future would rather pay occasional *loaded* fees or subsidize production to specialists than maintain a full-time staff commitment or production capacity of lesser capability, for occasional contribution to the service they are able to offer their clients. In fact, is this not what many principals and founders of some firms have already done, when they spend most of their time managing the firm and obtaining business? Have they not, in many cases, delegated production and development to their staff? The next step of delegating to specialists outside of the firm is a small one, and one many small firms can expect to benefit from in the future.

The most often quoted argument against this idea is that of control! This, however, is really not logical as a firm intent on building its own business by supplying the same expertise on an ongoing basis to other firms, will probably be more reliable than an individual within a large firm who has more personal career goals. It is possible, therefore, that as competition increases, the cost of employing full-time staff escalates, travel costs rise, and legal codes and professional bureaucracy multiply, the idea of bringing in specialists on an *as needed* basis, will become far more attractive to everyone. Therefore, both individuals and firms should take a long look at the potential of their capabilities to see if some form of specialization might not be advantageous before they embark on planning a marketing strategy. It might be wise to consider the need to specialize in the light of the comments and judgments of those most in tune with the future of business development. On top of the list of *most quoted* opinions you will usually find one of the following:

Government intervention into business has become a major consideration—codes of practice, consumer protection, energy conservation laws, standards for health and safety—means that the senior executive spends much of his or her time performing within set guidelines laid down by those outside of the firm.

Technology is moving so fast it will soon be impossible for anyone to keep abreast of all that is happening in anything on a broad scale.

With the increased complexity of new regulations, small firms may soon have to employ a full-time legal and contractual expert, as they today need to employ a full-time bookkeeper or accountant.

Many schools concentrate on teaching ''overviews'' and concepts—this leads to a surfeit of graduates with little knowledge of the real needs of their potential clients, which have to do with logistics, function, economics and time limitations.

Limited space, scarcity of raw materials, energy costs, etc., will soon reduce the designer's options to a point where design will be 90% pre-specified by availability of materials and legal codes.

There are many fundamental changes executives will need to face in the future, and it is probable that, in general, the successful will be specialists.

The only advice one is able to give to the individual graduate today is perhaps the following:

Investigate the trends in your field as you see them and isolate an area you could be comfortable in, and successful of course, and then concentrate upon honing your talent and skills to it. Whichever specialist area you decide upon, get your name on the mailing lists of the manufacturers in that sector if you can; subscribe to the magazines and journals that cater to your potential clients in that area of business as well, to keep up-to-date with their concerns and business trends. Then, keep your eyes and ears open for articles and seminars, etc., dealing with the subject you have chosen in the journals which serve your own professional field. As insurance, however, try to be involved in the occasional project outside of your chosen specialization, maintain contact with your peers in other fields, and take the publications which can at least give you an overview of your general profession. The firm or larger practice must give the matter far more thought in relation to financing, marketing, and the availability of trained staff.

Please refer to Checklist Number 3 on page 308.

"Dear Man I have a battle to fight. I have no time to hear you explain your new invention, the Machine Gun, or whatever it is!"

CHAPTER FOUR

METHODS TO AVOID

There are many methods a firm or individual can employ to promote new business. Perhaps the most depressing part of being in business is the constant worry, and hassle involved, in trying to make outdated or inefficient methods provide the flow of business required. If you think it is difficult for the president or principal, imagine how much more nerve-racking it can be for the sales manager or director. The idea of spending a lifetime trying to be successful with the wrong tools is soul-destroying, yet many people responsible for the sales in fact do just that. Perhaps this is because of the way they allow the situation to develop around them, and it is doubly applicable in the professions where the *product* must be sold before it can be *demonstrated.* Much of the sales training available today does no more than give tips on *how to close the sale.* This may be fine when one is selling small-cost consumer products door-to-door, but on large-cost or long-term sales it is all but ridiculous. Very few people are going to commit a massive expenditure on promises, unless you are able to gain their agreement to your ability, integrity and professionalism. Therefore, trying to organize a professional marketing program with the methods used to sell door-to-door is ridiculous, and if someone *should* buy from you on this method then you can expect trouble all down the line.

As stated earlier—identifying positive factors, while ignoring negative ones, can only be bad management. Therefore, in this chapter the *negatives, myths* and *out-of-context advice* will be concentrated upon, so that you can evaluate them before moving on to the positive factors of professional marketing.

Many of us have heard the advice to *get out there and sell, sell, sell,* which, like all sayings, can only be right when given context. Surely this war cry of some sales managers can only be right if it is preceded by advice on the **who—where—when—how** and **why** questions, to have any practical application. Another regular piece of advice to salespeople is the oldest one in the book, which comes in several variations, like:

> *You get the money/contract/order, etc., and we will decide what to do then, or....*
>
> *Never turn down an order, or....*
>
> *You get the money and then we will worry.*

The fact is that the best and most successful firms in any business turn away almost as many orders as they take on, or they restrict the type of business they pursue. If you cannot make a profit out of a job, do not waste your time. Worse still, if you take a job you are unequipped to handle, you might be sacrificing everything for the sake of *now* results.

In the end, all business success is based upon being "able to supply the goods." Promoting something beyond its capabilities, be it a person, a service or a product is, to say the least, unethical; at the worst, it is courting disaster.

MONOPOLY CLAIMS

Many salespeople, and sometimes even company presidents, state from time to time that:

> *We have no competition in our field or....*
> *No one is equipped to approach the problem as we are.*

The variations on statements of monopoly are many, however, in all but a very few cases they are wrong. If potential clients can supply their needs, or solve their problems by employing another product or service, then no monopoly exists, and asserting anything to the contrary is counterproductive to say the least. It just makes the salesperson look like a fool.

LACK OF CONFIDENCE IN ABILITY

Another common problem is the acceptance by many that *salespeople have no effect on creating the market size or demands, the clients decide—the salesperson serves the client.* If this were true, we would still be living in caves, or at the least, stepping over horse droppings every time we crossed the street. The professional salesperson or firm does have a great effect on the size and demands of the market, it is just that few ever use this capability to its fullest extent.

INTERGROUP EFFECT

Often finance which could be used for marketing (both research and promotion) is wasted on ego trips and short-term, local growth. Many firms suffer where money has been taken out of work to pay for a succession of *gadgets* and *toys* to keep staff or principals happy, or where a side-line business has been developed to gain a regular, but limited, return and then becomes responsible for effectively tying up cash and production time.

The obvious example of this method is "taking in" photocopying, and print work for other organizations because you need to have such equipment, and by selling time on them you can effectively reduce the costs involved. There are occasions when such an endeavor can help to off-set the costs of new equipment, but if not watched carefully it can, in time, be troublesome to control. Properly managed, this method of *covering costs* can *save* money sometimes, however it is unable to generate real profit or add to real sales volume, therefore, commitment of time by sales personnel on such *side lines* should be kept to a minimum. There can also be a problem in this method of management, that unless sufficient usage is generated, the capital required to keep up with technical innovations and developments in styles and expertise will not be available (due to the low volume involved). The lesson to be learned from all this is simply—do not be distracted from your main goals by short-term ambitions. Remember the sign that used to hang in every butcher's shop, "we do not cash checks, because the banks have agreed not to sell meat."

CULTURAL CIRCLE TRAPS

Many businesses are established employing some variation of cultural advantage to assist in gaining sales. Basically, it develops from an inherent need created by a particular culture or group demand.

In a service industry, especially where many firms rely upon *referrals* as their main source of business, it is possible to become *caught up* in such a circle which can eventually become a problem. The flaws in this sales method are of course as many as the advantages, for when one draws most business from a particular cultural or ethnic group, one normally always alienates another group. The executive, therefore, must watch for the possibility that the amount of business coming from one group is not preventing other business being developed. For no matter how bountiful the present, if it is possible that for some reason you should lose that circle, it might be very difficult to re-establish a new source of business fast enough to carry your costs.

ONE-FOR-ONE SALES

One-for-One Sales is a term used to describe business gained by providing a product or service at cost, or for free, to enlist the help of the receiver to gain an independent client to which he or she has access to, or influence upon. All in all, this method is rarely used where any other method can be employed, and offers based on the theory of reward for business generated in this way do not usually come from the competent or the professional business people. Basically this method is constructed around the theory of cheating one section of the community to benefit another (e.g., providing a service at a loss to one member of the community to gain their cooperation in winning a profit from some other party over whom they have influence or a relationship of trust). The danger in this system is that sooner or later a *real* client is made aware of a doubtful transaction, and a development of distrust begins. This leads to fall off in real business, resulting in the need to lean heavier upon the *one-for-one* method to supply new business. In the end, the net result is that the firm is effectively controlled from outside to ensure its survival.

In most cases where a firm suffers from being found out, the practice started in an innocent way and developed over a period of time, almost as a reward system. If advice is needed when an offer is put forward in this situation, then that advice must be—*smile, say ''not possible'' and walk away, quickly.*

BOUGHT INFLUENCE SALES

Bought Influence Sales. This term is a nice way of describing business gained by paying an employee or associate of a potential client to enlist his or her assistance in gaining a sale. There are two main ways that this business procurement theory operates:

1. Influential people are bribed by services or "slush" money.
2. Influential people are identified and converted into ambassadors by social meetings, friendship development, ego building, etc.

In some countries and cultures the first method is accepted, but in the Western World it is frowned upon, the reasoning being that only the desperate and the inefficient need to revert to such methods.

The second method is dangerous as it leads to the possibility of an overestimation by those introducing you, your product or service which, in turn, you would have to live up to. It is also an expensive method to operate in the long-term, as once employed, the system of reward will be expected by others who might not have otherwise required it.

This system of *closing the sale* must not be confused with employing agents or paying consultants, where the hired or commission-receiving agent has a working understanding of your business, represents you openly, and states that he or she *works for* or *is retained* by your firm.

PRICE UNDERCUTTING

Price Undercutting. Most of the people who employ this method have trouble in accepting the fact. Sometimes it is the result of pressure or desperation. In simple terms, it can best be described as business gained by agreeing to crop your price below the price of all other suppliers. The theory behind employing this method is that any profit is worth having, and any standard is acceptable as long as the invoice is paid. All one has to do is inform every possible client that you can undercut the prices of other bidders, then sit back and wait for a call. More often than not, a company will convince itself that this is not normal policy, and will turn a blind eye to salespeople who employ it. In fact, it should be forbidden by any firm or individual looking to build a long-term professional business, for once the word gets around your reputation will take years to regain. It can only result in lowering standards and professional image, and restricting long-term profitable growth. Ethically, this method is wrong, shortsighted and counterproductive; business gained this way can never really be worth having in the long run.

BLANKET CANVASSING SALES

Blanket Canvassing Sales. This method of lining up potential new business is practiced by many firms. It is even advised by some *consultants* as an economic method of promotion but, like most cheap things, it usually proves to be *nasty.* Managers who read someone else's public relations and suddenly decide that one industry or another is about to experience sudden expansion cause most of these problems. Whatever the industry, out come the *Yellow Pages* and every other directory available (out-of-date or not), and everyone is committed to *following up* for several days. It can be best described as business generated from canvassing (by telephone, letter or distribution of literature) as many potential prospects as it is possible to reach, without in-depth research beforehand. This activity is most common where no marketing program or professional marketer is employed. It is without doubt the most inefficient method of gaining business, and replacing it with true marketing will in most cases increase business activity and cost effective sales by at least a factor of five for the same expenditure of time and money.

The individual reasoning behind the employment of this system of finding business is motivated by the gambling instinct which exists in every extrovert personality. The theory is that one just might *hit* a prospect at the moment they enter the market, and thereby get a *large* order. The problem is that this does sometimes happen, but it is rare.

Untrained, over-ambitious or desperate sales personnel often use this method because they know of no other, and it helps them *look busy*. The greatest counterproductive factor in allowing this method to be used is that in time, more by luck than anything, any salesperson can build up a list of *contacts* at your expense. If they then become dissatisfied with their lot and move on (taking those contacts with them, of course), the person who replaces them is forced to follow the same path, as no system exists for exposing the basic failure of their predecessor. It is a chain reaction which goes on until the supply of contacts or sales replacements are used up, or your reputation is irrevocably damaged.

Whether the method employed is telephone contact using the Yellow Pages, or any other directory, or by continued and unmonitored mass mailing, it is inefficient and expensive and, like all gambling, the end product is to humble everyone involved in it, despite the occasional success.

The most counterproductive element in using this method is the insult many buyers feel at being treated as *one of a crowd*. Even worse is when the *letter* is a bad "mass-produced" one (sometimes even including a "printed" signature), with the addressing done in a different type face or more "intense ink" by obviously being typed at the top of the *circular*.

Looking at the situation logically, the idea of sending out hundreds of letters, or mass calling (which ties up the sales phones) can never be really justified. If everyone approached was to *come through*, the business volume would be too much. Also, consider the people who felt you had a real interest in their problems and then never heard from you again—or were approached later with a different story.

NON-APPOINTMENT CALLS

Non-appointment Calls (or Cold Calling). Simply described, this system is one which attempts to develop new business by visiting possible prospects without first making an appointment or having had any prior contact or invitation. It is mainly used by the same standard of sales manager as would employ the Blanket Canvassing Method, only he or she is normally the *I-like-to-be-out-there-working* type. Sometimes it is assisted by use of the Blanket Canvassing Method. More often, after reading or overhearing something, or having a hunch, the salesperson is encouraged to set off, like a knight on a charger, to present themselves at the door of a potential client, normally without checking to see if contact has already been made by someone else in the company and before researching the background information required. Nine times out of ten that type of salesperson gets no further than the receptionist, and if they do *get in* their efforts are normally wasted due to bad timing, lack of knowledge or not even seeing the right person. This method is applicable to selling brushes door-to-door, but it can do little or nothing for a professional organization, or anyone wishing to build a professional business reputation.

Please refer to Checklist Number 4 on page 310.

Please refer to Checklist Number 5 on page 313.

"You haven't been to one of our Sales Meetings before, have you?"

CHAPTER FIVE

THE PRIMARY METHODS OF MARKETING

The following methods can be instigated almost immediately to develop new business opportunities. They can be used effectively by any firm or individual to pave the way towards a complete marketing program. High capital expenditure is not normally involved and new contacts, ideas and development can be introduced in a very short amount of time.

OPEN CONTRACT MARKETING

Most companies operating in or supplying a service or product spend a great deal of time *giving opinions, explanations and advice* before they are ever hired or achieve *a sale.* The strange thing is that many people fail to recognize that this activity costs a great deal in time and money, which is normally written off in ''sales costs.'' The problem is that nine times out of ten no *invoiceable business activity* is developed from it.

In a profession like marketing where most individuals see themselves in a consultancy role, it is strange that most contracts are for very specific jobs and length of time. Those cases where an individual or company has *attached* their service on an *open-ended* advisory contract have proved, by experience, to be very worthwhile. Those involved in such an arrangement can also expect first chance at all future work. Therefore, by applying this logic, one needs to find prospects who will or may be contemplating a project or need in the future, and then to use the advantages you have available to become their aide for the *development stages.*

The theory behind this method of marketing is that it is offered to those clients who have already decided your company or product is probably something they need. Put simply, why does a potential client talk to you about services or products in the first place unless they:

1. Do not know enough to make an immediate decision about what they are buying.
2. Their previous supplier upset them or failed to meet their standards.
3. Their previous supplier let the relationship die or is no longer operating.
4. They are looking for alternatives.

Normally, every potential client is either looking for someone to ensure they will not have to take the responsibility for any mistakes that might be made, or they are intelligent enough to recognize specialist help can be a benefit to them. It is these basic needs of most buyers that **Open Contract Marketing** exploits in offering to act as a consultant on an ongoing basis, therefore taking responsibility off the buyer or providing expert advice in an area where the buyer needs such assistance.

How often have you approached a potential client to be told *we shall be doing something in the near future, we will get back to you when something definite is known?* Most of us have, and then of course they do not get back, so you begin the process of *follow-up* calls and telephone messages. In fact, you are doing one of four negative things from the moment they agree to *get back to you*:

1. Your continued *chasing* of their order makes them think you want the job too badly.

2. That your continued calling really means you are desperate for work.
3. That your continued reminding them of their promise really means you do not have confidence in their ability or their memory, or trust them to come back to you.
4. If you do wait for them to call:
   They think you do not care, you have gone out of business, or you have too much work to handle their project anyway.

All in all, the *I'll get back to you* answer means that you lose in nine cases out of ten. The price will be negotiated down, other bids will be entertained, or you will just not get approached to bid. It is possible, however, to employ **Open Contract Marketing** as a method to turn the *I'll get back to you* answer into an order there and then. Make an offer to help the potential client—offer your services, or rather some of them, at a reduced fee cost. Tempt them with the chance to impress their boss, friends and/or colleagues. The *I'll get back to you* answer implies does it not, that the speaker is short of facts and qualified information. So offer your *expert and specialized* assistance to help them gain the information they need, with the *hook* of making a decision implied, and tied to the supply of information you will help them establish. The fee, of course, must be relative to expected results.

The variety of possible services you could offer a hesitant client is unlimited, for example:

a) Offer to help them survey their existing equipment or premises and draw up plans for them to work with.
b) Offer to carry out an inventory for them.
c) Offer to hold instructional meetings for their staff.
d) Offer to design a research program.

Basically, you are helping them make a decision, but more important in the *peak and trough* situation that most firms live with, you are guaranteeing work to keep your staff employed in slow periods.

This is where being recognized as a specialist can be of enormous help in that even the purchasing or facilities management department within a firm will see you as an ally, rather than a threat. If you have any systems, experience or ability not held by the client in-house, then it can be presented as only logical that they retain you as an advisor, much as most firms retain lawyers and accountants. With the rising costs of all businesses, the need to employ highly qualified staff, and meet the increasing number of new laws and regulations, your fee will seem good insurance. To firms who have no *established* purchasing or facilities management department, your qualifications and experience are reason enough to retain you. If you want to use the easiest way to get retained, merely offer to give a talk on current laws, codes, regulations, etc., on your subject to your selected prospect. If you explain fully just how much they need to know to make the right decision, they will be likely to ask you to become their *retained advisor.*

For those clients with whom you have a close relationship, but for whom you do not, do not wish to, or cannot handle all of their work, there is another area open to you.

This method of marketing is built around the old belief that most people prefer *dealing with someone they know,* and the theory is that everyone likes to feel he or she can **trust** a consultant to follow through on stated requirements, unaffected by internal organizational politics their subordinates or ambitious fellows might play. What you effectively become is the ''client's aide'' when he or she cannot be there.

Let us take for an example a large organization with operations in several locations. The president (or whoever runs things) likes the way you work, and you have a good relationship. Therefore, he or she might be grateful for an offer from you to work (on a consultancy fee) to check the workmanship and services of others, and ensure that the *corporate image or goals* are maintained. The amount of business that this sort of relationship can generate, without capital outlay, is far larger than most people realize.

Please refer to Checklist Number 6 on page 315.

BUSINESS DEMAND SALES

This source of business is contained in the theory that whatever service or product you offer for sale, somewhere, someone wants to buy. In fact it can be said that all other methods are only tools to either "make" someone want what you have to offer, or to inform them where you are so that they can find you and discuss their needs. Assuming that someone, somewhere is looking to buy services such as you offer, it is obvious that you must make it easy for that person to find you. So, invest in good signs which make your store, offices or premises easy to locate and put name plates on your products (showing address and telephone number). Check the telephone directory and all other printed referral means your potential clients might use, and make sure *your* name is easy to spot and the details, numbers, etc., are correct. If you have company vehicles, compare them to your competitors fleet for "image" and advertising value.

CLIENT REFERRAL SALES (UNSOLICITED)

This source of business is a bonus for good management and professionalism. One cannot describe how it happens, reasons vary, but it should be the main source of new business for the efficient, and such ''referrals'' should always be given special priority, especially as they cost very little in marketing expenditure.

LINKED BENEFIT MARKETING

To employ your sales staff most efficiently, it is necessary that you reduce the time spent *prospecting* and increase the time used in *producing* business. To do this, there is a need to have more potential clients **coming to you** than possible clients you have to go out and find.

As the name suggests, **Linked Benefit Marketing** means that more than the normal two parties involved in a transaction will benefit. The list of potential partners who can assist and benefit from a *Linked Benefit* situation with your firm must be very long indeed. In most cases, the only reward these potential suppliers of new business require from you is the provision of professional, courteous, economical and fast service to their clients to help improve *their* image and professionalism. The smaller their operation the more they need to help you, as it will increase the total service they can offer to their clients.

The list can be very long indeed, it includes anyone, or any firm, who can sell your service as part of their own service (in a limited sense of course, because each of you retains complete control over your own operation).

When we buy a washing machine one of the key questions we ask is *how much will it cost to install and how soon can it be done?* This obvious example of Linked Benefit opportunity prompts the salesperson to recommend someone who will maintain his or her image with the client. So it is with almost every business, if another supplier or service is part of what your image is built on, you will always give the matter a lot of thought before taking the chance that you may be let down, but essentially, without *installation,* the *washing machine* could not be sold nor could the customer be satisfied. **Linked Benefit Marketing** then is finding and enlisting anyone who could recommend your service or product on an ongoing basis, and then creating a professional relationship whereby both parties benefit. Until you are able to increase the strength and/or standard of your sales force, this method of marketing can provide extra business potential in geometrical progression and increase your network of contacts. By linking your services to the service, products or expertise of another organization you would gain the benefit of introduction to their business contacts and their sales force activity, which could produce new business at very low initial overhead costs.

IMPLEMENTATION

a) Produce an audio-visual program or slide presentation, backed up by literature, which would explain your services indepth.
b) Train one of your salespeople in the techniques of introducing this to potential *partners,* and be available to train their sales staff to use this program to explain your service to their clients.
c) Develop a list of potential *Link Benefit Partners* and approach them in geographic order nearest to your location.

Quite often you will find that there are people and firms who have been looking for years to enlist services such as you offer, and they will not require any *return business* from you. As a last reminder in implementing **Linked Benefit Marketing,** ensure that every time you hand out a business card, you get one back, and enquire about the activities of its owner. If you think he or she has access to your potential clients, make an appointment to hear them explain further, as **you** are interested in what **they** do. Sometime during that appointment, the chance to make that person part of your sales introduction team **will** occur.

Please refer to Checklist Number 7 on page 316.

CHAPTER SIX

IMAGE MARKETING

Image Marketing is a tool to present you, or your firm, in the best light to those you have not yet had the opportunity to work for or with. Just like we are on our best behavior and dress up for certain occasions—so **Image Marketing** is used to present your talents to those who have not yet employed you. **Image Marketing** is used to make potential clients **want** to employ you because they can associate with your ability as a professional, or feel they will benefit with you as their advisor or supplier.

INFORMATIVE PUBLIC RELATIONS

Informative Public Relations can use articles, interviews, advertising, exhibitions, brochures, newsletters, marketing literature and letters. Its sole aim is to inform potential clients of your existence and capabilities. This method is an investment in the future. It relies upon planting the belief of your expertise in the minds of those who will one day be your potential clients.

ADVERTISING

There are many in commerce and the professions who feel that advertising is undignified or too expensive. If you can, and want to survive without it, well and good, but it is a little old-fashioned to throw business away. The more potential clients who know what you do, where to find you, or even that you exist, means the more probable it is your work will be commissioned. In fact, the only difference between advertising in a national business magazine and being interviewed by them (in the business-gaining sense) is that they are more likely to take your money for advertising than to interview you. In some cases, if you need to reach a particular audience you may well have no alternative but to advertise.

For those who do not already have a national or even international reputation, there is today, more than ever before, a greater need to consider advertising, due to the increase in competition we can expect in the future, if it does not exist already, from local and international sources. Perhaps more important is the mobility of business and people today, and the growing communication problems of urban centers. (Today, many of your potential clients are more likely to be newcomers to your area than would have been probable 20 years ago.) If you rely on word of mouth and recommendations, in the true sense, then you can expect to miss 90% of the business opportunities around you.

There can be no better advice than to suggest that anyone considering venturing into advertising should consult a professional, and always remember that you are marketing *quality, talent, service* and *profits;* and realize that bad advertising or grabbing the limelight can only harm the future of your profession. Points to consider, however, include the following:

1. Coupons on advertisements guarantee a savings in following up non-productive leads and can increase reply rates.
2. Make sure your reply to an inquiry is fast and of high quality, comparable to that which other advertisers in the same medium use. (If you want to know how high the quality is, just reply to several advertisements prior to placing yours, and check it out.)
3. Most major business magazines have *local* circulation editions which can reduce the cost.

4. Check out the smaller *specialized* journals in your catchment area for prices, circulation figures and readership evaluations.
5. Research where "the successful" advertise and who manages their account—not the firm, the actual person!

EXHIBITIONS

Designers design exhibition stands, but rarely occupy them. It is surprising that so many firms are against taking part in exhibitions, when you consider that most of their potential clients attend at least one exhibition a year. Perhaps, once again, it is seen as undignified. Consider for a moment, however, the effect a small stand at a trade exhibition or professional conference would have. Imagine the feeling of a footsore business executive invited to sit down and watch a ten-minute slide show on an alternative subject, after a day of wandering around looking at heavy machinery, row upon row of work stations, or whatever. It is not exaggeration to suggest that a properly organized traveling exhibition unit could double the business of any *specialist, quality* or *professional service* firm.

The cost would be relatively low because the size of stand you would need would be small, and the contact rate in one week should equal the work of a traditional salesperson for a year. In ten-years time it is probable that even very small firms with stands at exhibitions not put together for their "professions" will be a quite normal business practice, for the very reason of escalating sales costs in traditional sales methods.

There are few firms that do not consider they gain a definite advantage if they can entice a potential client to visit their offices. A good exhibition stand can do everything an office can do to excite or impress a potential client. A small stand equipped with an impressive desk and small seating area, a never-empty coffee pot, good quality chinaware and friendly talk, will impress anyone in an exhibition hall. Walls hung with pictures of completed projects, a prominent and varied client list, and the strategically placed model here and there will interest most people. Add a good supply of marketing literature and business cards, and you are equipped to talk to anyone and collect business cards from potential clients by the box full.

A good tip here is to instigate a coding system and mark the back of each business card **before** it is filed away, e.g., 1 = Immediate Business, 2 = Presently using a Competitor, 3 = Potential Excellent, 4 = Low Potential, 5 = Low Priority. Also have each salesperson put his or her initials on the card so you know who saw the visitor.

MARKETING LITERATURE

When a single sheet of paper with insufficient attention to detail or even quality is produced to describe a product or a high dollar expenditure project, the reaction of a potential client must be that the firm responsible just does not have enough pride or confidence in their work or product to promote it properly.

It is hard to understand why so many business people refuse to acknowledge the skills of others who specialize and are expert in the skills of print, graphics, photography, typography and presentation, and do all the things they complain of in their clients—as if there were two sets of rules. Many will state that they *have the talent in-house* to produce their own literature, and there are others who will announce that photography is their hobby, and then insist they shoot the photographs for their marketing and public relations.

The best and most successful firms and individuals in the world have always hired the best professionals available. The reason is simple, three good photographs of a project are worth 300 mediocre ones. A good photographer, in fact, can get shots which make the most ordinary product or job look fantastic as it jumps out at you from the pages of a magazine.

It is also a fact that many really talented people and firms lose opportunities because their portfolio is full of rather mediocre snapshots of their products or work.

It is worth remembering that few people ever actually walk around a building and make a definitive statement of opinion, just as few people ever study the trees which line the path they are walking along. However, show someone a photograph and they feel obliged to make a statement of their opinion. Therefore, unless the photograph is superb, it is counterproductive nine times out of ten, and as photographs also last longer than design schemes or products, study every photograph of your work that exists, and then lock all but the superb away (or simply destroy the bad ones!).

It would also seem logical that printed graphics should be left to experts who specialize in the subject, and yet those who spend most of their waking hours debating the need for *innovative thinking, courage to experiment* and *leading design development,* with few exceptions, produce brochures and descriptive literature that is geometric and simplified to the point of being plain and uninteresting to the potential client in most cases. Abstract treatments like counter-screening and cutaway images are all but unheard of in most firms, and it is rare when something is produced without neat little borders or columns of print balanced like bricks in a wall. If the aim is to impress your competitors, who think the same way, or just gather a personal record of your work, well perhaps it does not matter if your brochures are boring. But why should you care what your competitors think of the literature and brochures you produce? They are not likely to employ you, recommend you, or give you one red cent towards the costs of what you print. If marketing literature is unable to bring potential clients to your door, why bother to spend money producing it in the first place?

Make the client **want** to buy from you. Aim at the client—appeal to the potential client—that is how you gain success and grow. Put excitement and innovation into your brochures, employ the best photographers, delegate literature production to experts and, even if you do not like it personally, learn to judge by results. Be sensible, review the graphics of your potential clients, not those of your competitors.

SUCCESS PUBLIC RELATIONS

Success Public Relations—There is a lot of truth in the old saying that, *success breeds success,* but what is often overlooked is that ***apparent*** *success can breed real success.* The potential client is really looking for a firm or individual who has **proven** ability, trustworthiness and professionalism, and there are two main ways that you are able to *prove* success:

1. Your past clients recommend you.
2. Professional magazines publish articles about your work.

The first way is discussed in several of the other methods of marketing (especially **Organized Referral Programs**).

The second way of *proving* your success depends almost entirely upon your working to achieve publication as a regular marketing activity. There are three main tools you need to have:

1. excellent photographs
2. first rate writing ability
3. perseverance and hard work

If you do not have these attributes then you can hire a qualified photographer, a writer who understands your field, and a public relations agent to *place* the product. Remembering that few editors have the time to visit the actual project or to even ask to see your product, these three assets are even more important than the quality of the project itself. This may not be a happy or even a wanted state of affairs but, as it exists, perhaps it is wise to learn to live with it.

We have already covered the need for excellent photographs and renderings, etc., (the requirements of written communication are considered at the end of this chapter) so let us assume you have managed to overcome those prerequisites, and consider how to achieve success in getting your work published.

First of all, there are the *Trade* magazines and journals, which are devoted to your particular profession or business; that is, those publications which are read for the most part by your competitors rather than your clients. The real value of articles in these publications, from the marketing point of view, is their reprint value. Your potential clients are not likely to read these publications, their employees may, but the person who signs the orders and the contracts is rarely a reader. Therefore, to put your success before that person you will need to send him or her a reprinted copy. Obviously, you do not want to send the whole magazine. (The likelihood that a competitor who is also featured in it might get chosen is, of course, thereby made possible.) Nor can you tear out the relevant pages and still look professional. Therefore, it is necessary to plan your *reprint* as you produce the article.

The formula is simple:

1. Analyze the magazine you are aiming at, and study the way they lay out their feature articles. How many photographs do they use per page? Do they use more color, or more black-and-white photographs? How many columns do they lay out in a typical page? Do they tend to *run stories through the pages?* In other words, do you have to *turn to page* --, and have half of the page taken up by advertisements? What is the average word length of a feature? (This means counting the words so that you know how many to submit to the editor.) What subject matter or opinions does the editor seem to favor? When you have analyzed what a publication uses, you can then produce *your* article to meet the guidelines established.

2. Now you need to identify what you can use in reprint form. (A two-page feature article can be reprinted with your cover front and back, to tie it into your marketing program.)

3. The next step is to find out what the magazine intends to feature in forthcoming months. This is simple as most publications produce *editorial schedules* for anything up to a year in advance. Obtain a copy and try to match one of your recent projects to meet the magazine's needs. Remember, in most cases you will need your articles to be on the editor's desk at least two or three months prior to the issue it could be used in.

4. The most important part of any article is the *opening paragraph.* If you get that right, you are half-way to being published. Styles and approaches vary, so take a past issue and cut out all the *opening paragraphs.* Paste them onto a

board and read them over and over again until you can produce your opening paragraph to be indistinguishable in style and word usage from that used by the magazine's own writers.

5. To pick your title, study those used by the publication for similar articles, but only for style and approach. Remember always, that an article which is new or *aimed differently* is what all editors are looking for.

6. In your article take the stance of an observer, if you try to *boast* it will be counter-productive. *Describe* rather than list and try always to limit the number of times you use your name or the firm's title. It must not look like PR. Also, most trade editors like to list supplier sources, so make sure you include a separate listing of what materials were used and who produced or distributed them, and who else was involved in the project described. In the case of a product, send a list of major clients (three—five maximum) now using your product, the more famous the clients mentioned, the better.

7. An article is also the best inducement to a client to give you a reference, so obtain some *quotes* you can use in the body of the text.

8. Many firms retain publicity rights within their contracts with clients (a necessity in most cases), however, gaining the client's cooperation is always a wise move.

9. Remember all the points outlined in **Written Communications** (later in this chapter) and present your *copy* to the magazine in a way which will interest them from the outset.

1. Always mail your submission in a large **white** envelope.
2. Never fold copy to fit a small envelope.
3. All typed copy should be perfect (no corrections in ink or pencil) and it should be double-spaced.
4. Black-and-white photographs should always be 8'' x 10'' with a glossy finish.
5. Color positives or slides should be enclosed in see-through plastic protectors.
6. Descriptive titles of what the photographs are, and a return address, should be typed on white labels and affixed to the back of black-and-white photographs, or on the plastic covers of color positives or slides, so that they can be identified should they get separated from the main package.
7. The whole unit should be enclosed in a presentation folder, with a submission on your letterhead for identification purposes.

It is a wise move to ring the editor (or his or her secretary) the day before you post your submission. This way you can evaluate its chances and prepare its anticipation by the magazine concerned. Check a week later to see that they received it, and that someone will read it and get back to you.

Another valuable source of **success** image building is the constant announcement of contracts gained and completed. The reason being is that the more times potential clients see your name the more likelihood they will come to you is valid, and yet few firms use this tool to its full potential.

The formula is not difficult to employ and a regular program to use it will pay excellent dividends. There are three times when your work is **newsworthy**:

1. When the contract is signed or you are commissioned to supply your products or services.
2. When construction or installation begins.
3. When the project is completed.

The format accepted by most newspapers and business magazines is as follows: (You can forget most *Trade* magazines for the first two categories. In the marketing sense, their inclusion in *Trade* publications is, at the least, useless and, at the worst, invites your competition to try harder.)

1. Send press releases to every newspaper and business magazine or to the 'client's' professional *Trade* magazine in your ''catchment area'' or where you **want** to work.
2. Each press release should include one black-and-white 8'' x 10'' glossy photograph either of your rendering, artist's impression or model of the product or project, or of yourself, or a member of your staff *announcing* the fact.
3. Keep the word copy (text) short, a paragraph or two at the most.
4. The name of the client, a brief description of the project and your names. (A good point is to link your firm's title to the telephone area where you are, so that potential clients can find you in that directory, e.g., A & B International of Seattle announces ..., etc.)
5. Use the same standard of presentation as you would for a full-length article, and find out the name of the relevant editor so that you can address it to him or her personally.

IMAGE RESPECT MARKETING

Image Respect Marketing is the description or promotion of your image through academic articles, interviews, panel appearances and seminar speaking, etc. The aim of this method is to establish *expertise.* **Image Respect Marketing** is basically the activity which, if successful, can make someone famous faster than almost any other activity. Some people come by the talent as a birthright almost, the majority, however, have to work very hard to achieve success. The fact is that for every one person who manages to sustain the effort and becomes famous, there are at least a hundred who should have done so, but failed. The wonderful thing about **Image Respect Marketing** is that only achieving the first step of the ladder is success in itself. It is important, however, that you know, or have defendable opinions on, whichever subject you decide to use as a vehicle.

In all types of business, or any of the professions, *fame* will always bring you clients—and that is what **Image Respect Marketing** is all about.

FAME according to Webster's Dictionary has two definitions:

1. *Reputation, especially for good.*
2. *Widespread public recognition, usually highly favorable; renown; glory.*

RESPECT is gained by sharing your experience and contributing to the knowledge of your profession or business field, or by sharing your experience and expertise with others. The **Image** part of it is being seen and credited for doing something affirmative.

Image Respect Marketing is the tool for achieving fame, and if you are prepared as a firm, or as an individual, to put your opinions up for judgment, it is not as hard to achieve as most people would have you believe. The objective is to get the widest coverage of your opinions or knowledge amongst the body of your prospective clients. To do this, there are many outlets you can employ, including (but not restricted to):

1. Business magazines and journals
2. Trade-orientated publications
3. Seminars
4. Association meetings and conferences
5. Business luncheons
6. Academic research
7. Radio and television
8. Environmental and community programs
9. Trade and business conferences
10. Reference papers, reports and books
11. Advising manufacturers
12. Advising law-making bodies

The reason why so few become famous in any profession is that they are not prepared to give the time to research, or they pick subjects abjectly difficult, or enter an area with too many existing experts.

False modesty (or even real shyness) often prevents the most promising users of this method of marketing from carrying it through. Business opportunities which can develop from it, however, suggest that it should be carefully considered before being discarded. There is also the added advantage that while teaching others one cannot help but benefit as well, and this interaction alone can be worth a great deal to anyone in business today.

Business magazines and journals are interested in your knowledge if it interests and can assist their readers. The same can be said for all of the 12 opportunities listed above. If you can teach, explain or advise, add to or contribute something to those who you address, then **Image Respect Marketing** is open to you. Your efforts will be assisted by attention to your presentation. If you are going to use the personal approach of speaking, then lessons on communication techniques, presentation and public speaking would be an asset. Your visual image will also need attention; how you look, move, and unknown habits can ruin your presentation. Short of suggesting acting lessons, perhaps practicing in front of a mirror, or rehearsing in front of friends or colleagues is the best way to improve your visual image and delivery. If you decide to use a pen, then get help from a professional writer. The services of a good public relations consultant could also be helpful. There are, of course, several good books on the market which can help you develop speaking or writing "style," but possibly the most beneficial advice is to read everything you can find on your subject, and then go and listen and learn from those who are out there practicing this method.

If you are able to find a subject you can specialize in to your benefit, then **Image Respect Marketing** is made that much easier—if not, then you can work with what you already know, built with the lessons of experience.

Please refer to Checklist Number 8 on page 317.

EDUCATIONAL MARKETING

Educational Marketing is the establishment of a future cadre of clients, by teaching and assisting tomorrow's executives today. It can also be used to explain new methods, systems or services to existing or potential clients.

In many ways **Educational Marketing** is similar to **Image Respect Marketing** except that it is directed to an audience which has already been identified as probable clients (or those who can assist you in gaining business) now or in the future. **Educational Mar-**

keting can also be used as an ongoing program by a firm or team of people, whereas **Image Respect Marketing** normally is identified with an individual. This method of marketing demands the prior preparation of a presentation to *explain* a new product, concept, method or service being offered. Its aim is not to entertain more than necessary, but rather to teach to a small group of involved people.

There are many ways a firm can use this method employing in-house staff or consultants, or working with agents or manufacturers. Three immediately recognizable potential areas where this method could be successful are:

1. Individuals who have a need or want to gain a more in-depth knowledge of a particular subject.
2. Social or business associations who could use such in-depth state-of-the-art presentations as part of their own ongoing education program.
3. Commercial organizations who could incorporate your presentation into their training program.

The first method is one which can be used to good effect by someone who deals directly with the public (the housewares salesperson or residential designer, etc.). As the organizer you will need to provide or hire the meeting place, and develop a method of informing potential interested parties.

*(As a potential self-financing method of promoting your ability and increasing your network of contacts, consider the following as just one example of how **Educational Marketing** might be employed to your benefit.)*

a) Interior design is seen by the *general public* as an artistic and interesting subject.
b) When and where are the most promising (from a business

or contact point of view) members of the *general public* likely to be most receptive to hearing about interior design?

c) After a lot of thought (and discarding 90% of brainstorming development) the following progression of ideas developed:

Where do people spend money, dress for, are surrounded by, and take the time to examine in others ''good taste''?------
First class, international-standard hotels------
When they are: guests, out to dinner, in the evening------
Hotels in the evening have empty meeting rooms because the day's conventions etc., are over and delegates are in the bar or restaurant, or out on the town------
Which nights, and at what time, do people like not to be in the bar, restaurant or out on the town?------
Optimum day and time------
Between 6-7:30 pm Mondays and Tuesdays------
(A quick check revealed that on Monday and Tuesday nights most hotels had more unaccompanied or single business people in than couples.)

Conclusion

Approach the management of a large hotel and offer to give a one-hour presentation on your own subject at no charge, in the smallest meeting room, for no more than 16 people every Monday or Tuesday, between 6:15 and 7:15 pm; each week taking a particular subject within the overall scope of what you are presenting as a subject.

Point out to the management that:

1. Publicity would encourage new clients (of higher income bracket, of course) to enter the hotel.
2. The hotel might attract more ''doubles'' on these nights.

3. It would be an extra service for minimal costs to offer their clients.

Safeguards:

Ask for a 12-month concession from the hotel.
Make sure you pass out business cards or brochures at every opportunity, and gain press releases, etc. Offer to mail out the Hotel's brochure with your 'invitations!'

Another method could also be offered to individual buyers, office managers, etc., offering to give them in-depth discussion and educational opportunities in subjects which concern them most. (Titles for the half-hour or one-hour lunch time or afternoon sessions could be: e.g., Comparative values in health and fitness programs available today, or Acoustic Panels—applications to maintenance costs, etc.) Print up a small descriptive brochure and mail it to all the companies where you think there might be interest. Include with the brochure a reply card or coupon. These are, of course, only two of potentially hundreds of opportunities for gaining individuals to listen to you. This method of *public performance* can be applied to just about anything from Fire Safety Equipment to Oil Painting. Develop your subject as if you were a teacher, and then go out and convert your pupils into future clients or contacts to introduce you to new clients.

The third method needs little explanation, for once you have prepared a few half-hour or one-hour presentations, you merely approach any local organization which holds luncheons, or other meetings, and offer to *do your act.* From Chambers of Commerce to church institutions, all have a constant need for speakers, just choose which you are most likely to develop business from and approach them.

The fourth method is a little more difficult, but if you choose your subjects and titles well, there are many firms who will welcome you because new systems and equipment, plant care, maintenance realities and the like, well explained to staff, will be helpful to almost any organization.

Preparing your **Educational Marketing** presentation is something that should be given a lot of thought and experimentation. The reason being is that once you have created a presentation, you can go on using it for a long time and it can become a valuable sales tool.

1. Research relevant magazines, books on the subject chosen and manufacturer's literature, etc.
2. Develop a script and practice in front of a mirror, and against the clock.
3. Put together a slide program to illustrate your opinions and information. (You do not need to restrict yourself to examples of just your own work, manufacturers, or suppliers; other sources will normally be happy to loan you slides if you ask.)
4. Assemble a collection of samples or demonstration models.
5. Try out your presentation in front of friends, family or business associates to sharpen your delivery and organization.

Educational Marketing is grouped together with the other methods of **Image Marketing** for the reason that it can assist in the building of *believable expertise.*

BORROWED RESPECT MARKETING

Borrowed Respect Marketing is best described as improving your image by promoting your work, or product, in association with famous individuals, places or organizations. This method is probably the simplest and cheapest image-builder available to any company, however, it depends entirely upon you to generate the opportunity. The theory is that your image increases if you are able to link your name with the name of a famous company or individual with or for whom you have worked. The same benefits, of course, can also be gained by working in a respected or well-known geographical location which is recognized for high standards or innovation in your field. You then produce a program of public relations exploiting this partnership, which could be circulated in the form of articles or photographs with captions to the media. (Having first, of course, informed and gained the approval of your *Respect* partner in the venture you are exploiting.) In some cases it is possible to *link* your name with a famous location or individual, and incorporate it into articles which relate to your service without the article actually being about you, your firm or even the project in particular. An example of this would be an article dealing with an event in a city, where a shot of the skyline is used to identify it, pointing out your *association* with a prominent building on that skyline.

Another way of employing this borrowed respect method is to promote your executives to be participants in academic events with other famous names—i.e., taking part in seminars, etc., as *guest experts, panelists,* or *luncheon guests* where other well-known speakers will be in attendance.

One more source of business often overlooked by many firms is *shared promotion.* Many companies are usually only too pleased to pay the expenses of an "expert" to help them in promoting their product or service. Some will even welcome your assistance as a consultant in product development or specification. Obviously, professional limitations must be considered, but when a new product or innovation surfaces, an early approach will not only increase your way to obtaining a new network of contacts, but might even increase your value to clients by whatever you learn in the exercise.

In a reversed manner of this method, many manufacturers will *promote* your firm in their own marketing literature for the use of a good photograph of their product installed. The manufacturer benefits as well by your *recommendation* of their product in direct reaction to your publicity. Allowing others to use your photographs (even encouraging it) **with the provision that your name and your city appear** as a *credit,* is often beneficial, as their salespeople may see many of your potential clients. Insisting upon the inclusion of town or telephone district is, of course, 90% of the *cooperation;* that way interested potential clients have the key to finding you.

One can also use the project of a company that is a client of yours that has commissioned your services or products, unlike the majority of their competitors. You could then produce an audio-visual or slide presentation around it, describing the development of the project from conception to completion. What you, your product or service gain, in fact, is a complete case history indicating that only by using you, your product or service was the individual result gained made possible. This program could then be used in presentations to:

a) Chambers of Commerce
b) Potential clients
c) Given to the featured client themselves so that they can show it to visitors at their premises.

Many salespeople often forget that most clients approach a major project as a once-in-a-decade or, at the least, a very rare event. They are, therefore, understandably expecting a rewarding experience and a lot of problems, both at the same time. A prospective client for a major project once told me the feeling was similar to expecting a child, joyous anticipation and fear of the unknown mixed up to the point where the main effect was optimistic confusion. Reliving a similar project with such a client, good points and bad, problems and successes, is probably one of the best ways of establishing a mutual trust situation. Words alone, expensive lunches, even a portfolio of beautiful photographs can never be as effective as seeing a total report of a similar project from beginning to end.

RECEPTION MARKETING

Reception Marketing—the theory behind this method is that sooner or later everyone who visits the offices of an organization will give an opinion of that experience to a potential client, and should therefore be converted into an ambassador for your organization. The need is to promote the most professional, friendly and efficient image possible to **every** visitor to your place of business.

The key words about the facility itself are:

1. Cleanliness
2. Design and furnishings related to the professional image you wish to promote
3. Atmosphere

The key words about your staff as seen by a visitor should be:

1. Appearance related to a business image
2. Politeness, courtesy and patience
3. Efficiency and professionalism
4. Confidence

This method of marketing can do more to produce long-term clients and maintain cash flow than almost anything else. With concerted **Reception Marketing** you will achieve friends and ambassadors for your business on a geometric progression. Your aim is that everyone who enters your building, leaves with the conviction that he or she would be proud and happy to be part of your team, or to work with you.

It is well worth investing in a communications training scheme for your staff, to explain and implement this benefit to both them and the organization. For, if every other activity brings clients in, but you lose their confidence as they enter your store, building, office or studio, then it is to no avail that you seek to grow.

The reasoning behind **Reception Marketing** is the simple application of the fact that everyone wishes to associate with people they like and can feel comfortable with. So many of us in the day-to-day rush of business are tempted to forget the golden rule, that most buying situations end up at the last fence of *personality factors. The Personality Factors,* which influence buying decisions probably more than anything else, are continuous in their effect throughout any relationship, and writing out a list of how to overcome them is the oldest standby for all teachers of sales techniques. No matter how many photographs, samples, renderings or models you show the prospective client, or even how many past projects you walk them around, the buyer must logically see your offices or facilities as *the result of your success* and *the best of your character,* and they will examine every detail while you are concentrating on your presentation. The design profession has of course recognized this; the proof is in the neutral, non-controversial way most architects, etc., decorate their own work place in greys, neutral browns, olives or white and, nine times out of ten, the place looks like a public museum or college classroom, with a few plants and non-controversial sculptures.

With apologies for quoting the obvious, I would suggest that once a week you *walk through* your premises, **as a prospective client,** looking for anything that you could criticize if you were considering placing an order with or hiring your firm. Inspect the paint work, the woodwork and every other finish treatment. Consider the lighting and the state of cleanliness. Compare the signage, traffic lanes and furniture to what the client will see elsewhere. Then, when prospective clients are present, try to see your staff as the client sees them; rate them as assets or liabilities to your chances of clearing the *Personality Factor* fence.

Remember, your clients buy from or hire not just you, but everyone who is on your team, and they will consider everyone they meet in your organization in comparison to their own employees or friends and all the other *experts* to whom they go. (One firm I know used to hold a staff meeting every month, and I observed two of them before I realized that none of this open exchange of ideas ever mentioned how *potential clients* could be better received, dealt with or impressed by the firm's professionalism. I am well known for being blunt on occasion, and so my hand went up and when asked to speak, I inquired if anyone present knew of anything which might be beneficial to clients who visited the facility. The results were amazing and the clients who visit that firm today can thank my *innocent* question for the new reception area, the immaculate almost hotel quality of welcome, and even the new signs which direct the stranger to the restroom.) It is probable that every firm could benefit far more than they would ever think possible just by holding such a meeting every month. From the receptionist to the cleaner, there is no one who cannot contribute to such a program.

Some firms have instigated a *communication course* every three months, employing an outside communications expert to hold a series of one-hour meetings where staff attended in shifts. I have done many in my career and the outcome is that staff turnover usually drops, and a visit to these firms is pure enjoyment. You feel that they really do care about everyone and everything connected with the firm.

INTRODUCTION OR ANNOUNCEMENT MARKETING

Introduction or Announcement Marketing—Gaining interest by promoting an addition to your staff, products, systems or philosophy—or promotion of improvements or developments—or by introducing to potential clients a reason for doing something or buying something they have not done or used before.

We all know the new products section of most magazines which feature new, redesigned adaptations of existing products for the most part. Mass advertising has also discovered the interest which can be gained by the label *Improved.* True **Introduction Marketing** would concentrate only upon new products or services being introduced, however, it would be hard to offer almost anything in today's world as *new.* The human interest in *change* however is too valuable to ignore for the sake of semantics, so we use it to promote development and change in our world—hoping to promote interest which could lead to dialogue.

There are many tools one can develop to use this method of marketing, but experience has isolated three which would appear to the best:

1. The press announcement of new staff joining you or new services you have introduced. With new staff appointments, make sure you mention the competitors your new addition has worked for in the past; some clients do travel with people who have already served them well. With new services, end each press release with the paragraph:

''For further information and literature contact'':
Name
Department
Address
Telephone Number
Extension

If you are a large firm or operate more than one office, having a *Department* on the envelope helps speed up the whole process (e.g., the name of the new division, or just ''Marketing Department'').

Always use a new extension number (one which has not been published or used before). This way you, or your receptionist or telephone operator will know what the caller wants before the phone is even answered.

2. The second way is to write letters to newspapers and businesses or selected magazines in answer to previous letters or articles, e.g.,

Further to your correspondent __________________ who wrote to you last month complaining of cleaning costs, I would point out that there is much concern about this subject, and we have found our new service ________________ which was introduced recently has met great demand, etc., etc.,

or

In your article ___________ in ___________ issue I was amazed how little was said about ___________. We introduced a new service to meet this need a short while ago, and the demand has proved it is a very im-

portant issue in many peoples minds, etc., etc.

3. Another method is a **Newsletter,** which not only introduces new staff and services, but can describe your successes and maintain contact with past clients and friends. The newsletter is one of the most profitable tools a firm can employ to increase the general knowledge of their capabilities amongst existing and potential clients. As a marketing tool, it can be used equally well by the largest multi-discipline firm right down to the individual operating out of his or her home. The format and quality can be adjusted to fulfill the needs of any business operation and to justify the level of expenditure available.

NEWSLETTERS

To explain the impact of a newsletter, it is necessary to understand how the receiver of such a publication reacts. In most firms, newsletters are produced because the company employs so many people, or has so many clients, it is the only way to communicate with them. Receivers of your newsletter will, nine times out of ten, apply **that** reasoning to your newsletter! It is also worth bearing in mind that a newsletter every two or three months costs far less than a salesperson, and can reach many more people for the investment made. To the client or potential client, a newsletter *implies* you have more clients than you can reach by other means for the circulation of general information.

In human terms, the past or existing client will usually react with gratitude that you include them in the growth of your business. The reasoning for this can be explained in very simple terms, and in a way few executives even consider. When you realize that the supplier/client relationship is more intense on the part of the client, the use of a newsletter becomes a very important service. The supplier firm may have many clients, but usually the client only has one supplier in your field—you; therefore, the client has a vested interest in you or your firm. **The client wants to know you are successful,** mainly because it vindicates his or her belief in your ability. The newsletter both protects and exploits this singular interest and concern of your past and existing clients while, at the same time, helps you to increase your image and introduce other services to past or existing clients.

Format is, of course, important and the image you wish to promote must be the overriding factor of both content and design. Involving a consultant (public relations, graphic or your printer) can pay good dividends, however, insist upon seeing several examples of their work, comparing their past work and such things as cost, time involved and circulation factors.

There are several formats and levels of quality, and deciding upon the approach to be used is probably the most important factor towards producing a successful program. Of all the methods available there are five which can be generally recommended depending upon your size of operation and the budget you have available.

1. **Four-Color Magazine Format**
For the large firm, this impressive image-builder format may be almost dictated to describe international and prestigious projects. (For the small firm, however, a once-a-year publication on this scale is often valuable and very worthwhile.) Layout is usually "letter size" pages (8 1/2" x 11" for the USA, A4 8 1/4" x 11 3/4" international metric size for foreign markets) on quality gloss paper. In this case, where the majority of recipients will be business people, it is wise to follow the popular *Business* publication's layout and style for print and graphics.

It is also worth pointing out that important savings can be made by using *color separations* from published articles you have obtained in the past. Most publishers will allow you access to their material of your work, at a nominal cost, provided you allow them credits, as will your suppliers.

For the creative or high quality supplier, following the accepted format of the more prestigious magazines can add status to your work. The first item in such a newsletter should always be a *letter* from the principal or chief executive outlining progress and future goals.

2. **The Quality Two-Color Newsletter**

Experience suggests the tabloid format of a 11″ x 17″ page size for the USA (A3 11 3/4″ x 16 1/2″ international metric size) on a quality gloss paper to be the best vehicle for this newsletter. Using a grid of five columns of text 2″ wide, and a spot color for titles, backgrounds, or screenings allows a very professional effect to be developed at an economic cost.

3. **The Newspaper Format**

Using the same tabloid layout format as for example two, but on a cheaper non-gloss paper, and possibly with only one color.

4. **The In-house Format**

A letter size layout using only black and white, this is the cheapest method of all, and can be successfully run on a photocopier and then stapled together in-house. One tip for lifting the quality is to have the cover pre-printed in the company's color, with logo and title, before photocopying on the text. Even the typesetting in this case can be produced on an electric typewriter. If this format is chosen it must be obvious that it is an in-house publication, in content as well as format, so be sure to include news of staff, weddings, vacations, etc., to make this fact clear.

5. **The Journal Format**

Using a letter size format this production should be voluminous (20 pages at least) and cover every possible fact of interest since the last issue (new services, reprints, promotions, etc.). Its face value is to record every development since the previous issue. It is a reading piece, an educational tool, and should be academic in presentation.

Whichever format is right for you, the newsletter should be used to strengthen the relationship between your firm and your past clients, and to interest potential clients in using your products or service. Therefore, it is just as important to develop a mailing list of who should receive it, as it is to produce the newsletter itself. You should also produce sufficient copies so that you have enough to leave with potential clients after the first meeting with them.

Finally, and most important, make sure **all** the addresses and telephone numbers a potential client might use to make contact with you are prominently displayed in your publication.

POSITIVE CHALLENGE MARKETING

As everyone knows who is involved in marketing any product or service, there is always the point in the conversation with a potential buyer when he lays down his idea of 'perfect service.' It is also, of course, the ambition of every sales and marketing executive to get to that point where the potential client moves into the position where he is 'ready to hear what you have to offer.'

Taking that most basic of facts, I decided some years ago that if

I could come up with a method whereby I could actually challenge the potential client with an offer of 'perfect service' which met his guidelines rather than those of my own production and delivery people, then in theory he would have no alternative but to give me the chance to 'get in on a trial basis.'

Everyone also knows that 'perfect service' is a combination of many factors in the eyes of many individuals, but at the time I had some time to spare and I was meeting a lot of people through my lecturing engagements, so I started asking questions and sure enough, after several months I came up with a possible approach. The next problem was to find someone willing to risk a few thousand dollars to try the system out, because like the cobbler and his children's lack of shoes, I never felt that it 'was suited' to my own business. As it was, I got lucky, and I was approached by a company that did not have a lot of time or money to reverse a situation of falling sales. I made the offer, laid out the principles of the system, and the price was right.

The results were so much better than anyone had ever expected, including me, that I have since used the system several times with the same effect. I even proved that it did apply to my business, to my amazement I confess, and to date it has never failed. To those of you who have worked with 'mailing campaigns' it might interest you even more when I tell you that to date, the lowest response rate when the program was managed the way I am going to lay it out for you has never produced less than a **37% response rate leading to an actual meeting being arranged!**

To explain it completely I am going to use examples:

1. My own program, including the complete artwork for illustration purposes.

2. The 'Reasons' for a very specialized Non-Destructive Testing Service.

Warning: Be absolutely sure that everything you say you will do is well within your known and tested capabilities. Your own and your organization's future reputation depend upon it!

Step 1. The first step is a simple one. Call all of your clients and ask them what they like about your business, products, service, people, pricing policy, etc. (While you are doing this, you have a perfect opportunity to ask for references from those who say the best things about you and your organization, etc.).

(See **Organized Referral Marketing.**)

Step 2. Call some of the people you have recently lost on proposals when they awarded the contract to someone else. Ask them politely why they chose the other bidder. Ask them what they would consider to be 'perfect service' from a company such as your own.

Even ask them what they did not like about your way of trying to get work.

Step 3. Make a list of 'reasons to consider doing business with your organization' from your own experience in the business or profession you are in.

If, after this 'self-examination' you are still sure you want to be in the business you are in, and working for the firm that gives you your check at the end of the month, you can now develop a set of 'Reasons to Consider.'

Remember you are putting yourself on the line. You are making promises, or challenges if you wish, to get someone to listen to you explain why you are at least as good as, and probably better, than your competition. You had better be able to live up to, or be better than, everything you say about yourself!

The Program consists of four printed items:

1. A top-quality envelope. (If you have ever considered improving your stationery graphics, do it now!)
2. A custom-printed Rolodex Card.
3. A 'Return Paid' postcard.
4. A 'Fold-Over' card on quality stock that will measure 4'' x 8 1/2'' when folded.

Remember, the best quality is the most economical with this program. I suggest you use exactly the same card stock for everything except the envelope, which of course should be the paper-weight version of the same stock. The color of everything must match for visual effect.

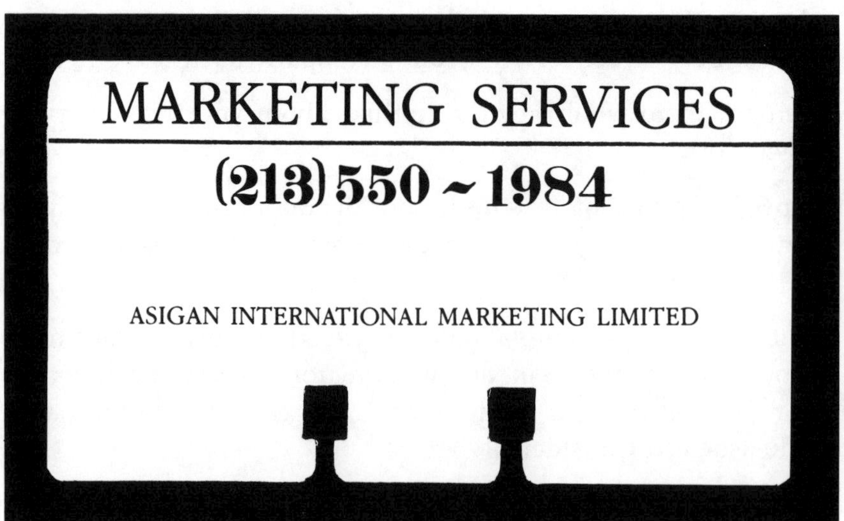

MARKETING SERVICES
(213) 550 ~ 1984
ASIGAN INTERNATIONAL MARKETING LIMITED

Increase the print size of your telephone number (which, incidentally, should be one or a series confined to handling this program).

Using the same ink color as you have used to print the main type content of the package, either use larger 'bold' typeface or reverse the words out of a solid color block that best describes the service or product range you are offering.

ASIGAN INTERNATIONAL MARKETING LIMITED

☐ I have received your material and would like to request further information, testimonials and details of the services you can provide.

☐ I have received your material and have placed it in our files for further reference.

Name ______________________ Title ______________________

City ____

State ______________________ Zip ______________________

Telephone ____

As you will soon recognize, either of the answers provided for your prospect to 'tick' give you the opportunity to call him or her. The first is to set up an appointment, and the second is to check that they have enough data to be able to judge you by when they come across a situation where they might consider your product or service.

The information asked for will also assist you and should they omit something, you have the perfect opportunity to call his or her secretary and establish a relationship for future dealings with them.

You will need to contact the Post Office to arrange a license to pay

No Postage
Necessary
If Mailed
In The
United States

BUSINESS REPLY MAIL
First Class Permit No. Beverly Hills, CA

Postage will be paid by addressee

ASIGAN INTERNATIONAL MARKETING LIMITED

for the cards that will be returned to you. This is a simple matter, but it should be done as a first priority as you will need the license number before you can even begin the artwork for this program.

The layout shown is (at the time of printing) exactly what the Post

Office demands; it is also to the exact size required. You can use this as artwork if you just change the Return Address and License Number details.

As I mentioned before, emboss, use foil stamping or the latest in print technology to make sure your cover is of the highest quality the receiver has ever had cross his desk.

Use the back page, if you wish, to list 'past clients,' 'references,' or any other data that will increase the 'belief factor' of the piece.

Make sure that the address and telephone numbers shown are as complete as it is possible to make them.

1. Use the complete postal zip code.
2. NEVER abbreviate words:
   'Avenue'—never 'Ave.'
   'Suite'—never '#' or 'Ste.'
   Every word must be as complete as it can be on the understanding that if you shorten words for convenience, you put visual proof in front of your prospective client that you will 'miss or cut things' for convenience or lack of oversight when doing their work.
3. Make sure that the folding process does not leave a bad appearance to the piece as a whole. Edges should meet at all sides, and the fold should not damage the ink or the cardstock itself.

Reasons To Consider

ASIGAN INTERNATIONAL MARKETING LIMITED

1 Results—that is the name of the game in Marketing. The only way to spend your marketing dollars is to relate them directly to results—the actual New Business they bring in.

2 You need to know you are getting the best your money can buy, that you can rely on us to produce results, on time and on budget. You need to know the price you are quoted is the price you will be billed; but above all you need to know that promises made will be promises kept. We invite you to test us, and to go on testing us; you will find that we really can do as well as we promise, everytime.

3 With us the exception is the rule. Present us with any marketing problem and we will solve it. In the very rare case that we can not deliver the specific results you need then we will help you to locate someone who can.

4 When you work with us you are always talking to the decision maker. They will rarely have to check back with the office, because we trust our specialists, and therefore you can too. We will not keep you waiting for an answer either. Whether your need is local, national or international, it is all handled in-house, so we are able to keep our promises and give commitments.

5 No extras, no excuses, no comebacks; when we quote you a price, that is exactly what you will be billed. We do not believe in expensive surprises, nor do we believe in wasting hard earned profits—we regard it as part of the service to keep your costs as low as possible.

6 Every now and then a rush job will come up. When that happens our clients can rely on us moving mountains to get them out of the hole. We regard our clients as friends and partners, and we work to keep it that way.

7 Your work will never sit around someone else's office while you are losing both time and money. In other words, if we say something will be done by Friday morning, then you can make plans for Friday afternoon.

8 Our services include: Marketing Audits, Business Analysis, Marketing Plan Development, Public Relations, Image Marketing, Advertising, Sales Training, Systems Implementation, Turnaround Services, Mailing Programs, New Product Launch, Market Research, Market Targeting, International Marketing and many others. If you have a marketing need, we can probably find the solution at a cost you can accept, and we will save you money, time and frustration when you work with us.

10 Reasons To Consider

Cedillos

TESTING COMPANY INCORPORATED

1 We want your business, and to keep it we will work harder, faster, more effectively and more efficiently. We never forget that the customer is the most important person in our company.

2 Service is important, so we guarantee to collect the product from you within 24 hours of you calling us to pick it up. You can call us 24 hours a day. In most cases during the working day we will be on our way to collect what you want tested within less than 2 hours.

3 If your product sits in our laboratory you are losing money. Therefore we offer an unusual guarantee; if we do not meet the delivery time we give you when we take your order—we will not charge you. If we say it will be done by Monday morning, then you can make plans for Monday afternoon.

4 With us the exception is the rule. Present us with your non-destructive testing problem and we will solve it. In the very rare case we can not do the work we will locate the establishment that can, because we really do care.

5 Certification of non-destructive testing is an important sales tool for your company, so we provide you with professional documentation, to hand on to your client, at no extra charge.

6 Every now and then a rush job comes up. Our clients can rely upon us to move mountains in such a case, our 24 hour call-in service is there to get them out of such holes. We like to think of our customers as our friends, and we try hard to earn their friendship.

7 When you place an order with us, the person you will be talking to is a qualified, and experienced, testing engineer. They will rarely need to "check back with the office," we trust our specialists...and so can you.

8 No extras, no excuses and no comebacks. When we quote you a price, that is what you will pay. If circumstances mean we have to run the test twice, or for that matter ten times, you will only pay what you agreed to pay when you placed the order with us. (Rework excepted.)

9 Non-destructive testing includes ultrasonic, x-ray, magnetic particle, penetrant, etching, passivation, grinding and sand blasting, we do it all, efficiently and professionally. We have a saying at Cedillos, "If a customer uses us once, they will never go anywhere else."

10 You need to know you are getting quality service; that you can rely on us when a rush job comes up; that delivery dates will be met; that the price quoted will be the price billed; but most of all you need to know that promises made will be promises kept...therefore we think you need Cedillos Testing Company.

Now you see the reasoning. You are offering your prospective client everything he or she ever dreamed of in service and assistance. You are challenging that person to use something they always stated did not exist. You are asking them to 'prove you wrong.' Who could resist such an offer? Could you do so if a potential supplier approached you in the same way?

All you have to do is develop your own 'Reasons to Consider,' along the lines of the examples given. To manage the program, use the Marketing Plan Control Sheet included in this book. You can make copies on a weekly basis for management purposes. Do not 'mass mail' these pieces, for if you were unable to follow-up on replies the total program will re-act against you. Instead, I suggest that you begin with ten a day for two weeks, and then re-evaluate the number you send out each week to maintain a level of activity you can service properly. Also, keep a check relative to the days you make mailings; you may discover that mailing on a particular day of the week or month will provide far better results than other days. As a last suggestion, I have found that by using hand-applied 'special issue' stamps I have achieved better results than by using a meter machine or ordinary stamps.

WRITTEN COMMUNICATION

The professions probably rely more upon written communications than any other type of business, and the most successful professionals realize this and develop the talent in every way they can, but all firms can benefit by utilizing the long lasting impact of the written word. Spoken words are said, and then disappear, to be forgotten or explained further until the true result is an understanding, an individual and singular creation of argument and exchange. The written word however stands on its own, is recorded, and can rarely be successfully denied or explained. Parents often urge their children to *put nothing in writing,* so do our legal and professional advisors— until it has been checked by them. So always bear in mind that your letters, articles about you or your firm, contracts and all other *written opinions* or explanations are vitally important to your image and your business.

Many firms go out and hire public relations consultants to write for them, but forget that it is unlikely that the person who writes their PR is as conversant with their business or profession as they are. The rule should always be—no release of anything until you have checked (and double-checked with your advisors) every word, statement and opinion. Without your **written** approval, nothing should be sent out for potential clients to read. If you are employed by a firm to produce written communication pieces, it is wise to clear everything with the principal, president, or your superior, and get them to *initial* the letter or release before you send it out. Whether you are writing an article, letter or contract (or delegating it to someone else), the following guidelines are important.

1. **Keep it simple and understandable.**

Professional people tend to develop their own *language* with which they converse with each other. The problem often forgotten is that the potential client usually does not understand the terminology. Therefore, keep such phrases and words to a minimum, dispense with them altogether, or explain what they mean where possible.

When communicating with a potential client, bear in mind their background and use phrases and words from *their* vocabulary or *business jargon* where appropriate. The foreigner (nationality or discipline) reading a proposal which he or she is mentally translating will be favorably impressed by your attempts to make understanding easier. (Never take anything for granted—for example, in working with clients on an international basis, I have even translated terminology; simple cases—even in English—exist to prove the point: a *saddle* in New York becomes a *threshold strip* to an English designer; *door hardware* becomes *door furniture* in the same exchange.)

Yet another laughable, but serious when fully considered example was a company director who was most upset after taking time to hear a lunch-time speech on *Space Planning* only to find it had nothing to do with *communication satellites.* Perhaps it sounds far-fetched and relatively unimportant—but the truth is that the client is paying, and therefore can demand that you talk in their language, or they can hire someone who will.

2. **Keep it short and interesting.**

While advising that all written communication should be kept short, to the point and interesting, it is also important that everything which needs to be stated is included. The easiest way to solve this paradox in advice is to rely upon editing to create the right compromise. Follow the steps below and, nine times out of ten, the improvement can double the effectiveness of your written communication.

1. Begin by adopting the frame of mind that you have been asked to *fully* explain whatever the subject is you are going to write about.
2. List all the subjects, statements and opinions you wish to include.
3. Allow the prose to take over and write for yourself, fully expounding everything you wish to, using analogy, metaphor and poetic license.
4. Go through your completed *masterpiece* and *underline* or *yellow highlight* the obvious mistakes, use of the same word

repeatedly, and spelling mistakes.

5. Have the *corrected* copy typed out and then *underline the main points* and *blue pencil* anything that is not necessary to your communication.
6. Use a thesaurus to make sure no words are used too often, and to make meanings stronger.
7. Type out the final proof—check it for spelling mistakes and layout.

You should then have a tool for communication which will do what you created it for.

3. **Keep it effective.**

In your initial synopsis for any written communication, there is a need to consider what all marketing literature, articles and letters are expected to achieve, and that is to interest the reader or convince potential clients to hire you. The three parts of all written marketing material can be summarized as:

i. **Ego-satisfaction** for the reader.
ii. **Hooks** to create two-way communication opportunities.
iii. **Window dressing** to hide or develop the former two parts.

Ego-satisfaction for the reader means simply that you should endeavor to build a situation where the potential client can *agree* with you, and feel that you **want** to work with them on the terms they wish.

Hooks are words or phrases which implant in the piece *satisfaction* with your ability, knowledge and professionalism. Hooks are also used to make the reader **want** to know more, to **want** to associate with you, and to believe you **know** the subject you are writing about.

Window dressing is used to soften these first two parts from immediate recognition, *hard sell,* or even rejection for disagreement on reasoning.

The reader should feel interested from the outset through to completion and find reasons to share your opinions. The potential client does not want to be told anything, even if they recognize that they *need* to be *told.* What they want is to be able to:

i. Learn for themselves.
ii. Increase their understanding and knowledge.
iii. Reach their own decision (based on good advice).
iv. Retain control of the situation.

Therefore, throughout your written material you should maintain the position of *advisor.* To explain these points consider the following:

Dear Mr. Whatever:

As you know, there is hardly a publication or authoritative report today which does not forecast severe difficulties ahead for what we have come to know as "the expansion economy."

Many businesses have, of course, come to rely upon the benefits such an economy produces, and any variation or setback to accepted patterns or developments could provide a reverse to the fortunes of those companies.

We have lately spent a great deal of time analyzing the best actions available to counter such a setback, should it take hold, and the results are quite interesting and in some cases, surprising.

We would therefore be most grateful if you would allow us a little of your time to describe our findings, and gain your evaluation of them.

This presentation could be used to gain interest in just about anything (I do not care what you are 'selling,' send out the letters and you will see for yourself). The **ego-satisfaction** assumed the reader is up-to-date, well informed and is important enough to receive such *authoritative reports,* etc. The **hooks** were *potential problems* and *we might have the answer* in return for a no-obligation short amount of time to listen. The rest was **window dressing**—nowhere did we mention what we were *selling,* although the letterhead of course told the reader who we were. There was no *hint* of low level (that is less than executive) contact. All the letters were title signed by an officer of the company; in other words, no *hard sales.* The letter was designed only to open the door; it was produced to be followed by a phone call to gain an appointment to explain the *ideas raised* on a face-to-face basis. Of course, just getting the potential client to see you does not mean they will hire you. However, unless you get to see people you will not even get the chance to sell your products, ideas or services.

Please refer to Checklist Number 9 on page 318.

Please refer to Checklist Number 10 on page 319.

FORMS

The forms in this book are the result of many years development and adaptation, and as far as forms are able to be general in application, they can be used to perform the management tasks of almost any marketing investigation. The need for careful analysis is essential in the development and monitoring of any marketing program, and using the examples described and illustrated as models, will enable you to create more precise forms and analysis programs to meet your own particular needs in any given situation.

PUBLIC RELATIONS DATA FORM©

FILE REFERENCE CODE

OFFICE | month | day | year | week number

1. Name of Client

2. Address of Client

Town or City | County or State

Postal Code | TELEPHONE

3. Corporation or Government Link

4. Link Liaison Address

Town or City | County or State

Postal Code | TELEPHONE

5. Name of Project

6. Address of Project

Town or City | County or State

Postal Code | TELEPHONE

7. Involved Party

DEALER ☐
AGENT ☐
ARCHITECT ☐
DESIGNER ☐
BROKER ☐
other

Address

Town or City | County or State

Postal Code | TELEPHONE

8. RELEASE DETAILS

NO RELEASE OF INFORMATION IS TO BE MADE TO THE PRESS OR ANY OTHER PARTY PRIOR TO OBTAINING THE WRITTEN PERMISSION OF THESE PEOPLE

Name

Address

Town or City | County or State

Postal Code | TELEPHONE

Name

Address

Town or City | County or State

Postal Code | TELEPHONE

9. IN-HOUSE RELEASE

NO RELEASE OF INFORMATION WITHOUT THE APPROVAL OF THESE EXECUTIVES

Name | TELEPHONE

Name | TELEPHONE

10. Project Description

11. Sales Executive

12. Production

13. Design by

Graphic Material Included — NUMBER

Black & White 10"x 8" GLOSSIES ☐
Color Positives ☐
Color Slides ☐
Artist's Impression ☐
Technical Drawings ☐
other ☐

14. Further information is available from:

Name
Contact | Telephone

Name
Contact | Telephone

Name
Contact | Telephone

15. Contract/Order signed — month | day | year

16. Construction/Delivery Start — month | day | year

17. Construction/Delivery Complete — month | day | year

18. Size of Project

19. Value of Project — $

20. Release Details

SUBMISSION DATE			NAME OF PUBLICATION	PUBLISHED		TEAR

PUBLIC RELATIONS DATA FORM

To assist your public relations effort it is wise to prepare a synopsis of every completed project, assembling all the relevant facts which are *releasable.* This report should be related by code or file number to the relevant files and photographs, etc., and then kept in a separate publicity file for use by the sales team, public relations department or consultant, and those engaged in research for new promotional programs.

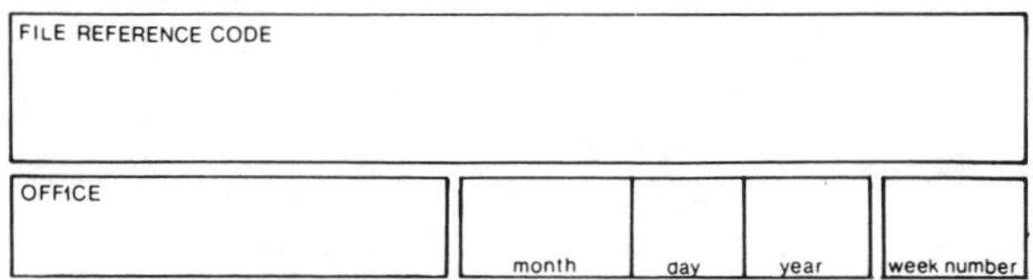
FILE REFERENCE CODE

OFFICE | month | day | year | week number

File Reference Code—This entry will relate each form to the relevant file and records, and it can use any series of letters and numbers to meet your requirements for fast information. For example:

CN	---4	---2007	---/81
initials of sales executive	office	proposal number in issue order	year

Office—If you operate from more than one location or have geographic territories for sales management purposes, enter the relevant office or territory in this box.

Date—Enter the month, day and year, and week number that this form was started.

1. Name of Client	

NAME OF THE CLIENT

Enter the full name of the client (as it appears on their letterhead).

2. Address of Client		
	Town or City	County or State
	Postal Code	TELEPHONE

ADDRESS OF CLIENT

The full postal address should be entered and the telephone number should include all dialing and extension codes. Remember, sometimes the editor or contact you send releases to will need to confirm details with your client.

3. Corporation or Government Link	

CORPORATION OR GOVERNMENT LINK

It assists your image and the importance of your release in the eyes of an editor if the project has wide appeal or importance. Therefore, if your client is *owned, involved with,* or *controlled by* a more well-known name, you can use this fact to gain attention.

4. Link Liaison Address		
	Town or City	County or State
	Postal Code	TELEPHONE

LINK LIAISON ADDRESS

As you have already noted the corporation or government *link* involved, the first box in this entry should be the full or official title. The address should be complete and the telephone number should include all codes. (This *link*, including the name of your contact and his or her telephone number and extension, should be entered in the first entry of Question 14 regarding sources of further information.)

5. Name of Project	

NAME OF PROJECT

Enter the name of the building, department, or a title that could be used for an editorial release in this box.

6. Address of Project		
	Town or City	County or State
	Postal Code	TELEPHONE

ADDRESS OF PROJECT

If the project is at a different location to the Client's Address noted in answer to Question 2, enter the details here, if the address is the same enter **N/A as for 2.**

7. Involved Party		
DEALER ☐	Address	
AGENT ☐		
ARCHITECT ☐	Town or City	County or State
DESIGNER ☐		
BROKER ☐	Postal Code	TELEPHONE
other		

INVOLVED PARTY

This firm or person could be who gave you the introduction, your agent or dealer, an architect or broker, or anyone who needs to be kept informed or can help in building your public relations release. Mark the relevant box as to their occupation or write it in the box **other** if it is different from the examples shown. Then enter their full address and telephone number.

8. RELEASE DETAILS NO RELEASE OF INFORMATION IS TO BE MADE TO THE PRESS OR ANY OTHER PARTY PRIOR TO OBTAINING THE WRITTEN PERMISSION OF THESE PEOPLE		
	Name	
	Address	
	Town or City	County or State
	Postal Code	TELEPHONE
	Name	
	Address	
	Town or City	County or State
	Postal Code	TELEPHONE

RELEASE DETAILS

It is often necessary, or even imposed upon you, that certain involved parties need to check your releases before they are submitted for publication or release. If this is the case, enter the details of these parties and ensure you receive **written** agreement releases, copies of which should be attached to this form before any release is made.

9. IN-HOUSE RELEASE NO RELEASE OF INFORMATION WITHOUT THE APPROVAL OF THESE EXECUTIVES		
	Name	TELEPHONE
	Name	TELEPHONE

IN-HOUSE RELEASE

If certain officers of your company need to agree or *check* your releases, enter their names in this section and follow the advice given in relation to Question 8 above.

10. Project Description

PROJECT DESCRIPTION

This entry should be as complete as possible and backup material should be attached to this form. Product numbers, codes, colors, etc., should be accurate and everything you might need in relation to information should be noted here, for example:

1. Project description
2. Brochures
3. Client's PR "news clippings"

11. Sales Executive

SALES EXECUTIVE

The name of the person who negotiated or was in overall charge of the project, order or contract should be entered in this box, including their extension number.

12. Production

PRODUCTION

The name of the executive in your firm responsible for production, installation or construction should be entered in this box.

13. Design by

DESIGN BY

The name of the person who designed the product, was responsible for the design, or drew up plans or working documents should be entered in this box. Include their extension number.

Graphic Material Included		NUMBER
Black & White 10"x 8" GLOSSIES	□	
Color Positives	□	
Color Slides	□	
Artist's Impression	□	
Technical Drawings	□	
other	□	

GRAPHIC MATERIAL INCLUDED

By noting what graphic material is available, there is less chance of it being mislaid. Extra material should be indicated by marking **other** and inserting the file numbers to show where it is held.

14. Further information is available from:	
Name	
Contact	Telephone
Name	
Contact	Telephone
Name	
Contact	Telephone

FURTHER INFORMATION IS AVAILABLE FROM

Enter the names of the firms, organizations, etc., who have more information, noting the name of the person to be contacted and his or her telephone number.

15.Contract/Order signed	month	day	year

CONTRACT/ORDER SIGNED

Enter the relevant date.

16.Construction/Delivery Start	month	day	year

CONSTRUCTION/DELIVERY START

17. Construction/Delivery Complete	month	day	year

CONSTRUCTION/DELIVERY COMPLETE

18.Size of Project	

SIZE OF PROJECT

Enter the number of items, area, etc., which constitute the contract, order or project.

19. Value of Project	$

VALUE OF PROJECT

Enter the *release agreed* sum which all parties involved have agreed to make public, or the words 'Not for Release.'

RELEASE DETAILS

20.Release Details						
SUBMISSION DATE			NAME OF PUBLICATION	PUBLISHED		TEAR

1. **Submission Date**
   The month, day and year a submission was made.
2. **Name of Publication**
   Enter the name of the paper, magazine or other media channel the submission was sent to.
3. **Published**
   Month and year of publication.

   If the article or release was rejected enter this fact across the last three boxes.
4. **Tear**
   Mark to indicate that a *Tear Sheet* or a copy of the published release or article was obtained.

This form is essential for efficient Public Relations Management and will make the systems described in Chapter Six, **Image Marketing** more controllable for all concerned.

"We can talk about your new mailer right now Sir, just let me dump this junk mail first."

CHAPTER SEVEN

CONSOLIDATION MARKETING METHODS

The following methods of marketing rely upon time and track record, so the sooner the gathering of material is put in motion, the sooner they can be implemented. These methods provide the *marketing tools* for your negotiations, or for your sales staff to use during business meetings with potential clients. The product of these methods will make it easier to convince the client to choose or commission your firm.

PRICE BENEFIT MARKETING

Price Benefit Marketing is based on the theory that everyone wishes to use their capital in the most efficient manner. It can be used to inform clients that for some reason (i.e., bulk purchase), it is possible to supply them at a price cheaper than other suppliers are able to, without loss of quality. It is not *price cutting,* but rather a *more quality for a reasonable price* reputation-builder. It can also be used as a system of purchasing management in that your clients are able to employ your experience and expertise to better manage their use of capital expenditure.

Many firms do in fact have a role they can play to the benefit of their clients in purchasing management, due to their experience in their own area of business. Contrary to the sometimes voiced opinion that professional buyers do not welcome advice from outsiders and suppliers, the fact is that buyers are usually very pleased to receive any help they can get in those areas outside of their own day-to-day experience. Most buyers specialize, to some extent or another, even if their methods have the same roots of education. Therefore, being able to rely upon someone with in-depth knowledge in a buying area they are not really conversant with, to ensure proper preparation of orders, specification of details, experience in delivery planning, and obtaining the best maintenance, service, installation or warranty contracts, etc., is a very valuable service that they are usually keen to employ.

Experience proves that many firms and individuals provide this service by way of friendly advice to their clients to some extent, but do not fully exploit its new business gaining potential. Most firms already have systems for organizing purchasing management and reference libraries full of maintenance procedures, relevant techniques, or advice listings. This information can provide assistance in many areas which the client will appreciate far more than any other long-term trust-building tool can provide. An occasional bulletin put out by your office on new products, maintenance methods or tools, or other such information will do as much good as any expensive lunch for the buyer, or bouquet for his or her secretary.

This method is in fact a strong strategy in long-term exposure, and will convince potential clients that your service is able to provide them with *better for less* than they might achieve employing another organization. The need is to constantly work to the point where you can assert (and prove) that the use of your service is at least economically sensible for the client to employ, and might actually reduce the clients capital expenditure without reducing quality or product life.

QUALITY BENEFIT MARKETING

Quality Benefit Marketing is aimed at the knowledgeable prospective client. The theory being that these people purchase goods or services to *lengthen* the return of their investment or to increase their status and image.

There are two methods of employing this system, the first is simple —issue a guarantee or warranty for a period of time longer than expected by the client and more comprehensive than the guarantee of your competitors or imposed codes and legal requirements.

The second method is to build a reputation for quality work, which is proven by documented examples well known to the client. You must be able to convince potential clients that:

1. Clients continue to use products or services in preference to your competitors because experience has proven that you are the best.
2. Experience shows that your products or work outlasts your competitor's work because the quality is higher.
3. Because of your experience and expertise, you are chosen by the most professional and successful companies and organizations more often than any of your competitors.

Implementation

Establish examples which fall into the three categories, with as many names as possible of international or well-known clients. Develop *explanatory sales plans* in an audio-visual or graphic concept, making up a *history of your performance* over a period of years. It should become something which can be seen as a history of your organization (and part of the history of the total philosophy of your profession or business) where you can show your development of expertise.

The problems which arise from the client talking *budgets,* while the sales executive talks about *aesthetics, function, and design considerations* are probably the greatest contributor to client/supplier frustration. There can be no quick or true answer to the client watching a slide show of past projects, who inquires the *square-foot price* of each shot as it appears on the screen. Few things can be judged on *quantity* or *price per square foot,* and yet if we exchange places with the potential client for a moment, it does seem to be the only logical question for them to ask to arrive at a budget. The point is that quality is something the client will always want—without writing a blank check.

Organized marketing should create a situation where the client **wants** to buy your product or to hire you or your firm, and to achieve this you must in turn create a *knowledge* rather than a *feeling* of trust in your advice. One of the easiest ways to show potential clients your interest in quality is to create a series of **Comparison Alternatives.** There are two ways to do this while your competitors are still trying to evaluate the client's *needs,* the first—**Comparison Boards** are relatively easy and quite inexpensive to produce. The second is far more effective, time-consuming and costly, and it is called **Model Alternative Comparison** (MAC for short).

1. **Comparison Boards**

Creation: (related to commercial interior design as an example here, but other services can be illustrated in the same way of course).

1. Draw a plan of a 1,000 square foot space.
2. Choose from relative cost examples—e.g., $45, $75, $100 per square foot.
3. Calculate your fee percentage (as an extra) in varying sizes of say 1,000, 3,000, 10,000 and 50,000+ square feet in each of these categories.

4. Choose the components, e.g., floor coverings, drapes, furniture, accessories, seating, plants, etc., which would total to the square footage costs you have established (Item 2) for each example.
5. Produce a schedule for each scheme, with probable delivery dates, etc.
6. Make up sample boards for each scheme.
7. Make up *available product Comparison Boards* for each price range. The reason you will need both *sample boards* and *Comparison Boards* is that the client might like the $45 scheme but reject it because of the chairs, or some other item. The *Comparison Board* takes each scheme and shows alternatives using manufacturer's photographs within the same price range. For example, let us imagine your $45 scheme, for which you paste up photographs of every item you have used, you would then need to also paste on that board (say) four other chairs of approximately the same cost, and so on for every item.

2. **Model Alternative Comparison**

This method is expensive but was long ago recognized as very productive by showrooms and stores. It merely transfers your *Comparison Boards* alternative schemes to real life (room displays). If you have the space, then the real thing is very effective; but few businesses or firms do have the space, therefore, either of the following methods can be used instead.

1. Rent a space and create a set like film companies do, and install your schemes. Then record them on film and dismantle them. Many manufacturers will loan you products to do this.
2. Build scale models of the schemes you have designed,

backed by an elaborate sample board for each showing your choice (and several alternatives) by using *Comparison Boards.*

Both the *Comparison Boards* and the *Model Alternative Comparison* systems allow the client to visualize why and how his or her money will be used, and the negotiator can more easily explain the reasoning for any budget and the design implications. You are not trying to sell the schemes used as examples, but just visualize for the client the relative cost factors.

There was study some years ago which concluded human understanding was influenced by our five senses to the following levels: ***SIGHT—****60%,* ***HEARING—****30%, and* ***TOUCH, SMELL*** *and* ***TASTE—****10%.* With this in mind, *Comparison Boards* should increase the potential client's recognition of your *quality awareness* by at least double.

There is always the tendency to credit a client with an ability to understand when in fact there may be less understanding than there is trust. Trust in your capability, taste, experience, etc., etc., which could mean that real communication breaks down. Therefore, if it is possible to create "visual explanations" of comparison, not only is communication made easier, but it also allows you to provide the very service you have assumed—true explanation.

IMAGE BENEFIT MARKETING

There are many potential clients who do not realize just how much they need your products or services, and some who think they cannot afford them. Obviously, you can make a case for both of them doing so—it would improve their image (it might also improve their efficiency, but that is of secondary importance with this type of client). What this category of client needs more than anything is an immediate *new image* or a *confidence statement.* The reason could be one of a thousand, or a variety of reasons, but usually the following are near the top of the list:

1. They have a terrible record of staff turnover.
2. Their shares are dropping faster than rain drops in a monsoon.
3. Their sales have dropped recently.
4. They are beset by rumors (take-over, bankruptcy, etc.).

In many cases, however, the potential client for this type of approach is not in any immediate financial trouble. Also, it is not unusual that the top management have never considered your solution to their daily problems. (If the company **is** in financial trouble, then obviously your invoices must be guaranteed by a third party or payments must be made 'in advance.')

In the business world in general, there are few company meetings that put the subject of *image generated by our facilities* high on their agenda of regular debate. Those that do we can all quote immediately, only to realize how few they are. The sources from which it is possible to predict potential business on the assumption of this method are readily available in the press everyday, and sales executives who do not take the financial newspapers are really restricting their ability to identify potential clients **before** they enter the general market. Of course, just walking in and talking non-specifics and generalities is counterproductive; you need to understand the background and needs from the business angle, as well as the humanistic and aesthetic viewpoints. Therefore, it can be very effective to be able to offer clients a way in which you can assist them to analyze the *differences* between what they have now and what their competitors have. Possibly the best method is to gain the input of everyone working in the firm or department you are aiming at. This method is far simpler than it at first appears if you can construct a program for behavioral psychology research—a set of questions requiring a choice from a selection of alternatives—which you can evaluate for the potential client as a true representation of what their staff, clients or users of their facilities actually **want,** and what they **need** to do to achieve those requirements, improve efficiency and *promote their image.*

Typical questions for staff members could be:

a) *Compared to other firms you have worked with, do you believe your present working conditions are:*

   FAR BETTER—MARGINALLY BETTER—ABOUT SAME—NOT SO GOOD—FAR WORSE.

b) *Of your reasons for continuing to work here, where would you rate "working conditions" in the following list:*

   1. Salary and benefits
   2. Company social program
   3. Pride in the company's work
   4. Pride in the company's reputation
   5. Friendship with co-workers
   6. Promotion possibilities
   7. Working conditions

c) *Which of the following do you believe would allow you to work better:*

   MORE NOISE—EXISTING NOISE LEVEL—LESS NOISE
   MORE HEAT—EXISTING HEAT—LESS HEAT
   MORE PRIVACY—EXISTING AMOUNT OF PRIVACY—MORE OPEN ENVIRONMENT

Obviously, the aid of a qualified and experienced behavioral psychologist to help you word your questions would be an asset, and if you wish to do the job fully, then such help is essential.

There is, of course, another time when the *image* of a potential client can be used to advantage. This opportunity to employ **Image Benefit Marketing** arises when a major unit of an operation is about to be sold. Spending a little to *improve* something prior to its being sold, can be a very small percentage of the actual selling price and can mean a faster sale and, in fact, command a higher price that could produce extra profit as well as covering your invoice. Once a promotion package has been developed, the most interested potential contacts would be other interested parties who would find such a service very helpful.

ORGANIZED REFERRAL MARKETING

Organized Referral Marketing is gathering and utilizing references of the expertise, quality and usefulness of your product or service from past clients to interest potential clients. First, it is necessary to identify those areas of business which you have recently found to be profitable, providing regular clients, or producing better than average payment. You then approach the highest executive you can in past client companies within this sector, with the sole intention to gain a written *recommendation of expertise.* There are several ways to do this, all usable and equally valuable:

1. You ask for the president's opinion of your work.
2. Explain what you aim to do and ask for a reference.
3. Collect all *news clippings* and media coverage, obtain *good* high standard photographs, and build case histories.
4. Produce articles and obtain reprints.

Then build an audio-visual or slide program, which consists of three parts:

a) A general introduction to your methodology and systems.
b) A selection of photographs of projects in this particular sector.
c) References from past clients produced in slide form, with the logo of the company concerned (providing that you have already gained the client's approval in writing).

The next step is to isolate potential clients in the given sector and write them a letter offering to show them the presentation, relying upon their curiosity and their wish to gain an insight into what the rest of their industry is doing, to encourage them to invite you to show your presentation.

This program of organized referrals can also be developed into an advertising campaign, beginning with a simple one-line hook, for example, *is your image the image you require?* followed by a list of logos and recommendations from your past clients, with a catch line at the bottom of the advertisement advising interested parties to contact you to see your presentation. These advertisements would then be placed in the relevant magazines of the industry concerned (for example, banks would be approached through professional banking magazines). Of course, and it cannot be said often enough, you must gain the permission of your past clients to publish their recommendations.

Consolidation Marketing can be summed up as *using your past success and experience in an organized manner to create trust with potential clients,* and the methods explained in **Image Marketing** can provide many tools for this ongoing activity. The need, therefore, for anyone who wishes to control growth is to also ensure access to past performance. Cataloging experience into types and categories from the outset of any business is the best way to ensure future access. Imagine that one day someone was going to write a history of your business, imagine what they would need—photographs, prototypes, models, project synopsis reports, etc., etc. Gather this material together and you have the components of **Consolidation Marketing** ready to be put to use.

Marketing is a Management Profession, yet more than almost any other it relies upon the ability and the imagination of individuals to open the way to innovative and conceptual thinking. If everyone followed the same path, or even style, then little would be accomplished. The exploration of new ideas, however, needs careful monitoring, analysis and evaluation if they are to make any return on investment. It all begins when one accepts that, ''where there are potential clients there is a Market to be developed''; then, all one has to do is evaluate which of the million or so opportunities that arise every day will be the most profitable (in every meaning of the word) to develop and accomplish.

Please refer to Checklist Number 11 on page 321.

Please refer to Checklist Number 12 on page 323.

Two tips for the founder -

Nepotism usually does for a business what inter-breeding does to a family.

Never credit others with having or believing what you have or believe, especially when it concerns your own future, or the future of your business.

John Hathaway-Bates
Princeton Club, New York. 1980

CHAPTER EIGHT

TREND MARKETING METHODS

The methods of **PRIMARY MARKETING, IMAGE MARKETING** and **CONSOLIDATION MARKETING** which have been covered so far, are easier to accomplish than the methods of **TREND MARKETING** which follow. The main reason for this being so is that this method of marketing needs a great deal of delegation of management to separate marketing units. In other words, an ongoing commitment is required to support the research and development of systems, tools and information base. Success, more often than not, is a matter of being *in the right place at the right time,* and this is what justifies the investment for the methods of **Trend Marketing.**

RELATED GROWTH MARKETING

Related Growth Marketing—this method is used to establish those areas of business which can be expected to produce potential clients for your organization due to the increase in activity or growth of their clients. Put simply, **Related Growth Marketing** isolates those organizations which are about to experience a sudden increase of business.

In any business, if you could know in advance who will need you, and *when,* before your competitors can find out, you would soon be number one in your field, if only in profits earned. **Related Growth Marketing** can give you advance knowledge of potential clients about to enter the market. The best way to describe it is *learning to predict by logical progression how events in everyday life can* *provide new business opportunities, or knowing and preparing for the right moment when your offer of services will be welcomed by a potential client, before they go out to search for such services.*

Later in this book I cover the system of **Analysis of Capability**—the value of keeping records, the methods of identifying past or existing clients, their main business activity and the dates involved, are also established as important. From such information it is possible to begin to answer the questions of:

1. Why did they buy then?
2. What market situation created a need for your product or service?
3. Who were their clients who provided the cash to pay you?
4. If they were expanding, why then?

The end result is that the decision to hire you is usually the result of many things which might never have been discussed, or even considered in depth, at the time. The main question is not why your clients picked you instead of your competitors (or your competitors instead of you) but **why they were in the market at that particular time, and what was the economic and need situation in their market at that time?** Very little business is done on a whim of the moment. Almost all business decisions are the result of a chain of events and associated circumstances ruling at the time. It is also very probable that if one firm increases, changes or contracts its operations, then the *domino effect* takes hold and many other firms are affected. So you need to know who will be in the market for help due to this action you are, will be, or were part of.

A simple example would be:

Company A sees its market increasing, so it decides to expand. Companies B, C and D supply parts and raw materials to Company A, so in time they will have to expand to supply the increased needs of Company A. The firms who supply services to Company A will also have the opportunity to expand to match Company A's growth (accountants, lawyers, cleaners, caterers, etc.) and can expect more business from Company A's expansion.

Therefore, by knowing that Company A is considering expansion, you can predict those associated with it will grow also. In some cases, you will find that Company A will be very helpful, if only to protect their own future.

One can also use *recognized* changes to promote business. For example (it is only an example, and very simplified):

> *If there was a lot of speculation that the increase in dental education and use of fluoride toothpastes might reduce the number of people seeking dentists' services—and it could be linked to the fact that the number of dentists graduating each year was increasing—and there was "belief" that the standard of managing and furnishing of dentists' surgeries had a lot to do with choice of dentist.....*

Then, by approaching dentists and informing them of these facts, you might interest them in buying your product or service to increase the standard of their surgery.

Another approach, and you were able to prove (or reason) that office costs and inflation would eventually mean dentists would have to *share costs* by uniting to form *dental centers,* it could be profitable to use some of the **Image Marketing** methods in this book to inform them of the *trend* and thereby expect to gain benefits by taking an active part in the creation of dental center buildings which could be purpose-designed and built. The information needed for **Related Growth Marketing** is readily available to everyone, including:

1. Newspapers
2. Trade magazines
3. Chambers of Commerce
4. New legal code publications
5. Radio and television news programs
6. Local and national government reports

By applying logic to present developments in relation to recent historical events, and maintaining a system of management and analysis to understand the implications of such development, it is possible to predict where your services will be needed before the potential client even recognizes the fact.

The display advertisements for executive staff appointments can often be a useful guide to change, and therefore potential business. Just by leaving it a week or so, and then calling the company involved can give you an introduction to a valuable new contact. The advertisement will give you the job title and responsibility and some background on the company itself. Call the company's general number and ask the receptionist something like:

> *I wanted to speak to your (whatever the job title) but I hear you are going to appoint someone new anytime now. I wonder if you could help me, and save me phoning every day. Can you give me some idea of when they are expected to take up the position?*

If you get put through to a secretary, run the same sort of introduction and try to establish as much detail as you can about developments in the company. Be open—and inventive, e.g., *Well, we are __ and I heard you were about to expand—is that right?* or *You seem to be taking on a lot of new staff, you must be expanding faster than anyone around here?* In other words, question, be friendly, take notes and prime your future approach to the new executive.

There are also the *New Business & Contract News* reports from which developments can be assessed. Of course, everyone approaches the listed names, but few firms delve into who else might be about to grow as a direct result—e.g., competitors, suppliers, distributors, agents, etc.

An often unused source of potential new business information is the staff of your firm themselves. The paradox of this situation is that the costs involved are so low, yet can be truly rewarding. To overcome the problem, organize a buffet lunch once a month for every member of your staff who can be considered intelligent, ambitious or mature (which of course means everyone in one of the categories or another), having prepared them to come ready to discuss "potential new business opportunities." Then, record the interchange and spend some time later extracting worthwhile comments and leads, never forgetting that "he who cannot link past, present and potential into a chain of understanding, has nothing save the moment in which he denies the link itself."

Please refer to Checklist Number 13 on page 325.

SYNERGETIC MARKETING

Synergetic Marketing—Creating a new market for a product or service developed for another market. This method is one of the most complex to instigate and can only be done where a company is flexible, and management are prepared to experiment and carry the investment. It depends upon examining your product or service in detail, to see if it can be used for another purpose other than for what it was developed. The problem is, of course, that when you take something (product or service) designed to meet the legal codes and needs of a particular situation and apply it to another, you could find yourself in trouble unless everything has been checked to ensure it is viable, legal, acceptable and economic.

Examining a product, service or manufacturing process to see if it can be used for another function or application to that for which it was developed, needs a different attitude toward examination than most of us were educated to employ. Most text books on market research instruct you to look for markets which *can* use your product or service. With **Synergetic Marketing** you need to do the opposite, try to evaluate markets which *cannot* use your product or service, and then answer the question of *why* those areas of business opportunity are closed to you. Most of the answers to the question, ''Why is our product or service *not* applicable to a particular market?'' just prove that by adaption or redesign they could be. Quite often of course, the necessary changes are economically too high, and in others, the time involved would not be justified, but occasionally whole *new* markets will come to light. For example, System Furniture has been around for a couple of decades in the office market, but it is only in the 1980's that we see the modular desking system evolve into light industrial work stations. This movement of a product designed for offices into the factory, is a perfect example of **Synergetic Marketing.** Soon, when the quality and benefits of light industrial work stations are accepted, we can expect to see ambient lighting, plants, carpets and other 'office equipment' enter the light industrial factory, and firms involved in selling to offices today will have a whole new market to exploit.

In other words, by examining the potential problems of going into a new market, we begin to see the possibilities of success, provided all other criteria is met.

Possibly the greatest problem you can encounter at a *Synergetic*

Marketing meeting, is the *"I-don't-want-to-look-a-fool"* syndrome. Therefore, it is worth dispelling this at the outset by establishing that you are looking for the *spark of genius* during a concentrated *brainstorming* and development of ideas session, and nothing is too far-fetched or science fiction to be considered.

ECONOMIC GEOGRAPHIC DEVELOPMENT MARKETING

Economic Geographic Development Marketing—This method is used to identify in which geographic location an organization can expect to find a high return of business activity for their product or service at any given time. This method relies upon accurate and timely information, and dependable systems to employ it. Most of the information needed is already in written form and easily available, but it must be collated from a variety of sources. This method can only be successful where an administrative research system is employed (a system which should exist in every company) to constantly analyze potential new markets (which is described later in this book). This method, although very important to anyone in business, can only really be employed by a firm with the required investment capital to support it during its development. Less in-depth, or even less specialized systems, employing the ideas of this method can, however, be used by just about anyone.

The most important tools are:

1. Large scale wall maps.
2. A system of coding, relating markings and color codes on the map to business activity, type of clients or other developments in the area concerned.
3. An extensive filing system which can be of the traditional

type, using cards and folders, or a computerized variable data analysis filing program.

The theory is that by plotting developments (political, institutional and commercial) it is possible to predict business activity in predetermined geographic areas.

As with **Related Growth Marketing,** a historical comparison is required in each and every case, unless you wish to work on unsubstantiated hunches. Then, by searching out every news item or other change related to a particular area, and relating it to your maps and historical counterparts, an overall picture develops from which some prediction can be evaluated. Most of the information is in written form and readily available from a variety of sources, including that obtainable from:

1. Chambers of Commerce
2. Government statistics (local and national)
3. Business and trade publications
4. City and state development reports
5. Contract information publications
6. Newspapers and other mass media

To be successful, one must motivate the executive management of a company to constantly analyze what the firm is doing, and why, in business activity. The results can then be compared to other areas (geographic or activity) to find similar developments which might be exploited. The most simple example would be that as the development of an oil economy led to building expansion in Iran, it should eventually mean the same in Mexico.

This is obvious and large scale, but illustrates the point well enough.

Proposals for new airports, roadworks or railroad routes, etc., are very important, as is curtailment of such services, for access has a great deal to do with the establishment of new business and the stability of established operations. Industrial development can also mean higher standards being needed in an area by existing organizations which need to keep or recruit staff. Such development continues with an expansion of service industries, retail and recreation facilities in most cases, causing an ongoing development of possibilities for business.

The simplest method of beginning this investigation is to *interrogate* your sales activity on a geographic basis every month. This is done by plotting the *sales calls* made each month, or the sales letters sent out by destination of each piece of such mail, and marking them both on a large scale map. Then by using different colors for each month, or by using overlays of previous months activity, patterns begin to emerge, showing different areas of activity, which can be used to stimulate questions and answers. This can soon identify areas of interest to be investigated further.

OFFICE NETWORK MARKETING

Office Network Marketing is employed to give an organization geographic expansion and access to the best markets without high capital expenditure in establishing independent offices. This method of marketing was introduced many years ago in *people intensive* service industries (for example, recruitment and management consultancy companies). It entails the establishment of sub-offices without the administrative or production overheads of fully staffed offices. From its implementation, it can improve your national image and increase your exploitation of new markets using a reputation you have already established elsewhere.

Most small companies and specialist organizations operate on a *local* scale. By *local* one can accept several definitions depending upon the size and degree of specialization of the firm involved. Restricting a firm in this way might have been realistic 30 years ago, but with today's technology, efficiency of communication, more efficient distribution and ease of travel, it is no longer necessary. Any firm or individual is now able to work on the other side of the world without moving the production, administration, equipment and all that goes to make up their firm. The main problem to such *long-distance* work is management's idea that it may not be possible to manage it effectively.

Having isolated the problems, consider the advantages of spreading your operations to more than one geographic area. It is obvious that the more markets you can tap, the more opportunities you will uncover. It is also obvious that if you can produce more quality business without increasing your costs/production/profit equation, then you are going to reap greater rewards in profit, image and satisfaction. The formula is simple and the implementation costs are acceptable to even the smallest operation, and there is no shortage of opportunities to exploit.

1. First, evaluate the possible areas of high development (using the methods of **Related Growth** and **Economic Geographic Development Marketing).**

2. Appoint someone (preferably from within your organization who knows your methods and operation) and give them the responsibility of developing that new area. In some cases, it will be necessary for that person to move to the new area, or it might be more feasible for him or her to merely supervise and provide liaison and training, in which case you will need to hire a manager or business development executive.

3. The next step is to hire a small *front* office, with a prestigious address in the best business area in the new city or area you

have chosen. If you have the available finance you could increase efficiency by installing a "linked" word processor system or, at the least, a telex link.

4. The new office will have to be manned at all times, so you will need to hire a secretary/receptionist. Preferably by recruiting this person from within that business community, you could then benefit from the knowledge he or she will have built up over the years.

5. The next step of course is to mount a high powered **Image Marketing** Program, and inform all of your past and present clients, and your network of contacts, that you are opening this new office.

6. In the first instance, your marketing program will be to contact and explain your services to the counterparts of your past clients in your original location. If you specialize in a particular field this will be easier, but if not, then many of your past clients will help you isolate their counterparts in the new area. They may even know them personally and might give you an introduction.

7. At the outset the new office will only be a "Marketing Operation," but when you gain your first contact you will need to appoint a project manager to supervise installation, delivery and so on.

As you can see, all that has been established is a sales office with a presentation room. *All production, accounting and the people-intensive work is retained at the original or head office.* This method of operation, using courier services, the mail, telephone and telex communication, can increase the area in which you can successfully operate, without having to establish fully staffed offices. By keeping all production capabilities in one location it is, therefore, easier to manage your total operation far more efficiently. More high profit work will allow you to hire better staff, and more work will allow you to grow faster. The objective is to open more *sales and presentation offices* by establishing a new office each time the previous one moves into profit-making. A side benefit of this system of marketing is that it allows staff members almost unlimited opportunities of advancement, and the personal satisfaction of being part of an expanding organization. It also allows you to operate in areas where a fully staffed office would be unfeasible.

There is also the possibility that "smaller" firms operating within your field, in another geographic location, might be interested in forming a "cooperative venture" with you. In this case, you would act jointly to increase your "purchasing power," but remain semi-independently in operation. If you could negotiate a major shareholding for such benefits, then link the two (or more) operations so that your public relations and marketing budget benefits both offices. The logic of such a venture is easily explained. Above all, geographic expansion is the best defense against having "all your eggs in one basket."

ASSOCIATION MARKETING

Association Marketing is the activity of developing new clients from areas associated with clients you have already dealt with successfully, to whom you have no other method of approach. This method of marketing is complicated, needs careful analysis of the possible reaction of your existing clients, and thorough investigation of that client's circle of associates. This method can be used to widen the business base of any organization, and thereby results in access to the most *profitable* jobs in many more fields than are presently being exploited for new business.

It is possible for a sales executive to concentrate on the needs of a client and the developing relationship to the point where the promotion of new business from the client's associates, clients and suppliers is not harnessed to its full potential.

In theory, **Association Marketing** should provide business in geometric progression, if it is properly employed, on the principle that every new client can provide at least two further clients. It is also possible to enter new fields of business with the aid of existing clients that might otherwise have been closed to you. The fact is that the employment of your services by a client is no less than an acceptance of your ability. Therefore, it is logical to expect that they should assist you, if only to share the benefits you give them with their circle of friends and associates.

The simplest way to employ your client's contacts is to develop a conversation with a client to the point where they will isolate those people or firms who **they** think could benefit from using your services. However, this is not always possible, and there is the chance that the client could believe that:

1. They might harm their relationship with anyone they recommend your product or services to, in the case that you might fail to satisfy them.
2. They do not completely understand **all** the facets of your product range or service, so they would rather not get involved.
3. They do not have the time to spare to get involved.

If the simple method is denied you, there are several alternative methods you can use to place the knowledge of your existence and capabilities before the acquaintances, friends and contacts of your existing clients.

The first, which costs less than a good lunch and will go on working for you for years, I call *signing the project.* Almost all projects and products are ''visible,'' some projects even have an official opening. It may be a prestigious affair, attended by local dignitaries, the press, and executives from head office, or it may just be a housewarming and get-together of old friends. Used wisely, this event, however it is organized, can be your introduction to potential business for many years to come. It entails you producing a *commemorative plaque,* and having it fixed (with ''everlasting, indestructible glue''?) in a prominent position so that every visitor will know of your involvement. Three tips to ensure it remains in place and that it works are:

1. Write its use into the original contract with the client.
2. Word the inscription to appeal to, or even flatter, the client.
3. *Link* your telephone directory area to your name so that potential clients can find you.

For those firms who supply products or ''unseen'' services, there are several ways of being seen:

1. Investigate the *labels* on your products—do they indicate where further items can be obtained.
2. Invest in desk calendars, ashtrays, desk ornaments, pictures, etc., to which you can affix your *presentation plaque.*
3. Make part of your contract the *display* of a plaque, for example:
   ''This building is protected by A & B Dust Cover Apparatus''
   ''This building is insured by A & B''

The second way of achieving your existing client's assistance in developing new markets (it can also apply to your business contacts) is to ask them questions, with answers which can improve your service and capabilities. The example given will of course need to be reworded and adapted to apply to your service.

1. *How did you first learn of our company?*
   a) *Recommended by one of our clients*
   b) *Recommended by a friend or business associate*
   c) *Reading a published article*
   d) *From a directory*
   e) *One of our staff contacting you*
2. *Why did you choose to employ our services?*
   a) *Price consideration*
   b) *Quality of presentation*
   c) *Preference of the examples of our work*
   d) *Our reputation*
3. *Of the staff you dealt with, whom would you single out as being helpful beyond the normal business expectations?*
4. *What single element of our service impressed you the most?*
5. *What single element of our service would you advise we improve?*
6. *Of your clients and associates, by business rather than by name, which would you think need the service we offer?*
7. *How would we have to adapt or change our service to be able to serve them?*
8. *Have you employed firms similar to ours?*
9. *Which areas of our service compare favorably to those of our competitors in your opinion?*
10. *Which areas of our service compare unfavorably to those of our competitors in your opinion?*
11. *What change in our service, or guarantee on our part, would you require before you would recommend employing our firm to one of your clients or business associates?*
12. *Were your original reasons for employing our services justified by the results?*

These 12 questions and their answers will assist you in developing a list of areas where, with your existing client's help, you could open negotia-

tions. Question 6 is the hook, a telephone call or informal meeting to discuss how the answer to this question (amongst others) intrigued you, will normally develop at least one *named* lead, with an introduction. Whether you include the questions in a questionnaire or ask them at a meeting arranged for that purpose, they will also help you to sharpen your total activities and the services you offer in everyday business.

Please refer to Checklist Number 14 on page 328.

CHAPTER NINE

INFORMATION ON POTENTIAL CLIENTS

The methods and systems of marketing which have been outlined in this book will all isolate potential new business prospects. However, to have a fully balanced approach to market development in any marketing endeavor, the marketing administrator or sales manager should develop a library of those publications which give details of all the potential clients in their catchment area. Many firms tend to limit their own market by not investing enough time or thought to this library of information, and it can be the most profitable tool available to a growing or ambitious organization.

The sphere of work, or potential catchment area of any sales team, is only limited by time and distance. Therefore, just knowing that on the route to one call there is another similar potential prospect, can double the effectiveness of the journey. This is where the use of a Business Activity Report can increase the efficiency of any sales team, for by checking the *routes* of each salesperson against the information held in a good reference library, the marketing administrator can soon uncover other potential clients in the area and make sure the next journey to a call includes two or three other potential prospects.

The establishment and implementation of marketing plans is almost impossible without a good reference library to isolate areas of business activity and potential clients for the introduction, mail program, etc. To help you draw up any list of prospects for a particular Marketing Plan aimed at an individual profession, business sector or industry, there can be no more useful source of information than the listing of the relevant association which those prospects belong to. First of all, you must establish if an association exists for your target area, and there are three ways which will usually achieve this.

1. a) Check a major city telephone directory under the heading "Associations" in the Yellow Pages and work through all the entries noting down those names and numbers you **think** might include your potential prospects.

   b) Then give each number a call and establish the following:
      i) Who does the association serve?
      ii) What is their present membership, local and national?
      iii) Do they hold listings of their members?
      iv) Can you obtain a copy of their membership listing? If the answer to Question iii is **yes** but the answer to Question iv is either **no** or at a significant price, see Method 2.

2. a) Go through your reference files and match up any of your contacts to the sector of business activity you are researching.

   b) Give them a call, or arrange a meeting, where you can ask them if they belong to a *specialized* association.

   c) If they do (or if you know the association and that they belong):
      i) Ask if there is a membership listing.
      ii) Ask if they could loan you their copy or obtain a

copy for you.

If neither of the first two methods can be used, there is another approach which can be employed, which is as follows:

3. a) Check the *Ayer Directory of Publications* (you should be able to find a copy in the reference section of your local library, although it is well worth buying your own for use in your public relations activity). Find the magazines or journals you believe would be read by your potential prospects.

   b) Obtain copies of those publications and study them for information on potential clients or associations.

   c) Or, you could advertise in those publications which reach readers in your catchment area.

   d) Or, call one of the editorial staff listed on the title page of the publication and ask them the relevant questions to identify the associations you need. Get the telephone number and then go back to the first method described to obtain the listing.

Belonging to the main **Chamber of Commerce** in your catchment area is very important. Not belonging is liable to cost you dear, as it can be one of your best reference sources.

a) Establish what *services* are offered that can help you in building your potential prospect lists. (Some Chambers will not only provide you with up-to-date specialized listings, but will also supply them on peel-off address labels to put on the envelopes.)

b) All main Chambers of Commerce issue directories to their members, which list addresses, telephone numbers and contacts. It is worth calling the contacts listed and asking him or her to whom you should direct your *letter* (remember you belong to the same *club*). If the listing indicates that the contact is the chairman, president or general manager, forget the phone call and address your approach on name basis.

Many of the major **commercial banks** maintain marketing services to assist their clients. Some of these services, especially in the field of foreign transactions and export/import dealings, can be very sophisticated and sometimes even more efficient than many government services.

a) Check with your bank manager as to what services are available and ask that someone from the marketing department arrange to see you.

b) If your bank is unable to help you, or you want more help, open another account with another bank and repeat the same procedure.

It is said that everything and everybody is listed somewhere in the records of **local government,** so consequently every single one of your potential prospects is there too. Therefore, you need to establish a link with those records. You help pay to keep them, and as long as everything is kept strictly legal, and you can survive stepping over, through and around the red tape and bureaucracy, you can help yourself a lot with those records.

a) Research from your past clients and your contacts the highest contact you can find with access to, or power over, local government.

b) Establish a meeting and learn what exists and how you could use such information.

c) Create a system for obtaining the listings of potential prospects you could use.

All of these **publications** should be available in the reference section of your local library, so you can either refer to them there, or after examining them obtain a copy:

1. *Ayer Directory of Publications*
2. *Congressional Directory*
3. *Dun & Bradstreet Reference Book of Corporate Management*
4. *National Trade & Professional Organizations of the U.S.*
5. *Standard & Poor's Register of Corporations, Directors and Executives*
6. *Standard Rate and Data Service*
7. *Who's Who in America*

Quite often directories are out-of-date because they are only published yearly, therefore, one has to keep up with developments by other methods. The Sunday papers carry situation advertisements (only those *boxed* or *feature* advertisements can be useful in identifying prospects). Checking the latest against your prepared listing, prior to launching your marketing program, can often throw up a few extra prospects to add to the list.

The methods of marketing outlined so far, can best be described as options available to the professional individual or firm to promote new business opportunities. The management systems and forms required to organize and direct a marketing program are described later in this book.

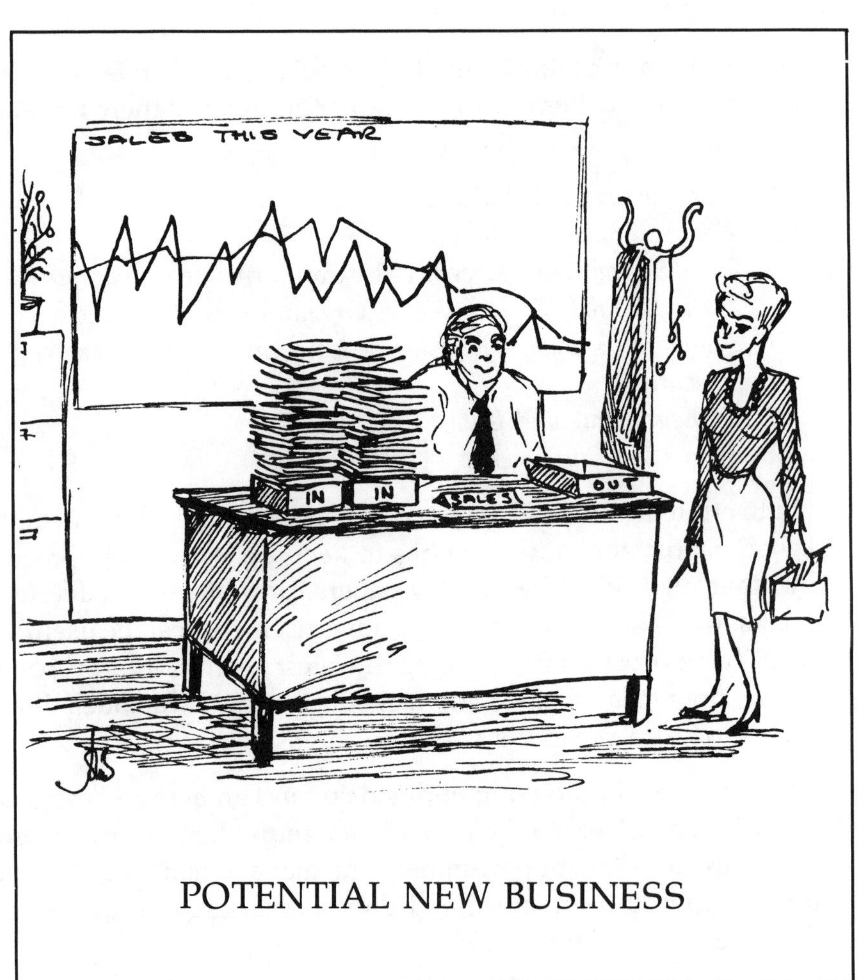

POTENTIAL NEW BUSINESS

CHAPTER TEN

THE MARKETING TEAM

There are those who say that everyone who meets, or has written or verbal contact with clients, or potential clients, is part of the sales team. In fact, everyone with such duties does contribute to the success or failure of any sales effort. Therefore, it is necessary to involve them in all developments and maintain the highest standards possible by ongoing education and training. Experience proves that once a month all the *client contact* staff should meet to bring to light ways to improve efficiency and the overall sales effort, for only by such ongoing involvement can the team be kept effective.

THE MARKETING ADMINISTRATOR

It cannot be stated often enough that gaining new business and keeping established clients is paramount to any undertaking, therefore, a concentrated application of ongoing management and control systems is a wise investment if planned growth and a stable business are to be achieved and maintained.

The need for control, research and promotion systems to be maintained and developed to a high level of efficiency means that the task of administrating a marketing program must be a full-time commitment and ongoing activity. To achieve this end, there are few firms who do not need a full-time Marketing Administrator. Experience proves that any firm which employs a full-time bookkeeper to deal with financial matters also needs a full-time Marketing Administrator to deal with management of the sales effort. The job description for such an appointment would include the following:

1. A high degree of bookkeeping ability.
2. An ability to communicate with people at all levels.
3. Writing ability and report-preparing skills.
4. An analytical aptitude and record-keeping capability.
5. Executive qualities of organization.

In status within the executive hierarchy, the Marketing Administrator can really only be outranked by the principals of the firm and the Marketing Director and/or Sales Manager in the firm's sales department. This authority is absolutely necessary to enable the Marketing Administrator to function, and the confidential nature of the facts involved also means that a high degree of privacy and security must be provided for the operation. The Marketing Administrator is responsible for: *bookkeeping* of the sales department, research for the marketing director, aide to the sales manager, and information officer to the president or principal when required. All sales records and compiling of statistics (using the forms and systems described later) are the responsibility of the Marketing Administrator.

Some firms seem to think that a full-time, highly qualified (and therefore well paid) Marketing Administrator is a luxury that is not needed as the duties could be shared amongst existing executives and staff. To date, I have been successful in proving the *economic necessity* of hiring a highly qualified, full-time Marketing Administrator by asking just three questions:

1. If it were possible to increase the management efficiency of the firm by 20%, would you hire someone?
2. If you could increase your sales activity by at least 20%, would you appoint someone?
3. How else could you obtain the information you need to manage your business more effectively, and provide controlled growth and strategic forecasting?

The fact is, that no matter how small a business, the need for a Marketing Administrator becomes necessary the moment you have more than two people selling. To provide an analogy—*a firm without a Marketing Administrator is like an automobile without the instrument panel in front of the driver, the size of the automobile is really irrelevant.* Being able to establish the facts about every aspect of your sales and marketing performance is the first step towards gaining real control over your future. Salespeople who operate in an undisciplined manner can never be as productive, or as happy, as those who *know* what is happening. It also makes it easier to decide who your best clients and contacts are once you have torn away all the camouflage and unnecessary bulk of *day-to-day* feelings and can evaluate the real details and results. If you want to succeed in anything, the motto must be *organize, analyze, plan, and carry through* and a controlled system of marketing management is really the only way to achieve success.

Everyone in a competitive society is totally reliant upon marketing themselves, what they can do, or what they produce, and there are six steps in the overall process.

1. Evaluate **what** it is you have to sell.
2. Establish **who** your potential clients are.
3. Establish **what** makes your product or service more desirable than what your competitors are offering.
4. Decide **which** methods will be most successful in convincing your potential clients to buy.
5. Evaluate **how** to use the staff, tools and communication channels that are available to you.
6. Decide **when,** or how often, you need to analyze your progress to reassess your methods, staff, products or service.

Having established this marketing procedure, the next step is *selling* whatever it is you are offering. In other words, if marketing is the *strategic planning,* then *selling* is the actual *enactment of the plans and strategy.* Therefore, if the Marketing Department is the *general staff,* then the Sales Force is the *combat troop.* Possibly the best description of modern business activity is the military one, which compares a successful business to a disciplined and purpose-endowed army, and an unsuccessful business as being a mass of individuals without purposeful objectives, or the organization or discipline for concerted effort.

In the late 1960's through the 1970's, liberalism in management, erosion of discipline throughout business and the general lack of rules for personal dress or behavior, it was going against the mainstream to suggest more discipline, more formality and a more *managerial* attitude by management. The cry then seemed to be *the more chefs, the better the soup.* In fact, if one takes an objective look at successful people, firms, or even nations now, and compares them to the unsuccessful, it soon becomes apparent that it is the organized, disciplined, objective and inventive who succeed in achieving their goals.

Anyone who believes that convincing someone to buy something is easy, has little understanding of the rules of business. No one pays full price if they can get a discount, and few people are prepared to hand over their own hard-earned profits from life just to make a salesperson happy. The reason for success in anything comes down to *attitude* as the bottom line. To be successful one must strive for it and be willing to apply oneself to continued effort and careful self-analysis. It does not matter if it is an individual, a company, a multi-national corporation or even a nation, the only real formula for success must be:

Organize, analyze, plan and carry through.

Organize yourself or your firm to be efficient and effective.

Analyze your market, your products or services, systems and methods, always with an open mind and allowing logical evaluation.

Plan your strategy, tactics, options and operations.

Carry through by application and attitude.

This book offers some of the methods and systems which experience has proved to be successful in implementing the above principles.

There are eight stages in gaining new business:

1. Assessing who needs, wants or can afford the product or service to be offered.
2. Finding a way to set up an opportunity to explain the product to potential clients.
3. Developing sales tools, sales plans, letters and presentation programs, promotional activity, etc.
4. Business development—making the first contact and assessing the potential for profit and success.
5. Negotiation—finalizing details, presenting a proposal and obtaining the order.
6. Account management—client liaison, continuing and improving the working relationship, and developing new opportunities for business.
7. Monitoring and evaluating the success and efficiency of the transaction, and developing ways to improve future business activity.
8. Marketing administration—improving the efficiency and effectiveness of all the previous stages by analysis and

monitoring of all business-gaining activity.

The need to establish a marketing policy and attitude to research has been outlined before, and the Chief Executive or Marketing Director, with the assistance of a marketing department (or committee in the case of a small firm) would cover stages **1, 2,** and **3** and oversee stages **7** and **8,** which would be performed by the Marketing Administrator. Stages **4, 5** and **6** are the responsibility of the Sales Manager and his or her staff.

THE BUSINESS DEVELOPMENT EXECUTIVE

In many cases, a lower echelon of sales personnel can bring many advantages to a firm and, although they must have a broad knowledge of the firm's capabilities, they do not need the experience of a top Negotiator. Their responsibility is to sift out the best potential clients so that the Negotiator can be introduced, thereby saving the Negotiator a lot of time and helping to keep costs in perspective. Public relations and marketing activity *should* generate a large number of leads, however, they will be geographically spread and unknown in potential when first received. It is the job of the Business Development Executive to investigate and evaluate every lead, and thereby ensure that every minute of the Negotiator's time is well used. It is possible (but not certain) that future Negotiators may come from the ranks of Business Development Executives, for their daily client evaluation and introduction activity is possibly the best training available to anyone. The Business Development Executive rarely *discovers* potential clients. Good public relations and marketing management isolates potential clients and passes the *lead* to the Business Development Executive, who must then evaluate the potential of possible business (there are forms detailed later to assist this activity). The Business Development Executive must be able to evaluate potential, and brief the Negotiator by providing enough information.

Information Business Development Executives should obtain:

1. Establish an in-depth knowledge of the potential client.
   i) Address of head office.
   ii) Name of ultimate decision-maker in that organization, in relation to the contract you wish to gain.
   iii) Which of your competitors have worked for the organization in the past, and what is their position with the potential client now?
   iv) Who will you need to deal with in the initial stages and what is their track record?
   v) Is your potential client financially able to complete the contract, and meet your fees or price within your normal terms and conditions?

2. Establish the total benefits for your firm in taking this client.
   i) How often does the potential client buy products or services such as you wish to offer?
   ii) What expenditure does the potential client make annually on products or services which you can provide?
   iii) What are the immediate/medium/long-term needs of the client which your firm can benefit from?
   iv) Does your firm have successful experience in the area this potential client is interested in (isolate examples with dates, client satisfaction levels, profit status)?
   v) What is your firm's track record in the geographic location of the potential project, or the client's locality?
   vi) What is the journey time from your office to:
      a) the client's present location?
      b) the proposed site of work or delivery?
   vii) Has a budget been established for the product/service

you can provide?

viii) What is the time scale involved:
   a) for contract signing?
   b) for commencement of project?
   c) for completion of project?

ix) How many levels of decision-making are there, what are they, and what procedures have been established?

x) What are your reasons for suggesting that your firm should or should not go after this project or order?

This information, passed onto the Negotiator, increases the chances of the right decision being made as to the value of this client's account and allows the Negotiator to develop a plan of action.

THE NEGOTIATOR

Experience proves that paying a good Negotiator commission on individual orders or projects is not really good management sense. In fact, in many small firms, the *Negotiator* is in reality the owner or Chief Executive and, even in large corporations there can be few members of the staff who are more important than the person who produces the business, which is the very reason for the firm's existence. A Negotiator who is influenced by the *what money is in it for me this month* attitude, will produce business which will only bring complications later. A Negotiator needs to evaluate every possible order or contract from many viewpoints, e.g., long-term effect, image, actual profit, production and delivery limitations, profit value and future potential business from the client or industry involved. Therefore, he or she should be salaried in the same manner as the President, Finance Director or Production Director. The idea that tempting a top level Negotiator with *commission* will make him or her work harder is outdated, and experience proves it is in fact counterproductive in the long term. The good Negotiator is worth a small fortune to any firm and should be compensated as one would reward any important executive. If a bonus is paid it should be just that, a bonus, and it should be paid in a relative amount to the successful *completion* of the project and the good will gained from the client.

It is best to give no hierarchy title to these most important members of your staff, for any title can be misinterpreted, and thereby can be counterproductive in results. The person entrusted with arranging the details of, and actually signing new business for the firm, must be a paragon of talents and virtues, and the objective is to have someone who will produce high income and important projects from respected clients.

THE ACCOUNT EXECUTIVE

Many firms waste a great deal of effort by concentrating so hard upon *new* clients that they lose guaranteed profits from established clients. Again, this is almost entirely due to the shortsighted system of reward for business development which, oversimplified, often works like this: The salesperson needs fast results, and therefore over-sells. The client works on the premise that what the salesperson said to gain the contract is true, and feels a *right* to continued use of that salesperson's time between contracts and in developing his or her needs. The salesperson knows that a client who has just bought, immediately reverts to a *long-term* prospect in the usual way of things. Eager for more *now* results, the salesperson then avoids the client, believing it to be a waste of time for the moment. The client then becomes annoyed, feels cheated, and begins to look around for someone else who will provide *better* service. The answer is to appoint a person within the firm whose responsibility is to maintain contact with, and provide service to, the existing client. It is an investment well worth the money, if only for the recommendation the client will be able to provide to potential clients when needed. One only has to look at the past client listings of a few of the top service firms to realize that few firms manage to keep their clients for long periods of time. The same names appear on almost everyone's lists.

Really well-managed client liaison is probably the most neglected area of business, and experience proves that the majority of complaints against firms are in the area of *follow-up service* and *ongoing* responsibility. Professional and service firms who sell *concepts* and *ideas* suffer even more from lack of organized client liaison, for no one will hire such services unless they feel they can trust and believe in not just the ability of the firm involved, but also the responsible back-up and care they are led to expect by the professional standards promoted by public relations, etc.

Effectively, therefore, the most efficient method of organizing and running the sales effort of any firm is to isolate the five basic levels of action and employ suitable staff to fill these positions.

1. The Marketing Director or Sales Manager.
2. The Marketing Administrator and Marketing Department and/or Sales Office Staff.
3. The Negotiator/s.
4. Business Development Executives.
5. Account Executives.

In a small firm, the responsibilities are the same, so although short-term variances might be necessary, the goal must be to achieve the right organization as soon as possible.

Please refer to Checklist Number 15 on page 329.

CHAPTER ELEVEN

THE 50-WEEK COMMERCIAL YEAR (THE 50-WEEK MARKETING YEAR)

Introduction: When I first introduced this system I called it The 50-Week Marketing Year, however after it was published it was suggested to me on many occasions that it applied to more disciplines within Business Management than Marketing alone, and so I have chosen to call it **The 50-Week Commercial Year** from now on.

The whole basis of Business Administration, and the total concept behind implementing an organized marketing program, is to be able to analyze performance, manage business activity, sustain growth, and increase efficiency and profits. These needs can only be achieved if it is possible to gather and organize factual (and usable) data. The problem is, however, that the basis of calculations relative to Commerce, Marketing and any other creative or production evaluation of time scales is different in its very conception.

All creative, production or manufacturing time is normally considered in *hours* and can be calculated on *short time-period cost factors;* whereas marketing results and activity are normally calculated in *weeks* and are judged as efficient or productive on *long time-period cost factors.* The real problem brought about by this difference in *acceptance values* where *costs expended* are judged against *value received* is that both have been regulated by bookkeepers to be *accountable* according to the calendar period of 12 months. In the 19th century, the bookkeepers gave some credence to the illogic of the system by adopting the *quarterly* accounting system, which has managed to give both parties involved (production and marketing) an equal *judgment* period of 13 weeks, but it is still cumbersome and 13 weeks is really too long a period to serve the needs of either party. Then, just to confuse logic and inquiry, political and social forces have thrown in many other negatives to *factual analysis.*

The Public Holidays. It is probable that there is no day of the year when industry and commerce are not closed somewhere on the planet Earth to celebrate some religious or national remembrance. So, what is the business owner or manager to do when he or she wishes to gather and compare facts about performance, efficiency and application for future planning? In my opinion, there is only one answer—adopt a **50-Week Commercial Year.**

The 50-Week Commercial Year is logical to the nth degree, in that it uses the basic number of days in the working week and graduates a scale upwards which remains constant for analysis and management purposes. (Even allowing two independent one-week (five day) accounting periods to do the analysis required without affecting the judgments.)

5 working hours	=	1 day
5 days	=	1 week
5 weeks	=	1 period
5 periods	=	half a year
10 periods	=	1 year

The 50-Week Commercial Year gives many advantages to any Business Management Program. The most important of which is the accuracy to all accounting data. To the marketing and sales staff, it gives two *free* weeks every year to analyze performance without losing *contribution* to overall sales figures. Obviously, it also helps production, accounts, and even personnel; and cash flow is improved if it is used for billing. Consider the implications compared to the traditional 12-month calendar and soon one starts wondering why everyone has not been using it for years (simple things—etc., etc.).

The two-weeks (ten days) accounting period *uncounted time* is not wasted or *lost*, it is working time, but it is just not counted in *results.* Therefore, an order signed in "uncounted time" would be credited to the period following, or the time could be used to catch up on production or targets; the numbers involved being transferred to the previous, or following, period as justified. These two weeks are used to *inventory* results, analyze performance and generally *to sit back* and evaluate the past and plan the future.

There are three ways experience has proved useful in *placing* these two weeks *uncounted time:* (Let us take 1981 as an example:)

1. In the case of professional services (architects, designers, lawyers, etc.) and those industries which *close for the winter,* these two weeks in the 1981 year would run from the 29th December 1980 to the 2nd January 1981 and the 21st to the 25th of December 1981.
2. In the case of small companies (wanting more regular total analysis input), the first week would be the same (29th December 1980 to the 2nd January 1981) and the second week would fall between the 29th of June and the 3rd July 1981.
3. Finally, for those companies who gain most business during *holiday seasons,* the weeks would be placed in either March or April and September or October.

The 50-Week Commercial Year is therefore not something that applies directly to the hours, days and weeks worked by the employees of the company. It is instead a method of Productivity Analysis and Quality Control used to 'account' for how the firm operates in its Marketing process, and what products or services the people and machines of the organization produce. Obviously, just because we are using the concept of five hours in a day, does not mean that everyone checks in at 9:00 a.m. and goes home at 2:00 p.m.! The people involved still work the full eight-hour day, however for management purposes we are calculating their activity or production by a divisional **Factor of 5.**

For example: Albert needs to sell 100 widgets a day, meaning his Sales Target for a Five-Day Period is 500 widgets. Fred works an eight-hour day at his machine in the shop, and in that day he is expected to produce 100 widgets. Therefore, in a five-day week he is expected to meet his target of 500 widgets produced. In the case of George, in a time billing service based industry, he may be expected to bill eight hours a day at say $25 per hour, which is $200 a day, and therefore $1,000 per five-day week.

So what we do for effective management control and 'Target and Budget Status' evaluation, is divide the daily and weekly requirements of everyone involved in Sales and Production by a **Factor of 5,** and establish more factual reference which will allow us to carry out more efficient analysis. (i.e., Fred would be entered into the calculations at 100 widgets divided by 5 = 20 per hour = 100 per day = 500 per week; and George will bill $40 per hour = $200 per day = $1,000 per week.) This provides basic digital information which can be managed far more effectively and with immediate understanding of the 'facts' at any given moment of time during the program.

Now let us say that Monday is a government holiday, and the whole operation is going to be closed for the day. Albert, Fred and George will therefore only work four days this week, however targets (and pay checks) have no way of allowing for this, and the organization will still have to pay them 'as if the holiday never happened.'

The 50-Week Commercial Year is not designed to get extra work out of people for less pay, nor is it a threat of any kind to anyone, employer or employee. It is merely a tool to analyze production and performance which cannot be 'cheated' or confused by answers based upon the illogic of the Gregorian Calendar which, incidentally, was designed to keep farmers in Italy happy in the 16th century when the shortest financial period of measurement was a year. Looking at it another way, it is also a way to take the political spanners out of business operations, which will continue to be thrown in for as long as the Business Community agrees to pay for Public Holidays, which is of course a far cheaper method for politicians to use than gaining votes with actual cash sent through the mail.

Have you ever wondered, as I have, how politicians and church authorities get away with increasing our overhead costs, and reducing our output, while making themselves 'look good,' or making us honor their beliefs and traditions? Did any of them ever come to us and ask if we minded making a 'donation' to their 'political image' or 'religious beliefs'? Seeing that businesses pay the bill 'as individuals,' surely it would be less of an imposition if they were allowed to 'individually decide' when such shutdowns of their business should happen based on the needs of the particular business itself. I admit though that as an employee I never thought to send a 'thank you' card to my employer for paying me not to work because someone else had 'given' me a 'free day off.' I wonder if anyone else ever has?

Whatever the idealistic logic and reality of financing a company for a year, there will never be a way that Christians will not want Christmas off to be with their families, nor will Jews quietly acquiesce to ignoring Yom Kippur, and it is doubtful that Muslims will agree not to fast when Ramadan comes round again next year. Religious Holidays are an undeniable cultural need of course, but

Public Holidays are another thing altogether, and if you put the two together I doubt that there is a day in the year when someone somewhere is not enjoying a religious festival or 'politically granted' day off.

When such a government given 'day off' comes round, or a religious holiday is celebrated, whatever the fairness to, or imposition upon the organization involved, the fact is **production stops**! In the practice of 'Management by Targets and Budgets,' the vacation logically cannot happen! In real life, however, the day 'disappears,' thereby providing perfect 'reasoning' for those responsible for production to 'modify' results. The fact is that we are still 'regulated' to operate on a one-year 'Financial and Production Cycle,' long after it has become redundant in the reality of Commercial Management, and despite the fact that it may actually harm our chances for success.

So what we have to do is re-align the responsibility for production as if no holiday or vacation occurred, otherwise all of our accounting and budgets, production and targets become absolutely unrealistic, and are no more than 'theoretical hopes and ambitions.'

This is where the **50-Week Commercial Year** becomes effective! Forget hourly or even weekly budgets and targets, and work on 'Production in a Five-Week Period.' Employees will understand the logic a great deal easier, and with far more clarity, than if you merely say, "The fact is we never worked Monday, so we docked you a day's pay!" In other words, Fred is set a target of 2,500 widgets to be produced in a Five-Week Period, and George is expected to 'bill his time' of $5,000 in the same Five-Week time frame. **That is all they have to know!** That is what they must do in five weeks! Remind them of the 'days out' which are coming up, and explain that their production quota must be achieved, or surpassed, if they wish to earn bonuses by the end of the five weeks involved. Ruling 'Gregorian Calendar Factors,' whether in their favor or against it, can have no bearing on the results demanded, and they must understand that fact. **The Five-Hours a Day, and Five-Days a Week Analysis tools that are imposed within this understanding are therefore achieved without anyone feeling that they are losing something.**

The **50-Week Commercial Year** then is a measurement of Production based upon 'Real Time.' No longer will everyone get excited when they 'have a good month,' not realizing that there were more actual working days in it than any other month that year, nor will they panic when February's figures are 'below monthly targets,' due to the forgotten fact that February had the least number of working days this year.

I worked with a Dutchman once who addressed his workers one morning with a simple statement. He agreed to pay full wages for a short month, providing his suppliers only billed him for three weeks and a couple of days. Everyone laughed at the 'obvious' joke, until he explained that if that did not happen then he would pay the bills, accept the lower production figures being projected and then share out the profits after taking his full salary out. He then added that that would mean a 25 percent cut in take-home money for everyone in the shop that month. Someone shouted that they were talking about Government Ordered Public Holidays—he answered, "Then send a claim to the Government for the difference." Someone else then shouted that it was not their fault that there were less days in the month this month—he answered that it was not his fault either. There was a particularly 'eloquent' shop steward present who, without shouting, explained that if full wages were not paid 'as was their right under the present contract,' he would have a strike on his hands. "Thank you, Pieter," replied the owner, "but could you call it now, then come back to work next month when I apologize and give in; it will cost me less than keeping the factory open with reduced production this month." The Dutch are a hard-working, high-ethics work force, and have a good sense of humor as well. The result was that everyone worked a little harder, took shorter breaks, and reduced the use of toilet paper that month. Production went up enough to cover the 'short days,' morale went up, and everyone 'felt good' about the outcome.

The point of the story is that someone pointed out the silly effect the Gregorian Calendar and Public Holidays have on business, and a solution to 'a bad month' was found and followed to the good of all. The problem is that this is not always possible, so therefore one has to find a way of 'managing' productivity and marketing that can be controlled and analyzed effectively throughout the year. It is my belief that the **50-Week Commercial Year** does this more effectively than any other method I have yet come across.

A New Philosophy for Management?

What the **50-Week Commercial Year** can do is allow you to control Production, Productivity, Billing, Marketing, Planning and Budgeting, and yet it is so simple my daughter, Sarah, mastered it at the age of seven. However you presently use the Gregorian Calendar Year, the application of the **50-Week Commercial Year** philosophy can be used to increase the efficiency of your management systems.

Let us say, for example, that your Operating Budget **for the year** is $1,000,000 and your Sales Need is 100,000 widgets. Instead of dividing those numbers by 12 months, or more likely just setting out to 'keep costs down' and 'make sales targets,' all you do is apply the **50-Week Commercial Year Factor of 5.**

With an operating Budget of $1,000,000 for the year, you have the following predictions of expenditure you can work with:

Per Year	— (10 Periods)	= $1,000,000
Per Half Year	— (5 Periods)	= $ 500,000
***Per Period**	**— (5 Weeks)**	= $ 100,000
Per Week	— (5 Days)	= $ 20,000
Per Day	— (5 Hours)	= $ 4,000

With a Marketing Target of 100,000 widgets per year, you have the following sales quotas to achieve:

Per Year	— (10 Periods)	= 100,000
Per Half Year	— (5 Periods)	= 50,000
***Per Period**	**— (5 Weeks)**	= 10,000
Per Week	— (5 Days)	= 2,000
Per Day	— (5 Hours)	= 400
Per Hour		= 80

* These are are the numbers you circulate to those people in your organization who carry responsibility for meeting this year's Budgets and Targets.

The fact is that machines cannot run any faster than they are designed to do, and workers cannot be expected to work like the machines they tend. People need to eat, to slow down occasionally, and visit the toilets when nature calls, and that is why there really is no such thing as the 'eight-hour working day.' However, if the machine is running, or in the case of service industry production, the hours are ticking by, then an hourly production rate can be calculated and demanded. The same applies with 'billing time' for lawyers, architects, doctors, and all other professionals who charge time on an hourly basis.

The fact is, however, that by using the numbers broken down to the **50-Week Commercial Year Factors of 5,** you will get more production if you set the hourly production rate at a 'day divided by 5 factor.' However, if you think, (I am talking to owners, managers, and principles), that you have just 'gained' extra work out of your people, then I am misleading you! All you have done is informed your people that production quotas have been set at 400 a week, and you have set this target to ensure the production of 100,000 by the end of the year. You also inform them that the target of 400 a week holds, no matter how many actual working days there are in any particular week. Another rule is that Targets are established to be met prior to any day off being taken, and that they should not fall into the false hope of 'catching up afterwards,' therefore you have recovered the public holidays and vacation time production loss (if your sales staff and production workers only get two weeks a year annual vacation).

The fact is that the average eight-hour a day worker actually works only six productive hours or less after you deduct lunch breaks, coffee breaks, social contact, and other 'time off the job.' I see no problem in asking workers, or salespeople, to 'prepare' for days off, and it is far less stressful and difficult than trying to catch up afterwards.

Only talk 'Weeks' in Production Quotas, while for Sales and Marketing staff you only talk about Five-Week Periods, and forget about days and weeks. That way, if there are three Public or Religious Holidays during those five weeks it does not matter to your targets or budgets for the purpose of management, and everyone must understand that you will totally ignore 'days out' from the calculation point of view for 'achievement of target' and 'bonus' purposes.

If you pay **Production Bonuses,** never do it based on anything other than the Five-Week Period. Quarterly Bonuses are temper-fraying for everyone in the last few weeks, and Annual Bonuses are based on so long a time frame that they soon become seen as 'un-earned perks,' especially if they are based on 'department,' 'division' or even (where the owner has really lost touch with reality) Company Performance. The latter, and to some extent all of these 'group rewards,' probably do more to sow staff dissent and jealousy, and cause morale problems, than they ever 'motivate' people, which of course is why they were introduced in the first place. 'Bonuses' are 'Rewards,' and the person who works the hardest should get the best 'reward.' Bonuses based on individual performance are the only ones that will increase productivity and profits. 'Shared Responsibility for Performance' only encourages the lazy, and victimizes the efficient!

The usual question is always, 'Well, how can I reward Freda in the Reception, she is very important to the company but she does not 'produce' anything, nor is her time 'chargeable'? Simple, establish a 'Bonus Fund' for all such people, and at the end of the Five-Week Period pay it out, either on Department Head recommendation or as a 'share basis,' and although the suggestion is enough to make most Chairmen and owners go white at the gills, I suggest you include a slip of paper which shows the 'percentage contributed by' basis of building that fund, showing 'Over-Target' achievement for all production units that contributed to the 'Fund.'

When this understanding has been established and accepted, then bring in the 'per week' targeting and budgeting explanation showing your people that by meeting or beating it, they are contributing to their income and long-term security with the firm.

Even Cash Flow can benefit from the **50-Week Commercial Year** philosophy! Send out invoices weekly, statements at the end of each calendar month, and letters at the end of each Five-Week Period after submission of invoice. Remember, everyone is now computerized when it comes to 'paying bills,' and the **50-Week Commercial Year** method of invoicing and reminders brings you 'out of the print-outs,' and can make a really amazing difference to cash flow.

"The more confusing the rules of the game, the more confused the players will be as the game is played." This is an old and true saying, and when you are trying to operate a business based on the rules of the Gregorian Calendar and the whim of various governments to impose 'days off' into your operation, then the **50-Week Commercial Year** can be the difference between light and dark when applied to Management Vision.

The 50-Week Commercial Year gives control to the manager who uses it, and takes away all of the old 'excuses' from salesperson and production worker alike, and actually allows them to better understand your business and how they can contribute to it, and thereby relax as they insure their own future in the organization.

The first two examples are explained and compared with the *traditional* calendar periods in the following pages:

COMPARISON ANALYSIS BETWEEN THE GREGORIAN CALENDAR YEAR & THE 50 WEEK COMMERCIAL YEAR.

WEEK Number	50-Week COMMERCIAL YEAR	S Sunday	M Mon.	T Tues.	W Weds.	T Thurs.	F Fri.	S Sat.	12 Month CALENDAR YEAR
52		1980 28	29	30	31	1	2	3	
1		4	5	6	7	8	9	10	
2		11	12	13	14	15	16	17	JANUARY
3	1	18	19	20	21	22	23	24	
4		25	26	27	28	29	30	31	
5		1	2	3	4	5	6	7	
6		8	9	10	11	12	13	14	
7		15	16	17	18	19	20	21	FEBRUARY
8	2	22	23	24	25	26	27	28	
9		1	2	3	4	5	6	7	
10		8	9	10	11	12	13	14	
11		15	16	17	18	19	20	21	MARCH
12		22	23	24	25	26	27	28	
13	3	29	30	31	1	2	3	4	
14		5	6	7	8	9	10	11	
15		12	13	14	15	16	17	18	APRIL
16		19	20	21	22	23	24	25	
17		26	27	28	29	30	1	2	
18	4	3	4	5	6	7	8	9	
19		10	11	12	13	14	15	16	
20		17	18	19	20	21	22	23	MAY
21		24	25	26	27	28	29	30	
22		31	1	2	3	4	5	6	
23	5	7	8	9	10	11	12	13	
24		14	15	16	17	18	19	20	JUNE
25		21	22	23	24	25	26	27	

Type 1

WEEK Number	50-Week COMMERCIAL YEAR	S Sunday	M Mon	T Tues	W Weds	T Thurs	F Fri	S Sat	12 Month CALENDAR YEAR
26		28	29	30	1	2	3	4	
27		5	6	7	8	9	10	11	
28	6	12	13	14	15	16	17	18	JULY
29		19	20	21	22	23	24	25	
30		26	27	28	29	30	31	1	
31		2	3	4	5	6	7	8	
32		9	10	11	12	13	14	15	AUGUST
33	7	16	17	18	19	20	21	22	
34		23	24	25	26	27	28	29	
35		30	31	1	2	3	4	5	
36		6	7	8	9	10	11	12	SEPTEMBER
37		13	14	15	16	17	18	19	
38	8	20	21	22	23	24	25	26	
39		27	28	29	30	1	2	3	
40		4	5	6	7	8	9	10	
41		11	12	13	14	15	16	17	OCTOBER
42		18	19	20	21	22	23	24	
43	9	25	26	27	28	29	30	31	
44		1	2	3	4	5	6	7	
45		8	9	10	11	12	13	14	
46		15	16	17	18	19	20	21	NOVEMBER
47		22	23	24	25	26	27	28	
48	10	29	30	1	2	3	4	5	
49		6	7	8	9	10	11	12	
50		13	14	15	16	17	18	19	DECEMBER
51		20	21	22	23	24	25	26	
52		27	28	29	30	31	1	2 1982	

	In the 50-Week Commercial Year	*In the 12-Month Calendar Year*
	Marketing Period 1	*January*
Holidays	Nil	1 day
Period Ends	Friday 6th February	Saturday 31st January
Working Days (Monday through Friday)	25	21
Weeks	5	4 (+ 2 days)
	Marketing Period 2	*February*
Holidays	2 days	2 days
Period Ends	Friday 13th March	Saturday 28th February
Working Days (Monday through Friday)	23	18
Weeks	5	4

	In the 50-Week Commercial Year	*In the 12-Month Calendar Year*
	Marketing Period 3	*March*
Holidays	2 days	1 day
Period Ends	Friday 17th April	Tuesday 31st March
Working Days (Monday through Friday)	23	21
Weeks	5	4 (+ 2 days)
	Marketing Period 4	*April*
Holidays	Nil	1 day
Period Ends	Friday 22nd May	Thursday 30th April
Working Days (Monday through Friday)	25	21
Weeks	5	4 (+ 2 days)

	In the 50-Week Commercial Year	*In the 12-Month Calendar Year*
	Marketing Period 5	*May*
Holidays	1 day	1 day
Period Ends	Friday 26th June	Saturday 30th May
Working Days (Monday through Friday)	24	20
Weeks	5	4 (+ 1 day)
		June
Holidays		Nil
Period Ends		Tuesday 30th June
Working Days (Monday through Friday)		22
Weeks		4 (+ 2 days)

	In the 50-Week Commercial Year	*In the 12-Month Calendar Year*
	Marketing Period 6	*July*
Holidays	Nil	Nil
Period Ends	Friday 31st July	Friday 31st July
Working Days (Monday through Friday)	25	23
Weeks	5	4 (+ 3 days)
	Marketing Period 7	*August*
Holidays	1 day	Nil
Period Ends	Friday 4th September	Monday 31st August
Working Days (Monday through Friday)	24	21
Weeks	5	4 (+ 1 day)

	In the 50-Week Commercial Year	*In the 12-Month Calendar Year*
	Marketing Period 8	*September*
Holidays	Nil	1 day
Period Ends	Friday 9th October	Wednesday 30th September
Working Days (Monday through Friday)	25	22
Weeks	5	4 (+ 2 days)
	Marketing Period 9	*October*
Holidays	2 days	1 day
Period Ends	Friday 13th November	Saturday 31st October
Working Days (Monday through Friday)	23	21
Weeks	5	4 (+ 2 days)

	In the 50-Week Commercial Year	*In the 12-Month Calendar Year*
	Marketing Period 10	*November*
Holidays	1 day	2 days
Period Ends	Friday 18th December	Monday 30th November
Working Days (Monday through Friday)	24	19
Weeks	5	4 (+ 1 day)
		December
Holidays		1 day
Period Ends		Thursday 31st December
Working Days (Monday through Friday)		22
Weeks		4 (+ 3 days)

	In the 50-Week Commercial Year	*In the 12-Month Calendar Year*
Working weeks of less than 5 days (not counting bank holidays) in a period.	None	Jan (1st) 3 days short
		March (last) 3 days short
		April (1st) 2 days short (last) 1 day short
		May (1st) 4 days short
		June (last) 3 days short
		July (1st) 2 days short
		Aug (last) 4 days short
		Sept (1st) 1 day short
		(last) 2 days short
		Oct (1st) 3 days short
		Nov (last) 4 days short
		Dec (1st) 1 day short
		(last) 1 day short

	In the 50-Week Commercial Year	*In the 12-Month Calendar Year*
Working Day Differences in Each Period	4 periods of 25 days (Marketing Periods 1, 4, 6 and 8)	1 month 23 days (July)
	3 periods of 24 days (Marketing Periods 5, 7 and 10)	3 months 22 days (Jun, Sept, and Dec.)
	3 periods of 23 days (Marketing Periods 2, 3 and 9)	5 months 21 days (Jan, Mar, Apr, Aug, and Oct)
		1 month 20 days (May)
		1 month 19 days (Nov)
		1 month 18 days (Feb)

	In the 50-Week Commercial Year	In the 12-Month Calendar Year
Last day of the period	Friday	Monday 2 (Aug and Nov) Tuesday 2 (Mar and June) Wednesday 1 (Sep) Thursday 2 (Apr and Dec) Friday 1 (July) Saturday 4 (Jan, Feb, and Oct) Sunday 1 (May)
Full Weeks (5 days) within the period	*Periods 1–5* 25 + 1 *Periods 6–10* 25 + 1	*Jan—Jun* 23 *Jul—Dec* 22

	In the 50-Week Commercial Year	*In the 12-Month Calendar Year*
First Half of the Year Comparisons to Second Half of Year		
Holidays	*Periods 1–5* 5	*Jan—Jun* 6
	Periods 6–10 5	*Jul—Dec* 5
Working Days	*Periods 1–5* 120	*Jan—Jun* 123
	Periods 6–10 121 (+ Two extra weeks)	*Jul—Dec* 131

WEEK Number	50-Week COMMERCIAL YEAR	S Sunday	M Mon.	T Tues.	W Weds.	T Thurs.	F Fri.	S Sat	12 Month CALENDAR YEAR
52		1980 28	29	30	31	1	2	3	
1		4	5	6	7	8	9	10	
2		11	12	13	14	15	16	17	JANUARY
3	1	18	19	20	21	22	23	24	
4		25	26	27	28	29	30	31	
5		1	2	3	4	5	6	7	
6		8	9	10	11	12	13	14	
7		15	16	17	18	19	20	21	FEBRUARY
8	2	22	23	24	25	26	27	28	
9		1	2	3	4	5	6	7	
10		8	9	10	11	12	13	14	
11		15	16	17	18	19	20	21	MARCH
12		22	23	24	25	26	27	28	
13	3	29	30	31	1	2	3	4	
14		5	6	7	8	9	10	11	
15		12	13	14	15	16	17	18	APRIL
16		19	20	21	22	23	24	25	
17		26	27	28	29	30	1	2	
18	4	3	4	5	6	7	8	9	
19		10	11	12	13	14	15	16	
20		17	18	19	20	21	22	23	MAY
21		24	25	26	27	28	29	30	
22		31	1	2	3	4	5	6	
23	5	7	8	9	10	11	12	13	
24		14	15	16	17	18	19	20	JUNE
25		21	22	23	24	25	26	27	

Type 2

WEEK Number	50-Week COMMERCIAL YEAR	S Sunday	M Mon.	T Tues.	W Weds.	T Thurs.	F Fri.	S Sat.	12 Month CALENDAR YEAR
26		28	29	30	1	2	3	4	
27		5	6	7	8	9	10	11	
28		12	13	14	15	16	17	18	JULY
29	6	19	20	21	22	23	24	25	
30		26	27	28	29	30	31	1	
31		2	3	4	5	6	7	8	
32		9	10	11	12	13	14	15	AUGUST
33		16	17	18	19	20	21	22	
34	7	23	24	25	26	27	28	29	
35		30	31	1	2	3	4	5	
36		6	7	8	9	10	11	12	SEPTEMBER
37		13	14	15	16	17	18	19	
38		20	21	22	23	24	25	26	
39	8	27	28	29	30	1	2	3	
40		4	5	6	7	8	9	10	
41		11	12	13	14	15	16	17	OCTOBER
42		18	19	20	21	22	23	24	
43		25	26	27	28	29	30	31	
44	9	1	2	3	4	5	6	7	
45		8	9	10	11	12	13	14	
46		15	16	17	18	19	20	21	NOVEMBER
47		22	23	24	25	26	27	28	
48		29	30	1	2	3	4	5	
49	10	6	7	8	9	10	11	12	
50		13	14	15	16	17	18	19	DECEMBER
51		20	21	22	23	24	25	26	
52		27	28	29	30	31	1	2 1982	

	In the 50-Week Commercial Year	*In the 12-Month Calendar Year*
	Marketing Period 1	*January*
Holidays	Nil	1 day
Period Ends	Friday 6th February	Saturday 31st January
Working Days (Monday through Friday)	25	21
Weeks	5	4 (+ 2 days)
	Marketing Period 2	*February*
Holidays	2 days	2 days
Period Ends	Friday 13th March	Saturday 28th February
Working Days (Monday through Friday)	23	18
Weeks	5	4

	In the 50-Week Commercial Year	*In the 12-Month Calendar Year*
	Marketing Period 3	*March*
Holidays	2 days	1 day
Period Ends	Friday 17th April	Tuesday 31st March
Working Days (Monday through Friday)	23	21
Weeks	5	4 (+ 2 days)
	Marketing Period 4	*April*
Holidays	Nil	1 day
Period Ends	Friday 22nd May	Thursday 30th April
Working Days (Monday through Friday)	25	21
Weeks	5	4 (+ 2 days)

	In the 50-Week Commercial Year	*In the 12-Month Calendar Year*
	Marketing Period 5	*May*
Holidays	1 day	1 day
Period Ends	Friday 26th June	Saturday 30th May
Working Days (Monday through Friday)	24	20
Weeks	5	4 (+ 1 day)
		June
Holidays		Nil
Period Ends		Tuesday 30th June
Working Days (Monday through Friday)		22
Weeks		4 (+ 2 days)

	In the 50-Week Commercial Year	*In the 12-Month Calendar Year*
	Marketing Period 6	*July*
Holidays	Nil	Nil
Period Ends	Friday 7th August	Friday 31st July
Working Days (Monday through Friday)	25	23
Weeks	5	4 (+ 3 days)
	Marketing Period 7	*August*
Holidays	1 day	Nil
Period Ends	Friday 11th September	Monday 31st August
Working Days (Monday through Friday)	24	21
Weeks	5	4 (+ 1 day)

	In the 50-Week Commercial Year	*In the 12-Month Calendar Year*
	Marketing Period 8	*September*
Holidays	1 day	1 day
Period Ends	Friday 16th October	Wednesday 30th September
Working Days (Monday through Friday)	24	22
Weeks	5	4 (+ 2 days)
	Marketing Period 9	*October*
Holidays	1 day	1 day
Period Ends	Friday 20th November	Saturday 31st October
Working Days (Monday through Friday)	24	22
Weeks	5	4 (+ 2 days)

	In the 50-Week Commercial Year	*In the 12-Month Calendar Year*
	Marketing Period 10	*November*
Holidays	2 days	2 days
Period Ends	Friday 25th December	Monday 30th November
Working Days (Monday through Friday)	23	21
Weeks	5	4 (+ 1 day)
		December
Holidays		1 day
Period Ends		Thursday 31st December
Working Days (Monday through Friday)		22
Weeks		4 (+ 3 days)

	In the 50-Week Commercial Year	*In the 12-Month Calendar Year*		
Working weeks of less than 5 days (not counting bank holidays) in a period	None	Jan	(1st)	3 days short
		March	(last)	3 days short
		April	(1st)	2 days short
			(last)	1 day short
		May	(1st)	4 days short
		June	(last)	3 days short
		July	(1st)	2 days short
		Aug	(last)	4 days short
		Sept	(1st)	1 day short
			(last)	2 days short
		Oct	(1st)	3 days short
		Nov	(last)	4 days short
		Dec	(1st)	1 day short
			(last)	1 day short

	In the 50-Week Commercial Year	*In the 12-Month Calendar Year*
Working Day Differences in Each Period	3 periods of 25 days (Marketing periods 1, 4 and 6)	1 month 23 days (July)
	4 periods of 24 days (Marketing periods 5, 7, 8 and 9)	3 months 22 days (Jun, Sept and Dec.)
	3 periods of 23 days (Marketing periods 2, 3 and 10)	5 months 21 days (Jan, Mar, Apr, Aug, and Oct.)
		1 month 20 days (May)
		1 month 19 days (Nov)
		1 month 18 days (Feb)

	In the 50-Week Commercial Year	*In the 12-Month Calendar Year*
Last day of the period	Friday	Monday 2 (Aug and Nov) Tuesday 2 (Mar and June) Wednesday 1 (Sep) Thursday 2 (Apr and Dec) Friday 1 (July) Saturday 3 (Jan, Feb, and Oct) Sunday 1 (May)
Full Weeks (5 days) within the period	*Periods 1–5* 25 +1 *Periods 6–10* 25 +1	*Jan—Jun* 23 *Jul—Dec* 22

	In the 50-Week Commercial Year	*In the 12-Month Calendar Year*
First Half of the Year Comparisons to Second Half of Year		
Holidays	*Periods 1–5* 5	*Jan—Jun* 6
	Periods 6–10 5	*Jul—Dec* 5
Working Days	*Periods 1–5* 120 (+ one extra week)	*Jan—Jun* 123
	Periods 6–10 120 (+ one extra week)	*Jul—Dec* 131

CHAPTER TWELVE

ANALYSIS OF CAPABILITY

Perhaps the most common problem in the relationship between marketers and corporate management is establishing just what both will accept as *success*. Therefore, the first task must always be the establishment of *goals* which everyone can recognize and be able to accept when they are reached. List what professional goals would satisfy you, then establish the goals you would like on a business or profit basis, and finally, list your personal goals related to family, friends and your needs as an individual. There are so many people who retire wishing they had done such an exercise the day they graduated from college or when they established their firm, that not to include it in this introduction to building a marketing program would be wrong. If the answers can be justified in comparison, then *success* can become a reality both on a subjective level, as well as upon attainment of the goals set.

COLLECTING THE FACTS FOR GAINING NEW BUSINESS

Most experts agree that records are the main tool of any business, and that careful analysis of what a firm or an individual has done in the past is the best foundation upon which to build growth and improvement in the future. For those firms or individuals just starting out, the following systems of analysis can be used from the outset to build an understanding of the progress as it happens. For those already established, it will help evaluate past performance and highlight potential growth areas to develop.

The most common *mistake* anyone can make when considering a marketing program is to base their plans solely upon the *successes* they have enjoyed in the past. To really analyze the capabilities of a sales force, firm or individual, it is necessary to take into account the negative factors discovered during the exercise as well. Most people can quote their past successes, contracts won, or projects completed; but it is human nature to forget the failures. Understanding why contracts were not won, why proposals failed, or why they did not earn the required profit, or even the minimum profit predicted, is just as important to the construction of a marketing program.

Whether one wishes to analyze a multi-office operation or just the success rate of an individual, the method is basically the same. To begin with, it is necessary to develop a formula so that events and data can be compared and analyzed when the process of collecting the facts is complete. The first step is to gather all the proposals of business made during the period to be analyzed. Many firms do not keep proposals that were *Lost* in readily accessible form, so it is necessary to first establish that **all** the proposals or bids (or as many as possible) that were made in the period are included. The easiest way to check this is to take the *copy letter file* and *appointment diary,* and produce a list (in date order) of all those people to whom a business approach quoting price or terms was made. Where a copy letter or entry exists to prove a proposal was made, or at least offered by way of suggestion, then the relevant information should be gathered from the staff involved in that proposal.

A Proposal of Business includes the following:

1. A meeting with a potential client from which business should develop, or where subsequently another firm or individual is employed.

2. Any *offer of services* in the form of letters, contract discussion or where price/fee is discussed.
3. Any inquiry from a potential client which led to business being offered (either to you or to a competitor).
4. A meeting, exchange of letters, or *offer to work* which resulted in a contract being given to you or others.

For those firms or individuals unable to raise all the answers included in the following *Proposal Analysis Data* listing, due to incomplete records or inadequate existing records systems, then only a part of the potential of real analysis can be achieved. Obviously, the comparisons and analysis described later can only be performed where every proposal involved has the relevant facts established to do so.

Going back too far into a firm's history can be just as counter-productive as not analyzing past performance at all. The usual period covered by marketing analysis is one year, however, where a firm is working on long-term contracts, two years, even five years, is sometimes required. Factors such as change in management executives or policy can be evaluated also by taking two equal periods and comparing results (e.g., the 12 months prior to the change and the 12 months since).

Where cash flow—sales volume—or profits are being evaluated, such factors as inflation, production costs and other overhead expenditure changes would need to be applied to the results to adjust *numerical results* to be applicable to analysis. (For example, a firm which increased its sales volume from 2 million dollars to 2.2 million dollars in a year where the inflation rate was 18%and all other cost factors remained constant in comparison, would in fact have suffered at least a $160,000 setback in real terms.)

Whether or not your existing records are able to produce all the details necessary, it will be beneficial if you are able to introduce the system for all future proposals. If it is only possible to go back to the beginning of the present financial year, then you can look forward to far greater knowledge of how efficient your Business Gaining Activity is before the next year begins.

PROPOSAL ANALYSIS DATA FORM

Few people *like* filling in forms, but once they are able to see the benefits of such activity, gaining full cooperation is not usually difficult. The few minutes it takes to complete the **Proposal Analysis Data Form** can save many hours, perhaps even weeks, of wasted effort (and professional frustration) which becomes an ongoing reward for the small amount of time required to fill out the forms. Experience has proved that most responsible people in a sales team are only too happy to assist analysis programs. It may be a little cynical to state, but more often than not, those who put up the strongest reasons for not doing so (too busy, etc.) are usually the ones who have the most to hide. Experience also proves that nine times out of ten the reluctant sales staff are usually the most disorganized—and inefficient—when the facts are analyzed.

PROPOSAL ANALYSIS DATA FORM©

PROPOSAL FILE CODE

SALES EXECUTIVE

COMPLETION DATE week month year

1. Name of Client

2. Address of Client
Town or City — County or State
Postal Code — AREA LOCATION

3. Address of Project
Town or City — County or State
City — State
Postal Code — AREA LOCATION

4. Description of work, products or services offered.

5. Have we submitted other Proposals to this client before? Yes No
NUMBER SUBMITTED — LAST PROPOSAL IN month year — FILE CODE

6. Have we worked with this client before? Yes No
FINANCIAL STATUS A B C D E — PAST CONTACT

7. Was a written Proposal submitted to this client? Yes No

8. Was this Proposal altered significantly during the negotiations? Yes No

9. Was this client referred to us by a past client? Referred by — Yes No

10. Overseeing Interest. out

11. Origin of this business opportunity

12. Who were our main competitors on this Project.

13. Negotiation period — FIRST MEETING week month day year — ORDER PLACED week month day year — TOTAL NUMBER WEEKS

14. Meeting locations — FIRST MEETING: OUR OFFICE ☐ CLIENT'S OFFICE ☐ Other — FINAL MEETING: OUR OFFICE ☐ CLIENT'S OFFICE ☐ Other

15. Main Client Contact — Name — Position

16. Time scale — PREDICTED DURATION OF PROJECT FROM DATE OF ORDER TO COMPLETION AND INVOICE
A B C D E

17. Profit potential — PREDICTED PRICE, PROFIT PERCENTAGE OR FEES
A B C D E

18. Size of Order — PREDICTED SIZE OF PROJECT IN NUMBERS, AREA, HOURS OR PRICE
A B C D E

19. Other staff/others active in Proposal

20. Status
PENDING DECISION — REVIEW DATE month day year week
REVIEW REQUESTED BY CLIENT — BY month day year week
ORDER LOST — ORDER GAINED

21. Business Activity.

ACCOUNTING	FILM INDUSTRY
ADVERTISING	FINANCIAL INSTITUTIONS
AEROSPACE DEVELOPMENT	FIRE PREVENTION
AEROSPACE MANUFACTURE	FOOD MANUFACTURE
AEROSPACE OPERATIONS	FOOD SALES
AGRICULTURAL RESEARCH	FURNISHINGS MANUFACTURE
AGRICULTURAL EQUIPMENT MANUFACTURE	FURNISHINGS DISTRIBUTION & SALES
AGRICULTURAL MANAGEMENT	GARAGING AND PARKING
AGRICULTURAL DISTRIBUTION & SALES	GOVERNMENT (NATIONAL)
	GOVERNMENT (LOCAL)
AIRCRAFT MANUFACTURE	HARDWARE MANUFACTURE SALES
AIRCRAFT SERVICE	HEATING & VENTILATION
AIRCRAFT OPERATION	HOMES (INSTITUTIONAL)
ARCHITECTURE	HOSPITALS
ASSOCIATIONS (CULTURAL)	HOTELS
ASSOCIATIONS (SOCIAL)	IMPORT/EXPORT MANAGEMENT
ASSOCIATIONS (PROFESSIONAL)	INDUSTRIAL PARK DEVELOPMENT
ASSOCIATIONS POLITICAL	INDUSTRIAL PARK MANAGEMENT
BANKING	INSURANCE CORPORATIONS
BOAT BUILDING	INSURANCE BROKERS
BOAT BUILDING MAINTENANCE	INVESTMENT MANAGEMENT
BREWERS & DISTILLERS	JEWELRY MANUFACTURE SALES
BUILDING FITTINGS & COMPONENTS MANUFACTURE	LABORATORIES
BUILDING MANAGEMENT	LAND MANAGEMENT
BUILDING PRODUCTS (HEAVY) MANUFACTURE	MARKET RESEARCH
BUILDING CONSTRUCTION	MATERIALS HANDLING
BUSINESS CONSULTANCY	MEDICAL EQUIPMENT
CAR RENTAL	MORTGAGE BROKERS
CAR SALES	MUSEUMS & ART GALLERIES
CATERING	MUSIC
CHARITY FUND ASSOCIATIONS	MUSICAL EQUIPMENT
CHEMICAL INDUSTRY	NEWSPAPERS
CHEMICAL SALES	OFFICE EQUIPMENT
CHILD-ORIENTED INDUSTRY	OIL & PETROLEUM PRODUCTION
CHURCH MANAGEMENT	OIL & PETROLEUM MANAGEMENT
CIVIL ENGINEERING	PACKAGING
CLEANING & MAINTENANCE	PAINT MANUFACTURE & SALES
CLINICS & HEALTH CENTERS	PHARMACEUTICALS
CLOTHING MANUFACTURERS	PHOTOGRAPHIC EQUIPMENT
CLOTHING SALES	PHOTOGRAPHY
CLUBS (SOCIAL)	PLASTICS
CLUBS (GENERAL)	POLITICAL ORGANIZATIONS
CLUBS (SPORTS)	POSTAL & DELIVERY SERVICE
CLUBS (POLITICAL)	PRINTING
COAL & SOLID FUEL	PROPERTY DEVELOPMENT
COMMUNICATIONS EQUIPMENT	PROPERTY INVESTMENT
COMMUNICATIONS OPERATION	PUBLIC UTILITIES
COMPUTER MANUFACTURE	PUBLISHING
COMPUTER SOFTWARE & SALES	RADIO & TELEVISION
CONFERENCE CENTERS	RAILWAYS
CONSUMER GOODS (APPLIANCES) MANUFACTURE	RESTAURANTS
	ROAD TRANSPORT MANUFACTURE
CONSUMER GOODS (APPLIANCES) SALES & SERVICE	SAVINGS & LOAN
COSMETIC MANUFACTURE	SCHOOLS & COLLEGES
COSMETIC SALES	SCIENTIFIC RESEARCH
CREDIT MANAGEMENT	SECURITIES
DEPARTMENT STORES	SOFT DRINK MANUFACTURE
DEVELOPMENT ORGANIZATIONS	STATIONERY MANUFACTURE
DOCKS & PORT OPERATION	STATIONERY DISTRIBUTION & SALES
EDUCATIONAL PRODUCTS	THEATERS
EDUCATION	TIMBER MANUFACTURE OR DISTRIBUTION
ELECTRICAL MANUFACTURE	TRAVEL AGENCY
ELECTRONICS	WAREHOUSING
ELECTRICAL INSTALLATIONS	WASTE DISPOSAL
ENERGY CONSERVATION	OTHER
ENTERTAINMENT & LEISURE	
EXHIBITIONS & DISPLAYS	

To successfully manage any sales force, or develop a real marketing program, all of the questions listed below must be answered for every proposal made in the period to be evaluated. How to collate the answers and develop an understanding of performance is explained later.

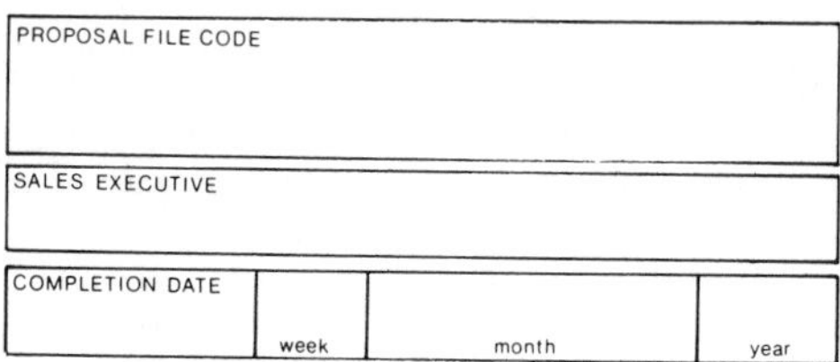
PROPOSAL FILE CODE

SALES EXECUTIVE

COMPLETION DATE	week	month	year

To assist in managing any Analysis Program every proposal should be given a **Proposal File Code** under which all details leading up to gaining or losing an order can be recorded. This number should be entered in the box provided on the form. It can use any series of letters and numbers to meet your needs, the following is an example only:

CN	4	2007	/81
initial of sales executive	office	proposal number in issue order	year

On every **Proposal Analysis Data Form** the name of the **Sales Executive** should be entered in the box provided. Someone always carries responsibility for directing negotiations, and therefore for gaining or losing a client, and that name should be noted. (Later you will read about methods to analyze the efforts of those involved in a proposal, their successes, and their weaknesses.) The **month** and **year** that the completed **Proposal Analysis Data Form** is passed in to be analyzed should be noted in the box provided. (Forms marked **PENDING DECISION** and **REVIEW REQUESTED BY**

CLIENT, Question 20, should not have this date box entered, as these proposals are not yet complete nor will be until a real decision is made by the client.)

1. Name of Client	

NAME OF CLIENT

The client or potential client's name or title. Simply explained, this is the firm or person's name that will produce the order and will pay for your products or services. It should be the **full** name or title as appears on the client's letterhead or in the legal contract.

2. Address of Client		
	Town or City	County or State
	Postal Code	AREA LOCATION

ADDRESS OF CLIENT

Again, the criteria of who places the order or authorizes payment will decide this answer.

3. Address of Project	Town or City	County or State
	City	State
	Postal Code	AREA LOCATION

ADDRESS OF PROJECT

The actual address of the project or delivery point is required if it differs from the answer to Question 2. Where there are several answers applicable to this question, you must decide whether a series of **Proposal Analysis Data Forms** are required, or you can enter the answer **Multiple** and note the addresses on the back of the form for more detailed evaluation if it becomes necessary later.

4. Description of work, products or services offered.	

DESCRIPTION OF WORK, PRODUCTS OR SERVICES OFFERED

Description of the work involved, or the details of the transaction you have proposed should be noted. To make analysis easier it will help, if it is possible, to develop a standard list of services offered, product codes or other contract titles so that in each case the answer to this question is one which is immediately understood.

5. Have we submitted other Proposals to this client before?					Yes	No
NUMBER SUBMITTED		LAST PROPOSAL IN	month	year	FILE CODE	

HAVE WE SUBMITTED OTHER PROPOSALS TO THIS CLIENT BEFORE?

This answer does not depend upon whether or not the proposal or proposals made previously were successful. The answer is simply **Yes** or **No,** and the relevant box on the form should be so marked. If the answer is **Yes,** then the further answers of *number* and *date/code* should be entered. *Number* is the number of times you have submitted independent proposals in the past, and *date/code* should be entered with the month and year of the last proposal made and its **Proposal Analysis Data Form** code number to allow further investigation later should that be required.

6. Have we worked with this client before?						Yes	No
FINANCIAL STATUS	A	B	C	D	E	PAST CONTACT	

HAVE WE WORKED WITH THIS CLIENT BEFORE?

The answer can only be **Yes** or **No,** and the relevant box must be marked. Sometimes it may occur that, although you have not worked for the company listed as *client* on this form, you may have worked for or with the person you are now dealing with at another company. In this case, the answer to the question is still **No,** but the box **Contact** should be marked to identify that fact for later evaluation.

In today's economic situation, bad payers can be as bad as having no clients at all and therefore it is wise to know the status of your success with regards to the credit rating of those you deal with. There are two methods of evaluating your position in this sector.

1. If you have had dealings with this potential client before, you have a history of payment to work with, and the average period of payment can be entered in the boxes **A** through **E.**
2. If you have not dealt with this potential client before, then retaining a credit search agency or utilizing your own in-house credit manager would be advisable. Entering the result in the boxes marked **Financial Status** will help you evaluate your actual or predicted cash flow situation. You must establish your own ratings for each of the categories involved to meet your business needs, for example:

   A = on presentation of invoice
   B = 1-14 days
   C = 14-30 days
   D = 30-60 days
   E = 60 days plus

7. Was a written Proposal submitted to this client?	Yes	No

WAS A WRITTEN PROPOSAL SUBMITTED TO THIS CLIENT?

Sometimes a proposal is made and accepted for detailed confirmation later (i.e., professionals are often hired by *letter of intent* on an hourly payment basis, or goods are ordered from catalogues without a formal written tender or bid). In such cases, no *written proposal* was made and the relevant box should be marked.

8. Was this Proposal altered significantly during the negotiations?	Yes	No

WAS THIS PROPOSAL ALTERED SIGNIFICANTLY DURING THE NEGOTIATIONS?

The answer to this question, when considered with the input from other answers, can do much to evaluate the standard of your business proposals. In short, it is necessary to decide for yourself what constitutes significant change—e.g., price change, extra services entered, etc., but it should be answered **Yes,** where by making the change you effectively reduced the profit involved or had to offer faster delivery or completion to gain the order.

9. Was this client referred to us by a past client?	Referred by	Yes	No

WAS THIS CLIENT REFERRED TO US BY A PAST CLIENT?

The answer to this must reflect whether or not the client *came to you.* If you gained the *recommendation* of past clients to assist the proposal, or showed examples of your work with the assistance of satisfied past clients, but you *introduced* the potential client to *them,* then that does not constitute referral in this case. Only where a past client directed this client to approach you, or introduced you to them, can you answer **Yes** to this question. If you were referred to this client by a past client, then their name should be entered in the box **Referred by.**

10. Overseeing Interest.		out

OVERSEEING INTEREST

Sometimes the name of the client on a proposal or contract can be misleading during later analysis. The reason for this is simple, but often overlooked. An **Overseeing Interest** is a person, company, or even government or corporation department who, in fact, has the ability to agree or veto awarding you the business. In some cases, the **Overseeing Interest** can be someone who refers the business to you or introduces you to the potential client. In other words, the **Overseeing Interest** can be anyone who has an interest in your being retained and who could possibly aid you (or obstruct you) in gaining business in the future.

Obviously, it can help your future plans if you know who *controls* the potential client, whether you won or lost this proposal. Therefore, if the client is part of a group of companies, a part of a corporation, or even an individual who works for a corporation, institute or other body, then this *link* must be established. Enter in this box the *link* by noting the corporation or body involved. If this answer relates to an organization outside of your catchment area (out of town, out of state, or foreign based) mark the box out for later analysis.

11. Origin of this business opportunity	

ORIGIN OF THIS BUSINESS OPPORTUNITY

All new business originated somewhere and you need to know the sources. If it came from an inquiry, discover what prompted the potential client to inquire. If you were told that the potential client was in the market, or were introduced to them, you need to know the name of the person involved and why they helped you. If you *researched* the potential for yourself, the sources from which you gained the information should be noted.

12. Who were our main competitors on this Project.	

WHO WERE OUR MAIN COMPETITORS ON THIS PROJECT?

Knowing who won the business you lost, or who you overcame in presentation and business activity, is the best way to evaluate your efficiency in sales effort. Later, ways to develop an understanding of this most important aspect of business are dealt with, but to enable you to do this you must know the facts. If you lost a proposal, the competitor who overcame your presentation should be marked as the winner on the **Proposal Analysis Data Form.**

13. Negotiation period	FIRST MEETING	week	month	day	year	ORDER PLACED	week	month	day	year	TOTAL NUMBER WEEKS	

NEGOTIATION PERIOD

Enter the date of the first meeting and the date the proposal was either lost or became a contract. These dates are important, as they can be used later to establish *lead-in time* trends and to pinpoint *periods of business activity.* Diaries, letters, telephone logs and many other methods can be found to ascertain these dates, if an organized call report system is not already in use.

14. Meeting locations	FIRST MEETING		FINAL MEETING	
	OUR OFFICE ☐	CLIENT'S OFFICE ☐	OUR OFFICE ☐	CLIENT'S OFFICE ☐
	Other		Other	

MEETING LOCATIONS

By noting the place where you held your presentations or meetings, can soon point to where you perform at your best. It can also give you some understanding of how your offices perform in assisting your success rate.

15. Main Client Contact	Name	Position

MAIN CLIENT CONTACT

This question is answered by the name of the most important person (or relevant individual) to whom you made your proposal or presented your abilities to.

For the next three questions (**16, 17** and **18**) a series of five categories should be developed, rather than entering the actual figure in each case. The definitions of these categories should be calculated according to your own experience and projections, and evaluated to best suit the purposes of your analysis.

16. Time scale	PREDICTED DURATION OF PROJECT FROM DATE OF ORDER TO COMPLETION AND INVOICE				
	A	B	C	D	E

TIME SCALE

The proposed or actual project duration. This question relates to the length of time of the contract or to the period between the client placing the order and the final invoice being rendered.

(As an example only:)

A = 1 month or less or 5 weeks or less
B = 1-3 months or 5-10 weeks
C = 3-6 months or 15-25 weeks
D = *6-12 months or 25-50 weeks*
E = 1 year or more or 50 weeks or more

17. Profit potential	PREDICTED PRICE, PROFIT PERCENTAGE OR FEES				
	A	B	C	D	E

PROFIT POTENTIAL

The proposed value of the project. This question can apply to gross volume sales, profits or a percentage in the case of fees.

(As an example only:)

A =	$100,000 or more	or	15% or more
B =	$50-100,000	or	10-15%
C =	$25-50,000	or	7 1/2-10%
D =	$5-25,000	or	5-7 1/2%
E =	$5,000 or less	or	5% or less

18. Size of Order	PREDICTED SIZE OF PROJECT IN NUMBERS, AREA, HOURS OR PRICE				
	A	B	C	D	E

SIZE OF ORDER

The proposed or actual size of the project. This question relates only to quantity, whether it is *square feet, number of items,* or *number of people* involved.

(As an example only:)

A =	100,000 sq. ft. or more	or	1 million or more
B =	50-100,000 sq. ft.	or	500,000-1 million
C =	20-50,000 sq. ft.	or	100,000-1/2 million
D =	5-20,000 sq. ft.	or	10-100,000
E =	5,000 sq. ft. or less	or	less than 10,000

19. Other staff/others active in Proposal		

OTHER STAFF/OTHERS ACTIVE IN PROPOSAL

Which staff members were involved other than the sales executive? The answer to this question could include members of the staff (or consultants, etc.) who were involved in the presentations or negotiations leading up to the client's decision regarding this proposal. Later analysis can use this information to increase the effectiveness of your marketing, sales and negotiation activity.

20. Status	PENDING DECISION REVIEW DATE		month	day	year	week
	REVIEW REQUESTED BY CLIENT BY		month	day	year	week
	ORDER LOST	ORDER GAINED				

STATUS

The status of this proposal. The most important question for which there are only four answers from which to choose:

1—**PENDING DECISION**
2—**REVIEW REQUESTED BY CLIENT**
3—**ORDER LOST**
4—**ORDER GAINED**

If the answer is **REVIEW REQUESTED BY CLIENT** then the date should be noted in the box provided. If the answer **PENDING DECISION** is noted, it may be because the proposal has only recently been issued and this **Proposal Analysis Data Form** should then be transferred to separate keeping until it can be completed. **Forms which fall into Categories 1 and 2 must be analyzed separately from completed forms, otherwise the evaluation cannot be truly accurate.**

21. Business Activity.

ACCOUNTING	FILM INDUSTRY
ADVERTISING	FINANCIAL INSTITUTIONS
AEROSPACE DEVELOPMENT	FIRE PREVENTION
AEROSPACE MANUFACTURE	FOOD MANUFACTURE
AEROSPACE OPERATIONS	FOOD SALES
AGRICULTURAL RESEARCH	FURNISHINGS MANUFACTURE
AGRICULTURAL EQUIPMENT MANUFACTURE	FURNISHINGS DISTRIBUTION & SALES
AGRICULTURAL MANAGEMENT	GARAGING AND PARKING
AGRICULTURAL DISTRIBUTION & SALES	GOVERNMENT (NATIONAL)
	GOVERNMENT (LOCAL)
AIRCRAFT MANUFACTURE	HARDWARE MANUFACTURE SALES
AIRCRAFT SERVICE	
AIRCRAFT OPERATION	HEATING & VENTILATION
ARCHITECTURE	HOMES (INSTITUTIONAL)
ASSOCIATIONS (CULTURAL)	HOSPITALS
ASSOCIATIONS (SOCIAL)	HOTELS
ASSOCIATIONS (PROFESSIONAL)	IMPORT/EXPORT MANAGEMENT
ASSOCIATIONS POLITICAL	INDUSTRIAL PARK DEVELOPMENT
BANKING	INDUSTRIAL PARK MANAGEMENT
BOAT BUILDING	INSURANCE CORPORATIONS
BOAT BUILDING MAINTENANCE	INSURANCE BROKERS
BREWERS & DISTILLERS	INVESTMENT MANAGEMENT
BUILDING FITTINGS & COMPONENTS MANUFACTURE	JEWELRY MANUFACTURE SALES
BUILDING MANAGEMENT	LABORATORIES
BUILDING PRODUCTS (HEAVY) MANUFACTURE	LAND MANAGEMENT
	MARKET RESEARCH
BUILDING CONSTRUCTION	MATERIALS HANDLING
BUSINESS CONSULTANCY	MEDICAL EQUIPMENT
CAR RENTAL	MORTGAGE BROKERS
CAR SALES	MUSEUMS & ART GALLERIES
CATERING	MUSIC
CHARITY FUND ASSOCIATIONS	MUSICAL EQUIPMENT
CHEMICAL INDUSTRY	NEWSPAPERS

CHEMICAL SALES	OFFICE EQUIPMENT
CHILD-ORIENTED INDUSTRY	OIL & PETROLEUM PRODUCTION
CHURCH MANAGEMENT	OIL & PETROLEUM MANAGEMENT
CIVIL ENGINEERING	PACKAGING
CLEANING & MAINTENANCE	PAINT MANUFACTURE & SALES
CLINICS & HEALTH CENTERS	PHARMACEUTICALS
CLOTHING MANUFACTURERS	PHOTOGRAPHIC EQUIPMENT
CLOTHING SALES	PHOTOGRAPHY
CLUBS (SOCIAL)	PLASTICS
CLUBS (GENERAL)	POLITICAL ORGANIZATIONS
CLUBS (SPORTS)	POSTAL & DELIVERY SERVICE
CLUBS (POLITICAL)	PRINTING
COAL & SOLID FUEL	PROPERTY DEVELOPMENT
COMMUNICATIONS EQUIPMENT	PROPERTY INVESTMENT
COMMUNICATIONS OPERATION	PUBLIC UTILITIES
COMPUTER MANUFACTURE	PUBLISHING
COMPUTER SOFTWARE & SALES	RADIO & TELEVISION
CONFERENCE CENTERS	RAILWAYS
CONSUMER GOODS (APPLIANCES) MANUFACTURE	RESTAURANTS
	ROAD TRANSPORT MANUFACTURE
CONSUMER GOODS (APPLIANCES) SALES & SERVICE	SAVINGS & LOAN
COSMETIC MANUFACTURE	SCHOOLS & COLLEGES
COSMETIC SALES	SCIENTIFIC RESEARCH
CREDIT MANAGEMENT	SECURITIES
DEPARTMENT STORES	SOFT DRINK MANUFACTURE
DEVELOPMENT ORGANIZATIONS	STATIONERY MANUFACTURE
DOCKS & PORT OPERATION	STATIONERY DISTRIBUTION & SALES
EDUCATIONAL PRODUCTS	THEATERS
EDUCATION	TIMBER MANUFACTURE OR DISTRIBUTION
ELECTRICAL MANUFACTURE	
ELECTRONICS	TRAVEL AGENCY
ELECTRICAL INSTALLATIONS	WAREHOUSING
ENERGY CONSERVATION	WASTE DISPOSAL
ENTERTAINMENT & LEISURE	OTHER
EXHIBITIONS & DISPLAYS	

CLIENT'S BUSINESS ACTIVITY

It is absolutely necessary to know what business provides the profit or reasoning to enable a potential client to consider buying whatever you are offering. This is probably one of the most neglected of market research options, and merely stating such business activities on first impression is not enough. There needs to be a statement of business activity of the type the potential client would use to describe themselves and the answer indicated against the listing shown or described in the box other. If the client is in several fields of profit earning, then the *prime* or *main activity* should be used and reference to the others noted.

To evaluate just *who* does *what* to carry through a Marketing Analysis upon past performance and to evaluate experience and capabilities, is dependent upon the size of the firm involved. There is no reason, in fact, why the analysis cannot be applied to an individual and, at the other end of the scale, its theories and applications could be used to analyze the same results for a multi-national corporation.

To begin with, the **Proposal Analysis Data Forms** must be completed and the answers established to be factual. For this purpose, the sales executive/negotiator responsible for a proposal can enter all the facts required with the possible exception of:

a) The Proposal File Code.
b) Question 5—where details may be required from records of a confidential nature.
c) Question 6—where records may have to be retrieved.
d) Question 18—where details may be confidential.

Other than the above possible exceptions, the majority of detail required will be readily available to the competent sales executive or will exist in company documents.

The next step is to collate and compare the answers to develop a full understanding—for as Shakespeare explained, *"All past is prologue."* It is for this purpose that a firm needs a Marketing Administrator (or someone who can take the responsibility) to devote the time and commitment to the task of the analysis procedure. Invariably, the results of a Proposal Analysis are somewhat surprising and, of course, should be kept confidential throughout the exercise for this reason. The fewer people who know the outcome prior to the formulation of policy or program, the better. It is usually a matter for principals alone, at least until the solutions to any problems raised have been established.

You can not win a battle you refuse to fight, and you only lose it when you give up fighting.

John Hathaway-Bates
University of Southern California. 1983

CHAPTER THIRTEEN

ORGANIZATION OF A MARKETING ANALYSIS

The reasoning behind the need for a **Marketing Analysis** is quite simple in that all too often an individual, firm or organization can be too *busy* to take the time to evaluate exactly what it is doing. The old saying about *being too close to the trees to see the forest* is true in many commercial undertakings, and probably even more so in the professions. The modern pressure of day-to-day activity can soon bring about an almost routine situation where it is possible to find oneself doing what is to be done today, and worrying about what tomorrow might have in store only when it comes. Concentrating completely upon the work at hand like this, the present project, or this month's problems, is something that can only be compared to the act of pulling string through a hole in a wall. If the string knots itself on the other side of the wall you will be unable to do anything about it, and if the end of the piece you are pulling suddenly comes through the hole, then you will have to find something else to do with your time. This analogy, which is used to describe *Management by Routine,* is far more complex than it at first appears in that knowledge of the reserve of string is completely outside of your control and judgment, yet the routine work is able to commit you to hours, if not years of activity. The real need is to dismantle the wall, of course, but as long as your total attention and both your hands are employed in pulling the string through the hole, then you are really controlled by rather than in control of the situation, as it would at first appear.

This is very similar to many business situations as well. Everyone is so involved in doing *today's task* they forget to analyze the situation or to do anything about the real objective—which is to make the future easier, more productive and safer for all concerned.

All a **Marketing Analysis** can do is allow you to see the real situation; what you decide to do then is dependent upon your goals and capabilities. Experience has proven that many firms welcome and accept the ideas which were outlined in the first part of this book, but employ them before they have invested the time to evaluate the **what, when, how** and **why** they can best use a Marketing Program and what it can do for them. (Reverting to the analogy again, it can only be compared to kicking the wall with your bare feet.) There is nothing mystical about Marketing and, with very few exceptions, no *easy luck* way to achieve ongoing success. Conceptual Marketing is made possible only by the application of certain systems and actions. *Pep talks, confidence meetings, other people's gimmicks* and *commonly known sales techniques* do far more for the ego than they ever do to create an ongoing stable growth situation. The staff turnover problem in many businesses is really due to these activities more than anything else. A firm will always benefit when it deals in facts regarding its sales management, rather than relying upon words of optimism and claims of unsubstantiated ability guaranteeing the future. Staff who never really know what is happening can never be expected to feel satisfied and secure, and this situation of constant change, new directions, hire one month—lay off the next, is the guaranteed future of any firm which operates without an established system of marketing administration and a controlled marketing program.

As was stated earlier, a **Marketing Analysis** which will evaluate the most comprehensive overview must be based upon the proposals made over a predetermined period. The reasons for this will become fully apparent as the possible evaluations are described.

All proposals must be included for the period it has been decided to analyze and, of course, these proposals will fall into two categories:

1. Those which have not yet reached a decision stage.
2. Those for which a decision has been reached.

Therefore, during the Analysis this situation must be identified to prevent misreading. It is of course possible to separate the proposals into two units and carry out an analysis on both independently, or one can color code the entries corresponding to the status of the proposal at the time of the analysis. Whichever system is used only one **Proposal Analysis Data Form** will ever have to be produced for a particular project.

To keep things simple, a color code should be established, e.g.,

ORDER LOST — YELLOW
PENDING DECISION — GREEN
REVIEW REQUESTED — PINK
ORDER GAINED — RED

All the entries on the **Proposal Analysis Development Sheets** should then be color coded relevant to their status at the time of the analysis.

How to use the facts you have gathered is really a matter of establishing what you want to know, and then collating the *analysis* to provide the answers. If you have been in business for more than five years, then perhaps the most surprising thing that you will have to learn is that you are probably *specializing* to some extent in an area, or to an extent you had not realized. The amount of factual information and management assistance which can be gained from a **Marketing Analysis** program is only limited by the number of uses you apply it to. The depth of the analysis is only limited by the time you can provide to it and, of course, that will be totally dependent upon the business you are in. The following notes will give you some ways of putting the new knowledge you have gained to work immediately, however, bear in mind, that this is only a fraction of what your analysis can be made to do.

BUSINESS RECORDS AND LISTINGS

All the proposals you have analyzed prove that the people or firms involved *recognized* the need for your help, just by listening to you. This implies that there could be business forthcoming from them in the future, on condition that:

i) Where you *won* the business, make sure you keep in contact with the decision-maker on a personal basis—place all those involved in helping you on your Christmas card list—and make sure the important names are added to your mailing list for reprints, in-house functions, etc., for even if they cannot give you more of their own business, they are a powerful contact to help you with referrals.

ii) Where you *lost* the business—endeavor to learn as much as you can about the firm and competitor that beat you—and why. Put the decision-maker on your mailing list—and establish the time period until the project will re-enter the market—and make sure you get the next project.

Using the answers to Question 1 *Name of client* and Question 2 *Address of client* on the **Proposal Analysis Data Form,** it is possible to prepare a listing which can save many hours of wasted work at a later date. Create two lists, the first being those people or firms for whom you worked (and invoiced), and the second being those prospects by whom your proposal was rejected. Both lists should be collated twice, the first time in *alphabetical order,* and the second time in relation to *geographic areas.* Every entry in these lists should be identified by the code number of the proposal or proposals involved, so that you can retrieve the relevant information from your files quickly should it be required. If an **Overseeing Interest (OSI)** is involved, that should be noted as well. A typical entry might look like the example shown:

A & B COMPUTERS, INC.
1234 Anystreet Avenue
WEST HOME TOWN,
California 90000
(213) 123-1234
Contact: John Johnson
V.P. Facilities and Purchasing
OSI—FRED BLOGGS & ASSN.
(213) 123-4321

PROPOSAL ANALYSIS DEVELOPMENT SHEET©

Subject of Analysis

A

Period of Analysis

month | day | year — month | day | year

date

month | day | year

C

	File Code	Proposal made to	Month	Detail	1	2	3	4	5	6	7	8	9	10
1														
2														
3														
4														
5														
6														
7														
8														
9														
10														
11														
12														
13														
14														
15		B								grid				
16														
17														
18														
19														
20														
21														
22														
23														
24														
25														
26														
27														
28														
29														
30														

11	12	13	14	15	16	17	18	19	20	21	22	23	24	25	26	27	28	29	30	31	32	33	34	35	
																									1
																									2
																									3
																									4
																									5
																									6
																									7
																									8
																									9
																									10
																									11
																									12
																									13
																									14
																									15
																									16
																									17
																									18
																									19
																									20
																									21
																									22
																									23
																									24
																									25
																									26
																									27
																									28
																									29
																									30

PROPOSAL ANALYSIS DEVELOPMENT SHEET

To evaluate the information you have collected on completed **Proposal Analysis Data Forms** is a simple process of cross-examination. For this purpose, the **Proposal Analysis Development Sheets** were created, however, these forms are merely a sophisticated time-saver and you can, of course, create your own tabulation to do the same task.

DEVELOPMENT OF THE MARKETING ANALYSIS

The development sheets are laid out to allow various projects to be collated against the various sets of answers to establish a trend or prove developments in the performance of an individual, sales force or total organization over a predetermined period of time. The sheets are subdivided to allow easy arrangement of similar projects, individual action or area answers which can thereby be grouped into sections for easy comparison. On the example sheet shown, the divisions have been marked for explanation.

Subject of Analysis								

Period of Analysis						date		
month	day	year	month	day	year	month	day	year

BOX A—contains the details of what or who is being analyzed, along with the period of time involved and the date of the analysis.

	File Code	Proposal made to	Month	Detail
1				
2				
3				
4				
5				
6				
7				
8				
9				
10				
11				
12				
13				
14				
15		B		
16				
17				
18				
19				
20				
21				
22				
23				
24				
25				
26				
27				
28				
29				
30				

BOX B—is used to list the projects being analyzed (proposal file code, name of client, and the month in which the proposal was made). The projects can be listed in respect to date of proposal, size, geographic area, sales executive responsibility or any of various combinations to make comparison easier.

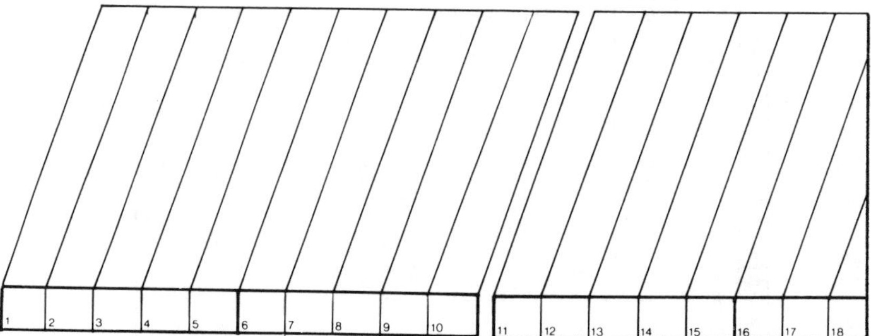

BOX C—lists the alternative answers available to the question being asked, or the facts being established.

The **grid** is then used to evaluate the relevant answers.

For example, if you wished to evaluate an overview of the success of your sales staff relative to size of project, the following collation would help:

1. Taking the **Proposal Analysis Data Forms** and separating them in relation to Question 18 *Size of Order* would give you five separate units.

2. Then starting at 01 in **Box B** you would list the lowest *size* project—proposal file code—name of client—month of proposal—progressively listing in size order continue through all proposals in the **E** answer unit. In the **Detail** Box enter the actual size figure. Then, in turn, enter the details for the projects in the **D, C, B** and **A** units in size order.

3. Then list in **Box C** all those members of your staff whose names appear in the *sales executive* box on the **Proposal Analysis Data Form.** To gain even more understanding leave a space in **Box C** and then go on to list all the names entered in answer to Question 19 *Other staff/others active in proposal* on the **Proposal Analysis Data Form.**

4. With these details entered you are able to examine each proposal in turn, and enter an **X** on the Grid against *Proposal* (horizontal alignment) and *Sales Executive* (vertical alignment). Further **X** entries linking the names of other staff involved will give you a more detailed study.
5. The last action required is to total the entries for each staff member involved, and you will have a factual record of sales performance relative to size of project.

Sometimes it is necessary to list proposals for which a true conclusion has been reached, **and** proposals which are still pending a decision or awaiting review. In this case, those proposals for which a definite conclusion has not been gained should be identified (by highlighting with a pink or green marker). Those proposals which have been *lost* should also be identified (by highlighting with a yellow marker).

PROPOSAL ANALYSIS DEVELOPMENT SHEET (LAYOUT 1)

To analyze the **Geographic Location Influence** on a firm's performance, a **Proposal Analysis Development Sheet** should be prepared as follows: First, divide up all the **Proposal Analysis Data Forms** into groupings for each Sales Executive involved. Then, enter each salesperson's group of forms (in size order) *NB in **Box B** of the sheet, leaving two spaces beneath each set for totals. **Orders Lost** should be highlighted with a yellow marker. **Proposal Analysis Data Forms** *Pending Approval* and *Review Required* should be analyzed separately. In **Box C** of the Development Sheet, enter in either geographic groupings or alphabetical order a listing including all *Locations* mentioned in the answer section of Question 2 *Address of Client* or Question 3 *Address of Proposal,* depending upon which set of facts you are evaluating at the time. In the Detail Section of **Box B,** enter the *size of order* for each project to be analyzed. This layout for the **Proposal Analysis Development Sheet** can be used for the following **Marketing Analysis Procedures.**

> *NB Effectively this normally means preparing separate sheets for each of the **A, B, C, D** and **E** categories of Question 18 *Size of Order* on the **Proposal Analysis Data Forms.** Thereby having a sheet, or sheets, for all proposals which fall into the **A** category, with the category letter (e.g., **A**) as relevant being entered for each project in the **Detail** Box provided. (This procedure being repeated for each of the other *Size of Order* categories.)

GEOGRAPHIC DEVELOPMENT EVALUATION

The geographic factors of an individual's or a firm's business activity can be of paramount importance to any marketing program or desire for growth. The first step is to establish what activity has transpired, been gained or lost relative to geographic location. For this purpose, Question 2 *Address of Client* and Question 3 *Address of Project* on the **Proposal Analysis Data Form** have been provided with an answer box entitled **Location.** The address alone is too singular to be used for the purpose of this stage of the Analysis, therefore, it is necessary to decide beforehand the geographic areas which will be used for this **Location** answer. Some organizations use postal code areas, others will use city limit boundaries, or county boundaries. The Marketing Administrator responsible for the Analysis must therefore evaluate the *Locations* to fulfil the needs required by the firm involved. The following procedures should be used separately for both **client** and **project** location data (Question 2 *Address of Client* and Question 3 *Address of Project* on the **Proposal Analysis Data Forms).**

GEOGRAPHIC DEVELOPMENT BY WORK DESCRIPTION

Providing that you have been able to develop categories for all the types of work you undertake, then you can now code all the answers given to Question 4 *Description of work, product or service offered* by number or letter, and can complete the prepared **Proposal Analysis Development Sheet** by entering the code in relation to *Project* (horizontally) and *Location* (vertically).

Then by totalling the entries under each *location* for each sales executive, you will establish what and where they are developing.

By comparing the **Types of Work** to the **Locations** you will begin to understand your strengths and weaknesses, relative to geographic areas of your catchment area. It could also prove that you might be drifting into specialization (or a reputation for specialization) in particular geographic areas.

GEOGRAPHIC DEVELOPMENT BY CLIENT USAGE

Often a firm can be presented with the opportunity for increasing its new business catchment area, and not realize it immediately, due to over-concentration on the work in hand. By coding the answers to Question 5 *Have we submitted proposals to this client before?* and Question 6 *Have we worked with this client before?* it is possible to get an insight on such potential, e.g., **New Client = X, Yes** to Question 5 = **P, Yes** to Question 6 = **C.** To sum up, if you cannot enter **C** or even **P** then mark each entry **X** for **New Client,** relating each *Proposal* (horizontally) with *Location* (vertically). The overview this will give you can be used to evaluate the potential of concentrating on certain geographic areas to seek new business opportunities. For example, couldn't the fact that a past client asks you to supply in a new location mean that there is perhaps a lack of your product, service or expertise in that area which you could exploit.

GEOGRAPHIC DIFFERENCES IN PROCEDURE

By examining the positive answers to Question 8 *Was this proposal altered significantly during the negotiations?* in relation to your prepared **Proposal Analysis Development Sheet,** it is possible to gain an insight to the standard of procedure and competition in different geographic areas. Quite often, a firm will spend a lot of time preparing proposals repeatedly for clients in a particular area, only to lose the business because the standards, terminology or terms, which are relevant elsewhere, are not accepted. The standard and content of presentations, procedures, contracts and everything else that goes to make up a proposal to a client varies drastically from location to location. It is obviously a great help to a firm if their proposal can be geared to the needs and acceptance criteria of potential clients in the area they are approaching.

By coding the answers to Question 8 (e.g., **Yes** = **Y, No** = **N**), it is possible to evaluate the success potential of your proposals relative to the geographic area where they are used. The entries should also be color coded to signify acceptance (e.g., **Order Gained** left uncolored; **Order Lost**—Yellow; **Review Requested**—Pink). In some cases it will be necessary to half-color the entry in this instance, as no matter whether the Order was **gained** or **lost,** it is important to know if the client requested that you review your proposal.

The relevance (and acceptance factor) of your proposal content is justified where a line of **N**'s appear under any location. If there is more than a scattering of occasional entries marked **Y**, and half colored Pink and Yellow, then your proposals, contracts, presentations and total sales procedures need to be examined.

Where any particular location has a higher than average number of **Y** entries and Yellow and/or Pink markings, then investigation is required into what your competitors are doing in that area. As a final conclusive check where this happens, see if the answers to Question 12 *Who were our main competitors on this project?* regularly produce the same name relevant to a line of **Yes** answers. If they do, then it is possible that the firm is using a better method of presentation, or you could be suffering from an effective *Price* disadvantage.

GEOGRAPHIC EXPANSION BY REFERRAL

The problem with *geographic expansion by referral* is that often a firm can expand *by chance* with the end result of fragmentation, or of staff leaving to establish a competitive entity to the firm which paid for the expansion. **Geographic Expansion by Referral** can only be beneficial in the long-term if it is seen merely as the first step in the growth process. All too often a firm will believe its sales activity is promoting expansion, when in fact it is only following up leads provided to it by past contacts. In this case, the expansion into new locations of business opportunity is not being exploited to its full extent. But that is only one side of the coin; problems can also arise where individual sales staff rush all over the country without organization or real objectives. Projects of a one-time basis, far from the center of control, are always more difficult to organize than a flow of projects from an area which is known by experience. By examining answers to Question 9 *Was this client referred to us by a Past Client?* it is possible to see if you are working in new areas due to client referral or sales activity.

The answers to Question 10 *Overseeing Interest* can also be employed in this evaluation where the **Overseeing Interest** is a longstanding contact, or one of your **Linked Benefit Partners.** First of all, you need to list all the names entered in answer to Question 9 *Was this client referred to us by a Past Client?* and Question 10 *Overseeing Interest.* These names should then be coded for entry on the **Proposal Analysis Development Sheet, Layout I.** When you have completed the sheet, look for locations where your salespeople developed the business without assistance or referral. Compare the size, profits, duration or type of work you are developing geographically in relation to *referrals,* and establish for yourself whether you like the picture from the point of view of long-term growth, image and security.

Locations where **all** the business activity stems from *referrals* need to be examined, and a sales effort to consolidate that area into producing new business should be instigated. Compare the relationship of **Orders Lost** to **Orders Gained,** relative to who gave you the *referral* (or did not). Experience has proved that there are occasions where a past client or a contact really wants to help you, but due to misunderstanding or lack of knowledge, continues to misrepresent your ability or refers you to work you will probably lose, until in the end they give up out of pure frustration.

GEOGRAPHIC INFLUENCE OF OVERSEEING INTEREST

Quite often, it is possible for a firm to continue trying to gain business in locations where they, for some reason or another, are regularly unsuccessful. Unless this situation happens at short-term intervals, a firm without a Marketing Administration program might not even realize the time they are wasting on such activity. In fact, the cost saving in this area alone can substantially justify the employment of a Marketing Administrator.

Most clients have preferences, even loyalty, to one supplier or another, and the larger the bureaucracy behind the decision-making, the more likely it is for a small cartel to exist in supplying that client. In the case of an **Overseeing Interest,** this *preference* to deal with someone they know or to stipulate the *type* of supplier they will deal with, can be of real importance to any Sales Effort by someone not in that *circle* or *category.*

There is also the possibility that you could be filling the position of *secondary bidder.* Few salespeople have not been on the positive end on this situation, where a prospective client will inform them that *the order is yours, but I have to get a couple of comparative bids.* Effectively, this can become a regular event with some buyers who request comparative bids merely to prove their judgment or validate the accepted proposal. By analyzing your **Orders Lost** and **Orders Gained** on a geographic basis, you can soon see if you are being *suggested* as an alternative without being in for real consideration of the order involved. There are, of course, many ways to combat *exclusions* from certain business opportunities, but first it is necessary to establish **if** they exist in your case, and **who** is effectively keeping you out of the arena.

In reverse, there could be certain **Overseeing Interests** who are assisting you, which if you knew about for certain, or could even establish a pattern, could be exploited more effectively to your benefit. By giving a code number to each of the names appearing in the **Overseeing Interest** answer to Question 10, you will then be able to identify which individual **Overseeing Interest** was involved in each project, relative to each location featured on your prepared **Proposal Analysis Development Sheet, Layout I.** Then by totaling the involvement relative first to **Orders Gained,** and then to **Orders Lost,** you will gain a knowledge of those who are predisposed to accept your services and those who regularly turn you away. You will also be able to establish if a particular geographic location is dependent upon the help or veto of any one *Overseeing Interest.*

To gain further insight into your reputation in any particular location, simply circle those **Overseeing Interest** entries where the **Out** box is marked for Question 10 on the **Proposal Analysis Data Form.** This way you may find a marked difference in acceptance levels where the **Overseeing Interest** is *absent,* meaning you either need to improve your *wider* image or your *local* reputation.

GEOGRAPHIC ORIGINATION RESPONSE

By examining the answers to Question 11 *Origin of this business opportunity,* it is possible to increase the efficiency of your overall marketing operation. Each answer should be given a code number which will relate to a particular origin of the introduction to this client (e.g., Name of Article and Magazine = **1,** and Sales Plan Letter Number 17 = **2,** and Referral by ABC, Inc., = **3,** etc.) repeated for each project the relevant *origin* introduced you to. Then, by entering this code number to link each *Client* (horizontally) to the relevant *Location* (vertically) you will have the basis for real evaluation of your marketing program from a geographic perspective.

The first fact to become apparent is invariably that different sales executives are able to *use* different methods of origin to better individual advantage. You will also usually find that certain marketing actions promoted a lot of interest, and generated many proposals, but brought less **Orders Gained** conclusions than other methods, which were judged less than effective at the time. Isolating the really *effective* marketing activity in this way, can save a firm a great deal of time and money. It can also prove which methods of marketing should be concentrated upon in the future.

TERRITORIAL COMPETITION ANALYSIS

The comparisons between expanding a business and mounting a military campaign are obvious in many cases, but when one begins to think about expansion, the lessons to be learned from military strategy can often be forgotten in the excitement and optimism as it begins to take place. By taking the answers to Question 13 *Who were our main competitors on this project?* and applying them to *geographic* locations, you will soon evaluate what changes are required to your presentations to be successful. First give a **Code**

Number to each of the competitors named in your **Proposal Analysis Data Forms** which were included as **an Order Lost.** Then, enter against the name of the *Lost Clients* (horizontally) and the *Location* (vertically) the **Code Number** of which competitor **GAINED** the order. By totaling the numbers of times you *lost* in any particular location to competitors (on a separate sheet of paper under the competitor's name) you will begin to appreciate your relative strength or weaknesses. If you continually *lose* to the same competitor in a certain location, check through your **Orders Gained** to see if you have ever *beaten* that competitor in that location. If not, then check to see if you have beaten them anywhere else. If you have, then you have a key to investigating their territorial control of the areas where you *lost.* If you have not beaten them elsewhere, then you need to set up a program to investigate their methods and products immediately, or retreat from their territory and hope they keep out of yours. Having established your strengths and weaknesses, you can turn to exploiting the territorial weaknesses of others.

GEOGRAPHIC ASPECTS OF NEGOTIATION PERIODS

Understanding the *think to buy* and *cash available* patterns of any geographical area, is something which can mean the difference between a sales program being a runaway success and a cold start. All areas experience certain times in the year where they first begin to think about stocking up, expanding, renovating or improving their operation. Then, there are those times when an area has a *localized payday.* Working out all the reasons, counter-reasons and trends is the task of the Economist or Financial Analyst, all the business person needs to know is the approximate date the *season* starts and ends, and then exploit that knowledge. This is a typical example of why an ongoing **Marketing Analysis** or Administration program can assist any firm. The longer the period it is used to establish the trend of *expand* and *consolidate* in any location, then obviously the more accurate the figures will be.

By entering the week number of the **First Meeting** and the week number of the **Final Meeting** given in answer to Question 13 (e.g., 29/37) linking the *Client* (horizontally) and the *Location* (vertically) a pattern will begin to build.

(The same process used to count inquiries against geographic location can assist in this investigation, for although all inquiries do not become proposals, they do indicate interest or activity in a particular area, relative to certain times of the year.)

GEOGRAPHIC MEETING REQUIREMENTS

The answers to Question 14 *Meeting Locations* can be important in planning sales activity, or expanding a firm by opening new offices. By giving a code to the two most common answers (e.g., our office = **1,** client's office = **2**) and then coding the *types* of meeting places contained in **other** as alternatives (e.g., hotel = **A,** showroom = **B,** exhibition = **C,** etc.) and then entering the relevant code against the name of the *Client* (horizontally) and *Location* (vertically) it is possible to gain an insight on the importance of location to successful meetings. Then, by comparing the results in relation to whether a proposal became an **Order Gained** or **Order Lost,** certain patterns will emerge that can help in planning future meetings.

RELATIVE STATUS/RESPECT GEOGRAPHICALLY

This little exercise in a **Marketing Analysis** can provide some real shocks for Management and Sales Staff alike. The first step is to grade the importance of the *contacts named* on the **Proposal Analysis**

Data Forms, and then to give them codes (e.g., Chairman = **1,** CEO = **2,** etc.) and enter these codes relative to the *Client* (horizontally) and *Location* (vertically). Entering the *value* of the project from the answers to Question 18 *Size of Order* in the **Detail** Boxes on the **Proposal Analysis Data Form** will complete the picture.

The first outcome will normally be that each of your sales staff has assumed a *character balance* and deals best only with certain levels of executive or individual importance. In other words, they will have decided what type of person they can best relate with, or feel comfortable with, and their success and failure rate (your **Orders Gained** or **Orders Lost**) will usually be dictated by this factor as much as anything else. Knowing these facts will allow you to take positive steps to overcome the problem.

Another factor which can be common is that the status, or importance of your *contacts* is different on average in your immediate geographic area to the more outlying proposals. Sometimes this is historical in cause, as when a firm is beginning in business it deals differently to how it does when the firm is established. Therefore, checking the various levels of contact relevant to size of project or location, can isolate some built-in restrictions dictated by the people involved, their image of your firm and of your importance to their own operation.

TIME SCALE OF PROJECTS RELATED TO LOCATION

(using the answer to Question 16)

To enable you to analyze this factor, enter the category (e.g., **A, B, C, D,** or **E**) against the *Client* (horizontally) relative to *Location* (vertically). By ascertaining where you are going to be occupied in the future can assist in developing sales plans to fully exploit your presence in that location.

PROFIT POTENTIAL ON A GEOGRAPHIC SCALE

(using the answer to Question 17)

By entering the relative category (**A, B, C, D** or **E**) against each *Client* (horizontally), and the *Location* (vertically) of the proposal involved, you can establish which areas promise the best profit potential on an ongoing basis. For once a client begins to upgrade expenditure, others in that area will have to follow to maintain an equal image or status.

SIZE OF ORDER RELATIVE TO GEOGRAPHIC AREA

(using the answer to Question 18)

By following the same procedure outlined above, you can evaluate which areas have the best expansion potential for your product or service.

CLIENT LIAISON FACTORS—GEOGRAPHICALLY

Many staff members who are otherwise effective, efficient and highly capable can create problems during negotiations with clients. More often than not, this is because they have not had the relative training or experience in social/business communication and standards. Sometimes it is not obvious to those who work with them, because they are used to the characteristics, behavior or other personal factors which upset the client. Familiarity with one's colleagues, often combined with lack of experience in other competitive sales teams, can cause some sales staff to think the approach which antagonizes the client is in fact normal. Also, a person perfectly at home and competent in one location is doomed to failure because of built-in prejudices in another location. Sometimes however, it is not staff members who cause the friction, but outside consultants, friends or mutual contacts.

By examining the data you have available, any real problem will become obvious in analysis. Give every name that appears in answer to Question 19 *Other staff/others active in proposal* on the **Proposal Analysis Data Forms** a **code letter** and enter them on the grid of the **Proposal Analysis Development Sheet** against the *Client* (horizontally) and *Location* (vertically). Then, compare the **Orders Gained** to **Orders Lost** geographically and decide if it might be possible that certain staff members seem to experience problems in certain locations, and you can establish those who seem strongest in certain locations relative to results of proposals, size of projects, etc.

ANALYSIS OF SPECIALIZATION DEVELOPMENT (LAYOUT 2)

To analyze the *type of work* of your firm, a **Proposal Analysis Development Sheet** should be prepared as follows. First divide up all the **Proposal Analysis Data Forms** into groupings for each sales executive involved. Then, enter each salesperson's group of forms (in size order) in **Box B** of the sheet, leaving two spaces beneath each set for totals. **Orders Lost** should be highlighted with a yellow marker. **Proposal Analysis Data Forms** *Pending Approval* and *Review Requested* should be analyzed separately. The next step is to evaluate all the answers for Question 4 *Description of work, products, or services offered* into type groups. These *type of work* titles should then be entered in **Box C** of the sheet. This layout for the **Proposal Analysis Development Sheet** can be used for the following **Marketing Analysis Procedures.**

IDENTIFYING SALES EXECUTIVE'S SPECIALIZATION

This is a simple matter in that all one needs to do is make an entry of *Profit Potential* on the grid corresponding to *Client* (horizontally) and *Type of Work* (vertically). This entry should be the **A, B, C, D** or **E** entry relevant to the particular client taken from the answer to Question 17 *Profit Potential.* Then total each vertical column (where an entry appears) for each sales executive.

The logical answers to sales performance this analysis produces are almost without argument, in that the value of projects relative to types of work can be compared with each other to suggest which sales executives excel in which areas of your business. It will also show where understanding of client needs, or specialist knowledge exist and, should you decide to promote any particular *type of work,* your *expert* will now be identified for you.

TYPE OF WORK—ONGOING CLIENT ANALYSIS

Consider the answers to Question 5 *Have we submitted other proposals to this client before?* and Question 6 *Have we worked with this client before?* Then by coding the **Yes** answers to Question 5 as **P** and Question 6 as **C,** it is possible to discover much about your *Type of Work* and its marketability. Mark each *client* (vertically relative to *type of work*) with a **C** or **P** as possible. (If both can be entered just enter **C**.) Then total the number of *Return Contracts* relative to *types of work* and calculate what percentage of every *type of work* is purchased by past clients. This may suggest that certain types of work could be promoted on a larger scale, or it may mean that continued use of your service or product could signify you have dropped below market prices. If some *types of work* or *products* are never reordered by past clients you should obviously investigate the reasons.

LEVEL OF PROFESSIONAL PROPOSAL AND PRESENTATION

Some firms, and many sales staff, use standard approach methods for whatever type of work they are negotiating. This can be counter-productive, therefore recognizing that proposals for certain types of work tend to be more subject to review or rewriting than others, can help isolate trouble areas. Investigation of what competitors are doing differently, and checking to see if the same points of objection arise regularly, can significantly improve your sales performance.

Use the answers to Question 8 *Was this proposal altered significantly during the negotiations?* and enter **Yes** or **No** against *Client* (horizontally) and *Type of Work* (vertically). If **Yes** answers come most often against particular sales executives in certain *types of work,* it could signify that perhaps more training should be given to the person involved. If the **Yes** answers predominate against certain *types of work,* irrespective of the sales executive doing the negotiation, it is probable that the *Proposal* or *System of Presentation* is at fault, and should be investigated further.

REFERRAL CONFIDENCE ANALYSIS

Often firms will believe that **they** are referred to new business as a total service, when in fact it is only **some** of their services, products or capabilities which benefit from referrals. Establishing which *products* or *types of work* your friends, contacts and past clients refer to you may be useful in establishing why other types of work are not referred to you, and could make you rethink your promotional plans for the future. Establishing a **code number** for each person, firm or *Linked Benefit Partner* who refers work to you, and entering these code numbers on the grid of the **Proposal Analysis Development Sheet** relative to the *Client* (horizontally) and *Type of Work* (vertically) will establish **who** gives you credit for being good at **what,** thereby proving your own evaluation or showing that you need to investigate your reputation in certain areas.

INFLUENTIAL INTEREST CONFIDENCE ANALYSIS

By following the same procedure outlined above for **Referral Confidence Analysis** and using the names which appear in answer to Question 10 *Overseeing Interest,* you can establish **who** credits you with **what** ability amongst the influential decision-makers in your area of business.

ORIGIN OF INDIVIDUAL TYPES OF WORK ANALYSIS

Establish a code number for each individual *source* from which a business opportunity arose that led to a proposal being submitted. Enter against each *Client* (horizontally) under *Type of Business* (vertically) the relevant **code number.** Then, by calculating totals you will be able to evaluate which Marketing Tools or methods produced the most successful response. Where one source led you to make many proposals, but did not lead to an **Order Gained** situation, it is probable that the source misrepresented, underpriced or overestimated your product or service. This analysis will also identify which *sources* are the most effective, thereby allowing you to develop them faster and to more effect.

LEVELS OF PROFICIENCY OF PRESENTATION ANALYSIS

Examine the answers to Question 12 *Who were our main competitors on this project?* and give each competitor a **code number.** Then, enter this coded number against every Proposal you **lost** under the relevant type of work. Sometimes the results of the **Territorial Competition Analysis** can be justified by finding you *win some, lose some,* only to find when you check the types of work involved, you always lost the same sort of project. This is a danger sign which must never be overlooked, for it means that in the eyes of potential clients you are second best in some sector of your business. If this analysis proves that a competitor *usually* wins certain types of work, mount an investigation to establish **why,** and develop ways to right the situation as fast as possible, or retire from the fray the next time that competitor appears and save time, money and face, which will allow you to concentrate on what you can win.

NEGOTIATION PERIOD RELATIVE TO TYPE OF WORK ANALYSIS

Obviously, the more complex the project the longer the **negotiation period** in the normal run of things. Therefore, to assist your long-term planning it helps if you can establish *averages* (relative to size) for negotiating certain types of work.

First, separate the **Proposal Analysis Data Forms** for each sales executive into separate groups for each of the answers to Question 18 *Size of Order.* Then produce five **Proposal Analysis Development Sheets** on the basis of that described on page 230 **(Layout 2),** one each for **A, B, C, D** and **E** categories. Then enter against each client under the relevant *Type of Work,* the **Total Number of Weeks** entry in the answer section of Question 13 *Negotiation Period.* Obviously the more examples (e.g., greater number of proposals), the easier it is to develop a *norm,* which once again proves the need for ongoing analysis.

ACTIVE PERIODS FOR TYPES OF WORK ANALYSIS

Maintain the groupings under **size of order** reference, and prepare five **Proposal Analysis Development Sheets** on Layout 2. Then, against each *client* and under the relevant *Type of Work* enter the **Week Number** for **First Meeting** and the **Week Number** for **Final Meeting,** as entered in the answer section to Question 13 *Negotiation Period.* Then check each *Type of Work* column to establish if there is an apparent *Active Period* for such projects. If you can establish such a pattern you are armed with a way to pre-empt your competitors next year.

LEAD-IN PERIOD ANALYSIS

Maintain the groupings under **size of order** reference and prepare five **Proposal Analysis Development Sheets** on Layout 2. Then enter the **Total Number of Weeks** answer for Question 13 *Negotiation Period* against each *client* and under the relevant *Type of Work.*

In the totals space at the bottom of each sheet, enter the **Minimum** and **Maximum** number of weeks taken in each **Size of Order** category. This particular analysis result is possibly the best way to lead a firm out of the *Peak and Trough* workload situation so many organizations experience. Having established the **minimum** and **maximum** number of weeks you can expect to have to negotiate to achieve an **Order Gained** or **Order Lost** conclusion for any particular *Type of Work* (without exceptional circumstances), you can now calculate the success rate for this *Type of Work* from the same sheets for each **Size of Order** category. Therefore, you are now able to determine how many prospects will be needed to develop the right amount of business, *all other factors* being constant. (As usually all other factors do not remain constant for long, you could insure your success prediction by doubling the number of prospects required.)

Checking back over the analysis results will soon establish the **how, who, when** and **why** details so that you can build a *Sales Plan* using methods outlined in the earlier part of this book. A little checking into records will determine the period between *first approach* and *first meeting*. Therefore, it is not difficult to prophesy new business of a *certain type* being signed up before a *certain date,* and be right nine times out of ten.

MEETING LOCATIONS RELATED TO TYPES OF BUSINESS ANALYSIS

Maintain the groupings under **Size of Order** reference and create five more Sheets based on Layout 2. Then, by entering against each *client,* under the relevant *Type of Work,* the answers to Question 14 *Meeting Locations* you can evaluate the result of which *location* is most productive relative to meetings discussing particular *Types* *of Work.* Code example: Our office = **H,** Client's office = **C,** and Other = **X.** Therefore, by adding a prefix to denote 1st or Final Meeting, e.g., **1** or **F,** a typical entry would read **1H/FC.** Then, by collating the totals under each relevant type of work you can establish where future meetings on similar Types of Work should be held to expect the best chance of success.

QUALITY OF BUSINESS ANALYSIS

Maintain the groupings under **size of order** reference and prepare five **Proposal Analysis Development Sheets,** Layout 2. The *size of order* data from the answers to Question 18 are provided in that each sheet covers one category. By entering the relevant category listing (**A, B, C, D** or **E**) from Question 16 *Time Scale* and Question 17 *Profit Potential* against each *client* under the relevant *Type of Work,* it is soon possible to establish which areas of business activity (and sales executives) are producing the best quality of business to contribute to the firm's growth, image, profit and overall success. Therefore, by taking the information gained and promoting the types of work most beneficial to all concerned, any firm can expand with confidence.

INDIVIDUAL STAFF NEGOTIATION ABILITIES ANALYSIS

Maintain the groupings under **size of order** reference and prepare five **Proposal Analysis Development Sheets** on Layout 2. Take the answers to Question 19 *Other Staff/others active in Proposal* and **Code** them with initials or numbers. Then, enter an **X** against each client under the relevant *Type of Work* heading. Next to each **X** enter the **Code Number**/or initials of those involved in making the proposal. Then, total the number of times each code number or initials occur under each *Type of Work.* By comparing success ratios of **Orders Gained** and **Orders Lost** conclusions, you will be able to establish **who** is good at **what** from another set of facts.

AREAS OF CONCENTRATION ANALYSIS

By comparing the **Orders Gained** to **Orders Lost** percentages under each *Type of Work* heading you will gain an insight into where your future lies. Sometimes a firm will be very successful with one type of work in small orders, but unsuccessful with large order proposals for the same work, or the other way around, therefore, regular analysis of success ratios in regard to *Type of Work* is very important.

ANALYSIS OF ACTIVITY RELATIVE TO PROFITS AND REPUTATION

It is an accepted fact that the *best costs more,* and every firm needs to ensure that it is getting the highest level of profit for the work or products it supplies. Short-term decisions to increase immediate sales volume by reducing the profit margin involved are usually made in relation to certain factors common to a *Peak and Trough* situation. For example:

a) Fresh food prices vary due to seasonal production.
b) Fashion changes in buying can lead to *end-of-line* production losing value.
c) Introducing a new product or service in competition with established firms can demand the use of lower price structures to provide the buyers with a reason to leave their previous suppliers.
d) When an existing product is up-graded, remaining models or items from the previous production run may need price

reductions to encourage sales.

e) Over-supply or strong competition can also have the effect of reducing profits.

However, a firm can reduce its own profits by lack of research, insufficient knowledge about competitors, over-ambitious growth plans, or simply by following traditional *Pricing Codes* when they no longer have any reasonable demands for application.

The need for careful analysis in this area is of course obvious, however, many individuals and firms believe that they do this by employing a bookkeeper or accountant. In fact, cash bookkeeping can only *prevent* real analysis which might make a positive contribution to management's need to increase profit ratios. A bookkeeper's job is to monitor and check financial facts relative to the firm's performance. Put more simply, a bookkeeper deals with *historical* facts, and there is little that can be done to change what is past. The actual effect a bookkeeper can have in *increasing* income is not very significant because many of the facts needed to do this are rarely available to the person *keeping the books*. However, if the bookkeeper and the marketing administrator can work together, and consult each others knowledge at regular intervals, the outcome can only be described as very productive.

PROFIT POTENTIAL ANALYSIS (LAYOUT 3)

Consult the **Proposal Analysis Development Sheets** to evaluate where profitable business is most often developed. Separate your completed **Proposal Analysis Data Forms** into groupings for each sales executive, and organize them into size of order.

Prepare **Proposal Analysis Development Sheets** for each sales executive with two sheets for each of the five (**A, B, C, D** and **E**) categories shown in Question 17 *Profit Potential* as described below.

In **Box B** enter (in size order) the names of the clients involved.

In **Box C** a series of entries are required to produce this analysis.

1. Have we worked with this client before?
2. **A**)
3. **B**)
4. **C**) FINANCIAL STATUS (QUESTION 6)
5. **D**)
6. **E**)
7. **A**)
8. **B**)
9. **C**) TIME SCALE (QUESTION 16)
10. **D**)
11. **E**)

In the **Detail** Box enter the actual **size of order.**

By entering either **Yes** or **No** for the first question and an **X** against each client under the relevant answer for **Financial Status** and **Time Scale,** you can then calculate percentages relative to the quality of *Profit Potential Business* during the period being evaluated.

The first prepared sheet for each sales executive will be used to analyze the **Pending Decision** and **Review Requested by Client Proposal Analysis Data Forms.** The second sheet will be used for the **Orders Gained** and **Orders Lost** data forms.

It is possible in any sales team that *success* may be related only to **size of order,** and this is dangerous as it leads almost inevitably into *overtrading* and cash flow problems associated with uncontrolled growth. The need of every firm is to balance its growth/cash flow situation, and to do this **size of order** is only important when related to the Financial Status of the client involved and to the Profit Potential of the contract negotiated. Possibly the best motto to hang over any salesperson's desk is the one which states *What have you given away today?*

SALES SUCCESS RATIO ANALYSIS (LAYOUT 4)

It is obvious that short sales meetings, or general management overview of a sales team, or individual salespersons are not able to judge the value of new business gained for the firm. More often than not, the extrovert or dominant personality can develop the admiration of fellow members of the staff by just quoting *size of order, important clients,* or by using words which hide rather than prove the facts of profit ratio. Knowing the real professionalism and ability of every member of the sales team is absolutely essential if an organized Marketing Program is to be successful. By consulting **Proposal Analysis Development Sheets** already outlined, a real evaluation should be established. The purpose of the following methods of analysis is to evaluate *work application* and *success ratios* for every member of the sales team.

First separate all the **Proposal Analysis Data Forms** into groupings for each of the five (**A, B, C, D** and **E**) categories relative to the answers to Question 17 *Profit Potential.* Each set should then be separated into groupings for each sales executive. Prepare **Proposal Analysis Development Sheets** for each of the five (**A, B, C, D** and **E**) categories of Question 17 *Profit Potential.* The client name, etc., from the presorted **Proposal Analysis Data Forms** should then be entered (in consecutive **Size of Order**) on the relevant sheet in **Box B.** After each sales executive's section of entries leave two spaces for totals to be inserted later. The actual **Size of Order** should be entered in the **Detail** Box.

In **Box C** enter the details from Question 6 *Financial Status* (e.g., 1 = **A**, 2 = **B**, 3 = **C**, 4 = **D** and 5 = **E**). Then enter the word **Proposal** in position 6 which will be answered by the answer to Question 7 *Was a written proposal submitted to this client?* Then enter the word **Referral** in position 7 which will be provided by the answer to Question 9 *Was this client referred to us by a past client?* Then enter the most common answers to the *Position Section* of Question 5 *Main Client Contact* in the last space *Other.*

With the exception of 6 and 7 in **Box C** (which should be answered **Yes** or **No**), the facts can be established by entering **X** against the client's name under the relevant headings. Then color code (by running a transparent marker over the relevant entry) each proposal to signify its present Status, e.g.,

ORDER LOST — Yellow
PENDING DECISION — Green
REVIEW REQUESTED — Pink
ORDER GAINED — Red

Calculate the total number of entries for each sales executive and you will have a factual evaluation of their performance, with and without assistance from others.

The examples shown in the Chapter for a **Marketing Analysis** are only the beginning, and depending upon what you need to establish or evaluate, the system and forms described can be used for almost any procedure or investigation you care to develop.

CHAPTER FOURTEEN

MARKETING MANAGEMENT

To **Manage** according to the primary description in Webster's New World Dictionary is: *"to control the movement or behavior of"*—and it is this simple fact which often causes some firms to accomplish less than they logically could expect to achieve. The reason being that because they do not have enough facts to *manage* they, therefore, *manage* despite the facts. Instinct and desire are not enough, however, to lead a firm, a department or even an individual to success. It takes experience, knowledge and a real understanding of the capabilities available; and as everyone knows, all of these attributes benefit from organization and applied evaluation. Whether the subject is an individual salesperson or a two-hundred-person international sales division, there can be no doubt that unless an organized system is used, the real reason behind success or failure can only be LUCK. Any organization, firm or individual which operates in today's world without an organized system of marketing or management can only be compared to an automobile without a driver. It does not matter what the situation or source of business, everyone needs to know what is happening, and if there is a rule to apply, it must be that you can never **know** too much about your past, present or future in business.

Some firms tend to neglect everything about their business-gaining methods and capability, except to question *how many new orders/jobs have we got this month?* Long-term planning, it would seem, is left to the very large firms, while the majority of people seem to only consider marketing when the existing workload begins to slacken. Many executives accept as a fact of life that they work in a *Peak and Trough* business, when perhaps they in fact create the situation. Many organizations also seem to believe they cannot afford the full-time commitment of marketing management, which is about as logical as cutting your head off to lose weight. Organized marketing not only increases the probability of higher profits, it can also increase public recognition and personal satisfaction, and thereby allow the individual to do more of what he or she is capable of doing.

Experience proves that a good sales executive spends his or her working time roughly in the following manner:

20% investigating who to approach.
20% recording the work done, processing orders, writing letters, proposals, etc.
20% gaining information and in liaison work with other members of his or her own firm.
25% traveling.
5% negotiating and in meetings with potential clients, past clients, etc.
10% wasted.
(Sometimes this number is far greater and all other percentages are reduced accordingly.)

Optimistically, therefore, the sales executive spends seven hours a day at this breakdown of activity every working day of the year. The calculation of how many hours per week, month or year that are used to actually perform the real task (explaining the product or service and gaining an order) can be seen to be relatively small and constitute the most expensive outlay of time any firm can invest. The objective of the sales manager (and the sales executives themselves) therefore is to increase the time available for explaining the product or service and gaining an order.

A professional marketing department using the methods outlined earlier in this book should be able to return to the sales executive much of the time spent *investigating who to approach* by developing inquiries from both investigation and public relations, and by the use of marketing plans.

Obviously, if the sales volume increases, then the time spent by each sales executive *recording the work done, processing orders, and writing letters, proposals, etc.,* logically should increase also. Therefore, there is much to be said for investigating exactly what is, and is not, really necessary for the sales executive to do, and what can be delegated to *less expensive* staff. The need to be up-to-date and to know such details as availability, production schedules, sales policy, etc., takes up a lot of every sales executive's time. The manager, therefore, has an ongoing responsibility to organize training and orientation meetings, rather than expect the individual to seek out information only when it becomes a problem. The marketing department, properly organized, can also supply at least half of the information required on a regular basis that otherwise the sales executive would have to search out personally.

Traveling time is probably the easiest area in which to *save time* for a sales executive. Usually, it is lack of time to organize that prevents real Route Planning, a problem which often loses its importance in the daily run of things. Therefore, everyone will benefit if *non-productive* tasks can be delegated away from the salesperson to allow them more time to do the job that they are employed to do. The opinion voiced above will normally be received by sales executive and management alike with total agreement, however, the problem is that there are many different opinions about *what salespeople are employed to do,* and some consideration is required to establish these responsibilities. Again, the military comparison is the easiest way to show the needs a firm have of their sales staff. If every soldier in an army decided to *operate independently,* only referring to the chain of command when in trouble or need of assistance, supplies or information, then it would not be long before they were defeated. As stated many times before, a sales effort without discipline is doomed to failure sooner or later. Therefore, the responsibilities of every sales executive (whether he or she be a business developer, account executive, negotiator or a member of the sales office staff) must be to carry out their function, record their actions, and supply the latest information available to the **Marketing Administrator** to collate and analyze. To continue the military analogy, the **Marketing Administrator** is to a firm engaged in business what the Information Officer, Strategic Planner and Communication System is to an army engaged in a war. Therefore, the **Marketing Administrator** needs a system to gather and analyze this information, and that is the subject of this chapter.

Today's sales executive is dealing with a more knowledgeable, better informed client than ever before, and the ease of travel has increased the level of competition in all areas of business. The tools employed by the sales executive are therefore more important also, and access to the right tools or assistance at the right time can mean the difference between an **Order Gained** and an **Order Lost.** Consider some of the basic tools which the salesperson can use to be more effective, efficient, and to increase the image of your firm. Begin with the everyday usage needs of the sales executive. The need to carry things into the client's office, the need to take notes, the need to communicate with and be reachable by his or her firm. With very little imagination, ways to help the person in the field, increase the company's image and improve the overall efficiency of the firm can be established which are well worth the expenditure involved, e.g.,

1. A small adhesive sticker affixed to the sales executive's car

at the rear to the right of the number plate, could put your name in front of every other driver who follows that car (e.g., Bekins Trucking, Petersburg, Montana, for Fast Delivery).

2. Offer as part of your *employment benefits* the loan of a large, well-made brief case for each sales executive to use. Put your logo on the outside in the form of a small, sophisticated medallion with a description of the services underneath in quality gold embossed letters, e.g.,

3. To save time on writing up notes, loan each sales representative a small electronic tape recorder. This will also mean that reports can be dropped off for audio typing while the sales executive does more productive work.
4. Many firms now install car phones in sales staff vehicles to allow fast contact. If this is not considered necessary, then invest in an electronic *paging system,* so that the sales executive can be notified to call into the office at the first opportunity. Lack of ability to communicate at the right time can often lose orders or anger clients waiting for an answer.

There are many ways a sales team can be assisted to increase efficiency, and often the cost is insignificant to the sales volume involved.

THE MARKETING LIBRARY

Collating all the available aids for sales executives to use is an important aspect of the **Marketing Administrator's** responsibilities. It is also worth pointing out that proper management of such items as photographs, color slides, models, samples, artists impressions, reprints, brochures, etc., not only ensures that such things are available when needed by the sales staff, but it also cuts down waste caused by misuse, damage and loss. These items cost a lot to produce and therefore looking after them makes good sense, but that does not mean locking them away in a cupboard or filing cabinet. Such sales aids have a limited life span as they date quickly, therefore they must be accessible to all salespeople and new sales staff members should be given a *guided tour* of what is available to help close a sale. A system of filing and storage should be established and a complete catalog of what is available should be produced and given to each member of the sales team.

When a salesperson takes out a particular report, photo or anything else, the fact should be noted as in any library system.

CALL MANAGEMENT

All sales staff can directly relate their success to the number of calls, telephone conversations, and meetings they are able to make in any day, week, month or year. Therefore, the better such calls are organized and managed, the better the chances of success, and in turn, the better the firm as a whole will benefit. Just making a lot of contacts however means little if these business opportunities are not properly organized and managed. Follow-up, relevant action at the right time and keeping records of such contacts are also important to a salesperson's success. The objective of **Call Management** is to fully exploit every contact the salesperson makes and to eliminate non-essential and time-wasting, non-productive effort.

BUSINESS ACTIVITY REPORT©

SALES EXECUTIVE	SHEET

DAY of the week	month	day	year	week number

Client 1	Project Location	Time In
Contact	Comments	FIRST VISIT
		COURTESY
Position		INQUIRY
		SERVICE
Business		BUSINESS
		POTENTIAL
Competition		NO POTENTIAL
Meeting Location		Time Out

Client 2	Project Location	Time In
Contact	Comments	FIRST VISIT
		COURTESY
Position		INQUIRY
		SERVICE
Business		BUSINESS
		POTENTIAL
Competition		NO POTENTIAL
Meeting Location		Time Out

Client 3	Project Location	Time In
Contact	Comments	FIRST VISIT
		COURTESY
Position		INQUIRY
		SERVICE
Business		BUSINESS
		POTENTIAL
Competition		NO POTENTIAL
Meeting Location		Time Out

Client 4	Project Location	Time In
Contact	Comments	FIRST VISIT
		COURTESY
Position		INQUIRY
		SERVICE
Business		BUSINESS
		POTENTIAL
Competition		NO POTENTIAL
Meeting Location		Time Out

BUSINESS ACTIVITY REPORT

The **Business Activity Report** is the diary of the day-to-day prospecting and follow-up on inquiries and sales programs. Every meeting, call or telephone contact with a new opportunity for business should be recorded on this report so that later analysis and discussion can evaluate further action, possible assistance and, of course, provide facts to improve the overall efficiency of the total sales effort. These Reports should be submitted to the sales manager or **Marketing Administrator** for comment, advice and assistance.

SALES EXECUTIVE				SHEET
DAY of the week	month	day	year	week number

IDENTIFICATION DETAILS

The **sales executive** completing the report should enter his or her name in the box provided, and each sheet should be numbered consecutively for each day throughout the week involved in the **sheet** box. To evaluate the quantity of work done on a daily basis (and to build an overview of levels of work relative to each day of the week), the **day** (e.g., Monday, etc.) should be entered in the box provided. The **date** of course is also important, and a separate box is provided to note the **week number.** Each entry requires only the basic information to allow discussion and investigation. The increase in efficiency by using this form rather than scribbling notes on odd pieces of paper and the back of napkins has to be experienced to be believed.

Client 1
Contact
Position
Business
Competition
Meeting Location

CLIENT

The full name or title of the client involved should be entered so that the **Marketing Administrator** can check through the records for past contact or information which might assist a successful result in this case.

CONTACT

The full name of the contact should be entered.

TITLE OR STATUS

It is important of course to know the importance of the contact relevant to his or her ability to place or influence an order.

BUSINESS

By noting the main business activity of the client, the **Marketing Administrator** will be able to check through the records for similar clients, etc., and may therefore be able to assist in the development by advice based upon past experience.

COMPETITION

If it is possible to establish who is competing for the potential business, or with whom the client dealt, or is dealing with, prior to your approach, the **Marketing Administrator** may again be able to offer advice based on past experience.

MEETING LOCATION

Where the meeting took place is important for sales call planning, etc. If the contact was made by telephone, then the full code and number should be entered in this box.

Project Location	Time In
Comments	FIRST VISIT COURTESY INQUIRY SERVICE BUSINESS POTENTIAL NO POTENTIAL Time Out

PROJECT LOCATION

Where the work will be done, or delivery made to is important to future planning.

COMMENTS

Any additional information, details of follow-up required, etc., should be entered in this box.

TIME IN

The time the meeting started, or the telephone conversation began should be entered in this box.

TIME OUT

The time the meeting or the telephone conversation ended should be entered in this box.

CALL INFORMATION

This is required for management purposes. By marking **X** against the relevant boxes at the top of each entry, e.g.,

FIRST VISIT

COURTESY

A call on a past client or contact.

INQUIRY

In answer to an inquiry from the potential client or passed for action by the marketing department.

SERVICE

A non-sales opportunity, a complaint to be dealt with, delivery, etc.

and

BUSINESS

Client expresses a firm wish to discuss business.

POTENTIAL

A good possibility of business but nothing definite having developed.

NO POTENTIAL

If in the opinion of the sales executive there is little chance of new business being developed in the foreseeable future, then mark this box.

When either **Business** or **Potential** is marked then a **Potential New Business Analysis Form** should be completed for this client.

POTENTIAL NEW BUSINESS© ANALYSIS FORM

PNB REFERENCE NUMBER

EXECUTIVE

week number	month	day	year

TRANSFERRED YES ☐ NO ☐ OLD CLIENT ☐ NEW CLIENT ☐

Client

Address

Telephone

Origin of Lead

Handover data

CONTACTS INFORMATION

Name	Position	Extension

BUSINESS DEVELOPMENT EXECUTIVE

NEGOTIATOR

1	2	3	4

WEEK

1	6	11
2	7	12
3	8	13
4	9	14
5	10	15

	month	day	year
PROPOSAL GIVEN			
BIDDING INVITED			
DELAYED UNTIL			
ABANDONED			

Comments

LOCATION

SIZE DATA

TYPE OF WORK

OVERSEEING INTEREST

1	2	3	4	5	6	7	8	9	10	11	12	13	14	15	TRANSFERRED

REVIEW DATE | month | year

POTENTIAL NEW BUSINESS ANALYSIS FORM

This form is used and kept by the Business Development Executive responsible for developing potential new business from the initial contact stage of a prospect through to the stage of presenting a proposal, and is designed to prevent time waste and to identify areas where special actions are required. It isolates all relevant information and actions to one piece of paper, which can be reviewed either in regular sales meetings, or when time is available. This form is the reference basis upon which both the executive involved and management can decide upon the best action for success. It is also, of course, able to indicate the performance ability of the Business Development Executive. Copies should be circulated to relevant persons in the organization on a pre-set schedule.

PNB REFERENCE NUMBER

EXECUTIVE

This form is used by the person in contact with potential prospects developing the business relationship (sales executives, etc.) and their name is entered in this box.

If there is more than one person working on sales development in the firm, then the **Potential New Business Analysis Form** number should indicate who is working with this potential client. (Initials/office/work number, etc.) More important, however, is that each form should be given a new consecutive number to help management judge volume of activity.

week number	month	day	year	TRANSFERRED YES ☐ NO ☐	OLD CLIENT ☐ NEW CLIENT ☐

WEEK NUMBER

The week number the form was opened.

WEEK OF ENTRY

Month/day/year.

TRANSFER

These forms are designed to be active for 15 weeks, sometimes they will run on for a longer period. They will of course keep the same **Potential New Business Analysis Form** number, so by marking this box one knows there are preceding forms to see.

OLD/NEW CLIENT

If the potential business is related to a client you have worked for before, the OLD box should be marked, if the client has not employed you before mark the NEW box.

Client

CLIENT

Full title of the potential client.

Address

ADDRESS

Full postal address (including zip code).

Telephone

TELEPHONE

Enter full telephone number including all dialing codes.

Origin of Lead

ORIGIN OF LEAD

This is self-explanatory. Every opportunity originates somewhere — articles, letters, or just a general inquiry — just enter where the client learned of you to make the inquiry, or to agree to see you.

CONTACTS INFORMATION

Name	Position	Extension

CONTACT INFORMATION

During the development of a new business one makes many contacts who later will prove, or could prove, important. This section is to ensure you know how to contact them all. Obviously, sooner or later, one name becomes the *prime* contact — and should be marked as such.

Handover data

HANDOVER DATA

Sometimes during business development a potential client will be passed to someone else in your firm. This box is to be used to make important notes relevant to the actions taken so far.

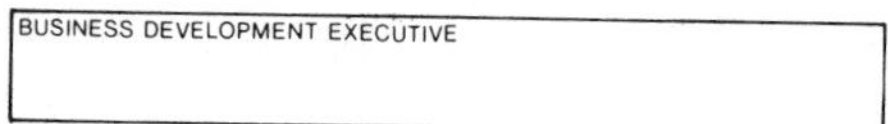
BUSINESS DEVELOPMENT EXECUTIVE

BD EXECUTIVE (BUSINESS DEVELOPMENT)

Whoever *opens* the potential new business opportunity.

NEGOTIATOR

NEGOTIATOR

The person to whom the *potential client* is handed over to, should the need to use someone else to close the sale be necessary.

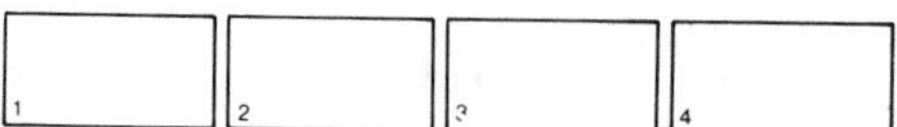

BOXES 1, 2, 3, 4

In some cases several people are involved in developing a potential client. The initials of these people and the date of their first involvement goes in these boxes.

WEEK 14	1

19	6

ACTIVITY BOXES

In the top left-hand corner of each of these boxes is a smaller box. The first is labeled **week number.** The week number entered in the week box below the PNB number, should be entered in Activity Box 1, and all other Activity Boxes should be consecutively numbered. Each week the main actions taken to gain this potential client should be noted in the box.

CONCLUSION

This form ends its active use when a conclusion is reached. There are only four possible true conclusions

PROPOSAL GIVEN	month	day	year

a) **A proposal was submitted,** in which case note the fact and enter the date it was sent in the provided boxes, month/day/year.

BIDDING INVITED	month	day	year

b) **You were invited to bid** with others — enter the date when the bid is required to be in by.

DELAYED UNTIL	month	day	year

c) **The project is delayed** — enter the date when it will become active again.

ABANDONED	month	day	year

d) **The project was abandoned** — or you were — again enter the date. Whatever the outcome, you may wish to comment in the box provided for later use.

REVIEW DATE	month	year

REVIEW DATE

Dependent upon your answers to the previous sections you will need to review this form at some date in the future — put the month and year in the boxes provided.

1	2	3	4	5	6	7	8	9	10	11	12	13	14	15	TRANSFERRED

PROGRESSION BOXES 1-15

This form is designed to help overcome the *Peak and Trough* situation, and therefore two important pieces of information can be gained here. If the form was handed over to a Negotiator, mark the week it happened with an **N.** The week you reached a *conclusion* should be marked with an **X.** There is also a small box at the end of the progression boxes marked **TRANSFERRED.** If the prospect on this form was transferred to another form because it went past 15 weeks, then mark this box.

Comments

LOCATION
SIZE DATA
TYPE OF WORK
OVERSEEING INTEREST

THE DATA BOXES

Location/Size Data/Type of Work should be completed for analysis later.

No sales meeting to evaluate performance can be productive or effective from the point of view of factual debate, without the use of these forms, for they constitute a synopsis of the progress on each prospect for new business.

MARKETING PLAN CONTROL SHEET

The **Marketing Plan Control Sheet** is a tool which the Sales Manager or Marketing Administrator can use to ensure *wasted time* is kept to an absolute minimum, and it can also be used to assist the *Sales Team Memory.* Used in conjunction with the **Business Activity Report** as a management tool, it can make the task of overseeing the day-to-day activity of everyone on the sales team much more efficient and analytical. Most Sales Teams either have weekly meetings or submit weekly reports, and it is with the facts gained in this way that the person in charge must make his or her recommendations. In the case of a typical Marketing or Sales Plan, a collection of names and addresses of potential clients must be carefully managed; and when the Plan is complete, conclusions must be drawn to better organize and manage the next one. When the names and addresses of the potential clients (or prospects) are collated at the beginning of the Sales Plan, it is not a difficult task to complete a **Marketing Plan Control Sheet** for each of the sales executives involved in the Plan. Then, when the weekly sales reports come in, or the sales meetings take place, the total undertaking can be managed *without omissions.*

DESCRIPTION OF PLAN	SHEET NUMBER

DESCRIPTION OF PLAN

In this box an entry of the *purpose* and *method* of the Plan must be entered.

Each sheet should be numbered consecutively so that none are *lost*

MARKETING PLAN CONTROL SHEET©

BUSINESS DEVELOPMENT EXECUTIVE				
Week of Entry				Authorized by
week number	month	day	year	

Case	Client Prospect	Address	Location	State	Post Code	Contact	Position
1 1							
2							
3							
4							
5							
6							
7							
8							
9							
10							
2 1							
2							
3							
4							
5							
6							
7							
8							
9							
10							
3 1							
2							
3							
4							
5							
6							
7							
8							
9							
10							

Potential New Business Cases ☐ **Cases Entered with Errors** ☐ **Cases Abandoned** ☐

DESCRIPTION OF PLAN

SHEET NUMBER

month	day	year	week	1	2	3	4	5	TO MAILING LIST

Cases Transfered to Mailing List

SUCCESS RATIO (Proposals Issued)

5 WEEKS	10 WEEKS	15 WEEKS	20 WEEKS	25 WEEKS

or *overlooked* during the period of the Plan. If more than one sheet is necessary for each sales executive, then a sub-number should be used (e.g., 1-1, 1-2, 1-3, etc.).

BUSINESS DEVELOPMENT EXECUTIVE

BUSINESS DEVELOPMENT EXECUTIVE

Enter the name of the sales executive who will be responsible for *managing* the *prospects* listed on the sheet.

Week of Entry				Authorized by
week number	month	day	year	

WEEK OF ENTRY

Enter the Week Number and month, day and year that the Plan commences.

AUTHORIZED BY

The name of the executive responsible for the management of the total Marketing or Sales Plan, and who designated the names on this sheet to be handled by the **Business Development Executive** named above should be entered in this box.

Case	Client Prospect	Address	Location	State	Post Code	Contact	Position
1₁							
2							
3							
4							
5							
6							
7							
8							
9							
10							

CASE

If more than one sales executive is sharing the *Prospects* in any Geographical Area, then these numbers can be used to collate several sheets, or they merely number the *Prospects* involved.

CLIENT PROSPECT

The name of the potential client or prospect is entered in this box.

ADDRESS

LOCATION

The town or city.

CONTACT

The name of the person to whom the letter is addressed, or who the sales executive is expected to contact. If no name is available at the outset, then the sales executive should complete this box when the relevant person has been established.

POSITION

The rank, title or responsibility of the *contact*.

DATE BOX

When a case or prospect is given a proposal or when it is abandoned as no business is expected, the date should be entered in this box with the week number. (Later, by reviewing these sheets, it is possible to establish some understanding of what time scale to expect in future Plans.)

ACTIVITY BOXES (1, 2, 3, 4 and 5)

These boxes can be used to note activity in each case for five weeks.

TO MAILING LIST

After five weeks it is possible to decide whether or not to include a *Client Prospect* in your Mailing List, those so chosen should be marked with an **X.**

Potential New Business Cases ☐

POTENTIAL NEW BUSINESS CASES

After five weeks it is possible to establish which of the potential new clients (client prospects) can be expected to provide some new business in the future. These cases should be *highlighted* with a red marker, and the total entered in this box. (Obviously, those which have already bought or received proposals should be included in this number.)

Cases Entered with Errors ☐

CASES ENTERED WITH ERRORS

Many otherwise excellent Sales Plans fail because of insufficient investigation before they are launched—letters sent to people who left the year before, incorrect address, no zip code, wrong company, etc., etc. Therefore, the number of cases which were handicapped by such a mistake should be noted and an **X** should be marked in front of the case number for each mistake.

Cases Abandoned ☐

CASES ABANDONED

Those client prospects from which no business is expected constitute bad research or low sales proficiency. The number of such cases should be entered in this box.

Cases Transfered to Mailing List ☐

Losing touch with potential clients because their need is not immediate can be an expensive mistake. Therefore, those prospects who can be identified as future potential clients should be placed on the mailing list.

	5 WEEKS	10 WEEKS	15 WEEKS	20 WEEKS	25 WEEKS
SUCCESS RATIO(Proposals Issued)					

SUCCESS RATIO

Success can only be achieved when proposals have been put before potential clients that could lead to new business. At the end of five weeks, the first entry can be made in the **5-week box.** After that, every five weeks review the results to date and update the figure in the next box. After 25 weeks you will have a factual determination of the success of the Marketing or Sales Plan involved.

"I think you should have looked at the product before you designed the box, don't you Sir?"

CHAPTER FIFTEEN

GROWTH ANALYSIS AND SALES MANAGEMENT CONTROL

Many businesses tend to waste effort, morale and profit when they are unable to organize the purchase and supply management side of their operation efficiently. Every day there must be thousands of sales which cannot be filled. Mismanagement of marketing, linked to supply, costs billions every year and yet experience proves that in most cases it need not happen. Marketing **and** Purchase & Supply Management can be simple if the firm or individual involved is prepared to accept the basic principle of applying a monitoring system based on uniform time management (e.g., the **50-Week Commercial Year**).

THE NUMBERS GAME

Perhaps the most unnecessary failing in **Marketing Management** is the reliance upon *numbers sold* as a yardstick for success, rather than *profits generated*. How this situation evolves is complex in development, yet simple in cause, but there is no doubt that its time is coming to an end and it is possible that many companies will disappear if they fail to recognize the problem. It is business revolution to suggest that the days of the *Numbers Game* are coming to an end (especially as so many influential business princes and economic professors continue to preach its application), but coming to an end it definitely is—and every branch of the media continues to make known new examples every day.

Marketing as a profession has suffered when it refuses to face in business what its individual members accept in their private lives. The age of cheap labor, raw materials, transportation, finance and restricted competition is over. The changes in the world marketplace are in some measure also the result of the change in the buyer's status over the last few years. The buyer today is better educated, more experienced and far, far better informed than his predecessor of just a few years ago. Add to this situation the relative youth and inexperience (or naivete) of today's average salesperson, and one understands the problems with which the sales manager or marketing director has to work.

In the *boom years* and the expanding market which followed World War II, the demand situation was so great that many firms were able to send out younger and younger representatives who were, of course, less experienced and less qualified, but they were willing to work for lower salaries and promises. Since the mid-1970's, however, the market has turned around and **the suppliers** are now finding that their sales team is often weaker in the marketplace than **the buyers** they have to deal with. The problem is that management got used to a *low-salaried, commission-based, young, inexperienced and transitory sales staff* and it could be a long time before the situation is recognized and corrected on a general scale.

Faced with all these problems there is only one real answer for the sales manager or marketing director, and that must be to develop more *controlled* analysis and management than was necessary in the past. The **GROWTH ANALYSIS AND SALES MANAGEMENT SHEET** can provide the management control needed in today's business climate. It is a multi-purpose system which can be used for the following management tasks (it is, however, not restricted to these examples only.)

1. DISCOUNT MANAGEMENT
   If all sales managers were issued with a constant price list (one product—one price) then there would be a first class case for applying the *numbers game* and judging results on *numbers sold;* however, quantity discounts, privileged client, dealer, agency and other discount tabulations makes analysis of *True Results* essential.
2. INVENTORY AND PRODUCTION MANAGEMENT
   Having a warehouse full of widgets and an order book full of wodgets is the sales manager's nightmare, but by careful analysis and management, this can be avoided.
3. TERRITORIAL MANAGEMENT
   Keeping sales expenditure in line with sales results is one of the sales manager's most difficult responsibilities, but for the best results it must be done.

It is obvious, therefore, from the marketing point of view, that a **50-Week Commercial Year** is the easiest to use from a professional management standpoint. Each week can be compared and each period is able to evaluated without calculation of *day difference,* etc., as is necessary in the awkward traditional calendar month year.

GROWTH ANALYSIS & SALES MANAGEMENT SHEET

	1							2							3				
	1	2	3	4	5	Total	AVERAGE	1	2	3	4	5	Total	AVERAGE	1	2	3	4	5
1 TOTAL to date AVERAGE B/F TARGET DIFFERENCE																			
2 TOTAL to date AVERAGE B/F TARGET DIFFERENCE																			
3 TOTAL to date AVERAGE B/F TARGET DIFFERENCE																			
4 TOTAL to date AVERAGE B/F TARGET DIFFERENCE																			
5 TOTAL to date AVERAGE B/F TARGET DIFFERENCE																			
6 TOTAL to date AVERAGE B/F TARGET DIFFERENCE																			
7 TOTAL to date AVERAGE B/F TARGET DIFFERENCE																			
8 TOTAL to date AVERAGE B/F TARGET DIFFERENCE																			
9 TOTAL to date AVERAGE B/F TARGET DIFFERENCE																			
10 TOTAL to date AVERAGE B/F TARGET DIFFERENCE																			
	1	2	3	4	5	Total	AVERAGE	1	2	3	4	5	Total	AVERAGE	1	2	3	4	5

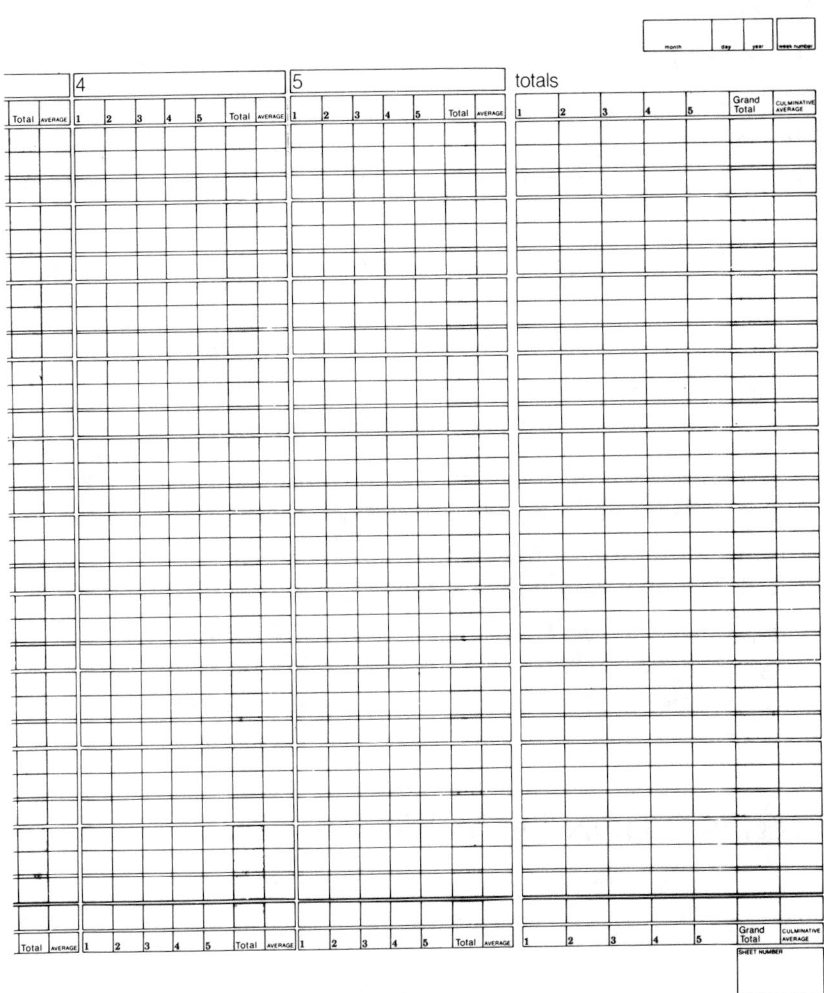
month
day
year
week number
4
5
totals
Total
AVERAGE
1
2
3
4
5
Grand Total
CULMINATIVE AVERAGE
SHEET NUMBER

DISCOUNT MANAGEMENT OF PRODUCT SALES

For this purpose the Sheet is applicable to five weeks (or 5-Week Periods) and five *levels of discount,* and should therefore be prepared as follows:

1 JAN. 5-9, 1981						
1 0%	2 2½%	3 10%	4 15%	5 20%	Total	AVERAGE

a) In the long box at the head of each column enter the week period (e.g., Jan. 5-9, 1981) with the week number on the right-hand side of the box (e.g., 01).

b) In the small boxes (1 thru 5) enter the discounts involved, (e.g., NIL—2½%-10%-15%-20%). These discount percentages should apply to a *base price* (e.g., the maximum price obtainable) or to your effective price list in use at the time of analysis.

IDENTIFICATION DETAILS

1	
	TOTAL to date
AVERAGE B/F	TARGET DIFFERENCE

c) In the *title* box enter the name of the product or item involved.

d) In the *code* boxes enter the product code, computer code or work number as applicable.
e) Total to date—enter in this box the number sold prior to the date of this analysis in the year so far. (This figure must be based upon the *base price total* system as explained in Note 1.)
f) Average—enter in this box the average number sold per week up to the date of this analysis (see Note 2.)
g) Target difference—enter in this box the number difference (either plus or minus) between what *has been sold* (e.g., total to date) and the number that *should have been sold* to meet the target figure (see Note 3.)

Note 1

The requirement of this analysis is to increase profits gained overall (or at least to identify true profits). If each product sold at Base Price gives a return of 25% gross (e.g., 25 cents on the dollar) then a product sold at 20% discount returns only 5% gross (e.g., five cents on the dollar). Therefore, five products must be sold to make the same *monetary* profit if a discount of 20% is made on all sales.

If the target set for sales is five products per week *at Base Price,* then at 20% discount, 25 products must be sold. (Obviously, the *actual* profit is *less* overall if the gross profit per product is reduced.) So it can be seen that with a sales target of 25 products per week at Base Price—the actual sales will be as shown below:

(Cost $100 each, gross profit = 25% or $25 per product)

11 products @ 2½% discount earns a price paid of	$1,072.50
7 products @ 10% discount earns a price paid of	$ 630.00
7 products @ 15% discount earns a price paid of	$ 595.00
10 products @ 20% discount earns a price paid of	$ 800.00
TOTAL 35 products sold at discounts earns an income of	$3,097.50

Therefore, the 35 sold at discounts averaged a price per product of	$ 88.50
Making a profit on each product of only	$ 13.50
Giving a gross profit earned of	$ 472.50
Whereas the sales target of 25 products @ Base Price would have returned a profit of	$ 625.00
Therefore there is a difference of **lost** gross profit of	$ 152.50

Therefore, sales are **below target** by $152.50, or 6(+) products, or almost 25%.

Therefore, the *total to date* would **not** be 35, but would in fact be 19 when the discount factor is considered relative to gross profits.

Note 2

If the situation described in *Note 1* continued for five weeks with the same sales each week the *number of products sold* would be 175. However, compared to the sales target which is calculated at Base Price gross profits, the actual *average number per week* would only be 19.

Note 3

If the situation described in *Notes 1* and *2* existed, then after five weeks the target would have been established for 125 products, but the actual sales (on Base Price returns) would only be 95 products. Therefore, the *average difference* would be MINUS 30 products relative to *Base Price Targets* and **not** PLUS 50 as the *numbers sold* would indicate.

The *Entry Grid* for each product each week is divided into two entry lines for five categories, each with a *total* box and an *average* box, and a further entry line for *running* totals.

This allows a cumulative total to be kept throughout the five-week period of the SHEET for judging *Target* performances.

The following progression describes five weeks sales on a Mark I Widget:

1						
1 0%	2 2½%	3 10%	4 15%	5 20%	Total	% AVERAGE
24	57	53	28	46	208	10.51

TARGET DIFFERENCE

On the face of it, these figures seem satisfactory when explained on a *Numbers Game* basis, for example:

1. The Target was 170 WIDGETS
   208 WIDGETS were sold

However, when the sales figures are analyzed on a *Base Price true profit* factor the sales manager is actually still in trouble.

208 widgets (sold at an average discount of 10.51%)	=	$ 89.49 each
Total Income	=	$18,613.92
208 widgets (production costs @ $75 each) total costs	=	$15,600.00
Gross Profit	=	$ 3,013.92
per widget Gross Profit	=	$ 14.49
The Target however predicted:		
170 widgets (sold at Base Price)	=	$ 100.00 each
Predicted Income	=	$17,000.00
170 widgets (production costs @ $75 each) total costs	=	$12,750.00
Predicted Gross Profit	=	$ 4,250.00
per widget Gross Profit	=	$ 25.00

Therefore, despite higher *numbers* sold, the sales are now $1,236.08 **below** target (29%) Gross Profit
or 49+ widgets below target at Base Price
or 85+ widgets below target at an average discount of 10.51%

Assuming that production costs remain the same and demand continues at the same level, the sales manager now faces several problems—the most immediate being:

1. Production will now have to produce nearly 60% more widgets to meet profit income at the discounts being offered.
2. Administrative paper work and bookkeeping will be increased and cash flow could be harmed by the increase in *numbers* relative to *profit.*
3. If this discount average of these two periods (10 weeks) is projected through the year the sales manager must:
   a) Increase targets from 34 to 59 per week, without increasing sales costs or staff.
   b) Increase the Base Price of a widget to $111.75 (11.75%) to return $25 at the same discount of 10.51%.
   c) Increase the targets (and sales performance) a little and work to reduce discounts offered.

DISCOUNT MANAGEMENT BY SALES STAFF RESULTS

If discount management proves that there is a problem relative to targets, experience proves that the sales manager should not approach his or her team of sales executives *en masse* to rectify it. A further step in the analysis will usually prove that the problem is often an individual factor, in that some of his staff contribute to it more than others. To discover who sells *by discount* and who does not (or put another way, who *sells* and who *gives the product away*), the following use of the **GROWTH ANALYSIS AND SALES MANAGEMENT SHEET** is available to the sales manager.

In this case the SHEET can apply to 10 weeks (or a year, 10 periods of five weeks) for five sales executives, and should be completed as follows:

1. The Identification Section is entered as for **Discount Management of Product Sales,** except that the title box becomes the date.
2. Enter the name of the sales executive (5) involved in the long box at the top of each vertical column. (One column per sales executive.)
3. Enter the discounts involved in the small boxes (1 thru 5), (e.g., NIL—2½%—10%—15%—20%).
4. The date of the first entry is entered into the date entry box 1 and the box at the head of the SHEET.

By entering the TRUE SALES in each discount category, for each sales executive, and making the following calculations, the true worth of each member of the sales team can be established.

The lesson to be learned by every sales manager is that he or she must be aware of discount effects, for numbers are only important if they produce the required profit.

As can be seen from the example, the TRUE SALES calculated this way present a very different picture to what the *number of products sold* figures show.

Base
Price $100 = NIL discount = $25.00 Gross Profit = 100%
Predicted Profit/Income

Discount
Price $97.50 = 2½% discount = $22.50 Gross Profit = 90%
Predicted Profit/Income

Discount
Price $90.00 = 10% discount = $15.00 Gross Profit = 60%
Predicted Profit/Income

Discount
Price $85.00 = 15% discount = $10.00 Gross Profit = 40%
Predicted Profit/Income

Discount
Price $80.00 = 20% discount = $ 5.00 Gross Profit = 20%
Predicted Profit/Income

Therefore the previous totals calculated at these percentages give the TRUE SALES relative to targets calculated at Base Price.

Base Price $100	24 numbers sold	= 24 true sales
Discount Price $97.50	57 numbers sold	= 51.3 true sales
Discount Price $90.00	53 numbers sold	= 31.8 true sales
Discount Price $85.00	28 numbers sold	= 11.2 true sales
Discount Price $80.00	46 numbers sold	= 9.2 true sales
TOTAL	**208 numbers sold**	**= 127.5 true sales**

INVENTORY AND PRODUCTION MANAGEMENT

In this case, the GROWTH ANALYSIS AND SALES MANAGEMENT SHEET can apply to 10 products for five weeks (or five periods of five weeks). Complete the sheet as follows:

1. The long box at the head of each vertical column is entered with the date of the week involved and the week number (or period and date).

2. Each unit in the Identification Section is entered with the details of the product sales of which are to be analyzed.
   a) Name of Product.
   b) Total sold prior to this analysis.
   c) Average sales to date relative to the period of this sheet (e.g., how many did you sell over the previous two, five or 10 similar periods).
   d) Target to be sold each week (or period).
3. The sales results are entered in the first line of each grid entry under the relevant discount heading.
4. The TRUE SALES are calculated and entered in the second line of each grid entry.
5. The total is calculated by adding this entry to the previous total each week (or period).
6. The **Average** box of the totals entry line is used to show the difference (plus or minus) between TRUE SALES and TARGET.

TERRITORIAL DISCOUNT MANAGEMENT

Knowing which geographic areas produce the highest profit is something every sales manager should know, for then he or she can develop those areas more efficiently. This can be done by completing a GROWTH ANALYSIS AND SALES MANAGEMENT SHEET as for **Discount Management by Sales Staff Results** except that the Territories are entered in the long boxes at the head of each vertical column. The sales results for each territory are entered in the same way as explained in Discount Management for Sales Staff Results.

TERRITORIAL INVENTORY AND PRODUCTION MANAGEMENT

Some products or services will always do better in certain areas than they do in others, and to maintain overall sales it is necessary to know how high a percentage of the business, in any given area, is dependent upon certain products. Experience has proved that looking only at *total* sales can sometimes mean discontinuing the sale or production of an item or service when it only constitutes a small percentage of *total sales,* only to find later that it made up almost all sales in one particular area. This type of sales management can also identify, immediately, if a particular product or service suddenly experiences ''acceptance'' in an area where it could not be sold before. This is done as follows:

Complete the GROWTH ANALYSIS AND SALES MANAGEMENT SHEET as for **Territorial Discount Management** with the following exceptions:

a) Enter the Week Numbers involved in the small boxes at the head of each vertical column.
b) The first entry line of each vertical column will be used for five entries of a five-week period. These entries will be totaled to show sales numbers for the period in the **Total** entry, and an average number of products sold per week will be calculated and entered in the ''Average'' entry. This means that the sheet will cover five weeks for five geographic areas, on the sales results of 10 products or services.
c) In the first box (week 1 of this period) in the second line entry, enter the *Target* (sales required number).
d) When the *sale numbers* for the first week are entered compare the entry with the *target* and enter in the total entry line the difference. This plus or minus figure should then be added or subtracted from the next weeks *Target* (sales required) number.
e) Total the five geographic *sales numbers* into the first line entry box 1 of the *totals* section.
f) Total the five geographic *Target* (sales required number)

into the second line entry box 1 of the *totals* section.

g) Calculate the difference between *total sales* against *total target* and enter the plus or minus figure into the third line entry of the *totals* section.
h) Add or subtract the difference to the next week's total *target* (sales required number).

The **GROWTH ANALYSIS AND SALES MANAGEMENT SHEET** can be applied to any task of comparison which needs a continuous analysis of performance or sales. It allows the Marketing Director or Sales Manager a way of peeling away unsubstantiated statements and misinterpretation of scattered facts and results.

CHAPTER SIXTEEN

TACTICAL SUPPLY AND DEMAND CONTROL

Conceiving and creating a successful Marketing Program is not difficult, however, it can be very dangerous if adequate systems for managing that program are not in force to administrate it.

There is absolutely no doubt whatsoever that the most important objective in any business is to 'sell' the product or service that the business is built around. Without adequate trading performance, any business will sooner or later have to close its doors. Another reason to have control systems in place that allow maximum marketing effort is something many business people overlook at the outset of any Marketing Program, and that is 'Overtrading.' Sales, just like cash flow, must be predictable as far as is possible, and must be achieved when and where they can best be serviced. Many business ventures have ultimately failed not because they could not sell their product or service, but because they were unable to deliver what they initially promised to deliver. Reputation is everything in the marketplace; if you promise 14-days delivery your client will expect delivery in 14 days; and if you promise to deliver a widget, then substituting a wodget will cause your business a lot of problems.

We live in a world where responsibility and authority have become individual domains, a world where each vice president is a separate steppingstone between the purchase order from the client and the delivery of that product or service to the client. Why create an organization to pass buckets of water to the fire when existing technology and systems allow less people to man the pumps and

	Week No.	SALES ANALYSIS			TURNOVER ANALYSIS				STOCK CONTROL				DISCOUNT ANALYSIS					DELIVERY		AREA SALES ANALYSIS			
		Sales	Total	Target	Sales	£	Target	%	Despatch	Forward Order	Available Stock	W/house Stock	Trade	7½%	15%	25%		Agent	Direct	1	2	3	4
Average	B/F																						
New Average																							
%																							
TOTALS																							

	Week No.	SALES ANALYSIS			TURNOVER ANALYSIS				STOCK CONTROL				DISCOUNT ANALYSIS					DELIVERY		AREA SALES ANALYSIS			
		Sales	Total	Target	Sales	£	Target	%	Despatch	Forward Order	Available Stock	W/house Stock	Trade	7½%	15%	25%		Agent	Direct	1	2	3	4
Average	B/F																						
New Average																							
%																							
TOTALS																							

	Week No.	SALES ANALYSIS			TURNOVER ANALYSIS				STOCK CONTROL				DISCOUNT ANALYSIS					DELIVERY		AREA SALES ANALYSIS			
		Sales	Total	Target	Sales	£	Target	%	Despatch	Forward Order	Available Stock	W/house Stock	Trade	7½%	15%	25%		Agent	Direct	1	2	3	4
Average	B/F																						
New Average																							
%																							
TOTALS																							

	Week No.	SALES ANALYSIS			TURNOVER ANALYSIS				STOCK CONTROL				DISCOUNT ANALYSIS					DELIVERY		AREA SALES ANALYSIS			
		Sales	Total	Target	Sales	£	Target	%	Despatch	Forward Order	Available Stock	W/house Stock	Trade	7½%	15%	25%		Agent	Direct	1	2	3	4
Average	B/F																						
New Average																							
%																							
TOTALS																							

	Week No.	SALES ANALYSIS			TURNOVER ANALYSIS				STOCK CONTROL				DISCOUNT ANALYSIS					DELIVERY		AREA SALES ANALYSIS			
		Sales	Total	Target	Sales	£	Target	%	Despatch	Forward Order	Available Stock	W/house Stock	Trade	7½%	15%	25%		Agent	Direct	1	2	3	4
Average	B/F																						
New Average																							
%																							
TOTALS																							

	Week No.	SALES ANALYSIS			TURNOVER ANALYSIS				STOCK CONTROL				DISCOUNT ANALYSIS					DELIVERY		AREA SALES ANALYSIS			
		Sales	Total	Target	Sales	£	Target	%	Despatch	Forward Order	Available Stock	W/house Stock	Trade	7½%	15%	25%		Agent	Direct	1	2	3	4
Average	B/F																						
New Average																							
%																							
TOTALS																							

	Week No.	SALES ANALYSIS			TURNOVER ANALYSIS				STOCK CONTROL				DISCOUNT ANALYSIS					DELIVERY		AREA SALES ANALYSIS			
		Sales	Total	Target	Sales	£	Target	%	Despatch	Forward Order	Available Stock	W/house Stock	Trade	7½%	15%	25%		Agent	Direct	1	2	3	4
Average	B/F																						
New Average																							
%																							
TOTALS																							

	Week No.	SALES ANALYSIS			TURNOVER ANALYSIS				STOCK CONTROL				DISCOUNT ANALYSIS					DELIVERY		AREA SALES ANALYSIS			
		Sales	Total	Target	Sales	£	Target	%	Despatch	Forward Order	Available Stock	W/house Stock	Trade	7½%	15%	25%		Agent	Direct	1	2	3	4
Average	B/F																						
New Average																							
%																							
TOTALS																							

Month	Weeks included	Last Month

£	£
£	£
Sales (Cash)	Difference (Cash)

	Week No.	SALES ANALYSIS			TURNOVER ANALYSIS				STOCK CONTROL				DISCOUNT ANALYSIS					DELIVERY		AREA SALES ANALYSIS			
		Sales	Total	Target	Sales	£	Target	%	Despatch	Forward Order	Available Stock	W/house Stock	Trade	7½%	15%	25%		Agent	Direct	1	2	3	4
Average	B/F																						
New Average																							
%																							
TOTALS																							

	Week No.	SALES ANALYSIS			TURNOVER ANALYSIS				STOCK CONTROL				DISCOUNT ANALYSIS					DELIVERY		AREA SALES ANALYSIS			
		Sales	Total	Target	Sales	£	Target	%	Despatch	Forward Order	Available Stock	W/house Stock	Trade	7½%	15%	25%		Agent	Direct	1	2	3	4
Average	B/F																						
New Average																							
%																							
TOTALS																							

	Week No.	SALES ANALYSIS			TURNOVER ANALYSIS				STOCK CONTROL				DISCOUNT ANALYSIS					DELIVERY		AREA SALES ANALYSIS			
		Sales	Total	Target	Sales	£	Target	%	Despatch	Forward Order	Available Stock	W/house Stock	Trade	7½%	15%	25%		Agent	Direct	1	2	3	4
Average	B/F																						
New Average																							
%																							
TOTALS																							

	Week No.	SALES ANALYSIS			TURNOVER ANALYSIS				STOCK CONTROL				DISCOUNT ANALYSIS					DELIVERY		AREA SALES ANALYSIS			
		Sales	Total	Target	Sales	£	Target	%	Despatch	Forward Order	Available Stock	W/house Stock	Trade	7½%	15%	25%		Agent	Direct	1	2	3	4
Average	B/F																						
New Average																							
%																							
TOTALS																							

	Week No.	SALES ANALYSIS			TURNOVER ANALYSIS				STOCK CONTROL				DISCOUNT ANALYSIS					DELIVERY		AREA SALES ANALYSIS			
		Sales	Total	Target	Sales	£	Target	%	Despatch	Forward Order	Available Stock	W/house Stock	Trade	7½%	15%	25%		Agent	Direct	1	2	3	4
Average	B/F																						
New Average																							
%																							
TOTALS																							

	Week No.	SALES ANALYSIS			TURNOVER ANALYSIS				STOCK CONTROL				DISCOUNT ANALYSIS					DELIVERY		AREA SALES ANALYSIS			
		Sales	Total	Target	Sales	£	Target	%	Despatch	Forward Order	Available Stock	W/house Stock	Trade	7½%	15%	25%		Agent	Direct	1	2	3	4
Average	B/F																						
New Average																							
%																							
TOTALS																							

	Week No.	SALES ANALYSIS			TURNOVER ANALYSIS				STOCK CONTROL				DISCOUNT ANALYSIS					DELIVERY		AREA SALES ANALYSIS			
		Sales	Total	Target	Sales	£	Target	%	Despatch	Forward Order	Available Stock	W/house Stock	Trade	7½%	15%	25%		Agent	Direct	1	2	3	4
Average	B/F																						
New Average																							
%																							
TOTALS																							

	Week No.	SALES ANALYSIS			TURNOVER ANALYSIS				STOCK CONTROL				DISCOUNT ANALYSIS					DELIVERY		AREA SALES ANALYSIS			
		Sales	Total	Target	Sales	£	Target	%	Despatch	Forward Order	Available Stock	W/house Stock	Trade	7½%	15%	25%		Agent	Direct	1	2	3	4
Average	B/F																						
New Average																							
%																							
TOTALS																							

Turnover through Agents	£
Turnover by Sales Staff	£

Area 1
Area 2
Area 3
Area 4

use a hose to solve the problem much faster and more efficiently? Vojin Hadzi-Pavlovic of Decision Management Company, and one of the world's experts on project management, gave me a quote which explains the problem succinctly: ''Management tends to operate like roosters in separate chicken coops, they all know what they are doing and what they have authority over, but they feel no responsibility over the grand plan which needs to bring the production of the many chicken coops on the farm into efficient total production.''

I, therefore, suggest that every marketing professional should take on the role of Commercial Tactician as a necessity. A Commercial Tactician ''looks for, and removes all negatives in achieving a successful business outcome.'' It is, of course, very difficult to predict all possible negative factors that 'may' arise, but by being on the look-out for them, and preparing for the 'idiot factor' possibility, can more often than not turn an average or failing business into a fast-turn-around success story.

I have always believed that having 'capability to supply' is the most important asset a marketing manager has in his business portfolio, yet it is my experience that most people only realize this fact after they find they do not have it. It is essential that marketing people 'know' stock levels on hand and delivery schedules for what they do not have available. As a client I have ceased to be shocked to discover that a telephone call can often prove that the 12-week delivery statement given to me by a salesperson can be converted into two weeks from stock delivery in a matter of days. However, I do still wonder if it is the firm's fault for not keeping the salesperson informed of stock levels, or the salesperson's fault for not making it their business to investigate the facts.

PRODUCT/CAPACITY ANALYSIS SYSTEM

Like all of my systems, this one operates within the guidelines of a digital five unit, within and usable to the **50-Week Commercial Year** concept. It is also a way for the Marketing Administrator to manage the sales effectiveness of both market areas and sales staff employed.

The form shown is one that was designed to do the following:

1. Manage four separate 'Sales Areas' or 'Territories.' If necessary, the number of Sales Areas could be as high or as low as meets your Geographic or Marketing needs involved.
2. Evaluate Discounts given, either by Sales individuals or dictated by competition or Market traditions. This alone can be used to increase profits by removing or changing discounts relative to order volume and the profits in other areas. For example, if no discount is needed to sell product 'A' in Area 1, whereas a large discount of 20% is needed to sell the same product in Area 2, it is obvious that Area 1 should be exploited and offered faster delivery, whereas Area 2 should be placed in a Supply to Demand mode for effectiveness.
3. Evaluate Profit Generation through Agents relative to Direct Delivery methods of supply.
4. Provide the complete Sales Effort with accurate Stock Availability information. So, if the warehouse is filled with Widgets Type 1, the salesperson will most probably try to convert the client from buying Widget Type 2, which is short in supply at this time and subject to delivery delays. This may not be possible if the client is adamant about what he wants, however it will be impossible if the salesperson is unaware of the facts.

	Week No.	SALES ANALYSIS			TURNOVER ANALYSIS			
		Sales	Total	Target	Sales	£	Target	%
Average	B/F							
New Average								
%								
TOTALS								

AVERAGE—In this box write the 'Average Sales to Date ' (i.e.: the number of sales divided by the number of days, or weeks, five-week periods, etc., to date.)

NEW AVERAGE—In this box write the New Average after the completion of the period involved (i.e.: the existing average multiplied by the weeks to date, add on the new sales and make a new division adding one to the division factor.)

% (Percentage)—In this box write the increase/decrease between the original AVERAGE and the NEW AVERAGE. To emphasize the changes highlight the increases in yellow, and the decreases in red.

SALES ANALYSIS

WEEK NUMBER—This entry will show the week/period which has passed prior to the present entry (i.e.: if you are entering the 15th week's figures then 15 should be entered in this box).

SALES—This box is negated in the top line because the 'Total Sales to Date' number should be entered in the *TOTAL* box beside it.

TARGET—In the top line box the Target figure should be entered as it stands subject to the sales performance of the period to date. (i.e.: in this box enter the plus or minus figure that was the result of the previous entry. For example: if the Target was 25 to the present date but only 20 had been sold, then this entry would read 5 + this period's target, resulting in a Target for this period 5 units higher than predicted at the beginning of the program.) Again, I suggest you highlight the 'over-target' entries and the 'under-target' entries.

SALES—In this box enter the 'actual sales made' during the period we are reporting.

TOTAL—In this box enter the number gained by adding the entries from the previous period.

TARGET—Enter in this box the predicted Target shown in the top line box minus sales made for the end of the period being reported.

TURNOVER ANALYSIS

How often has a salesperson been sent out with information on delivery and specifications available, only to find after the sale has been made that these 'facts at the time' no longer apply? How often have Production Numbers been given to prepare for 'expected orders' which resulted in the sale not being made and expensive products going into 'Inventory' or high cost man-hours being wasted? How often have the following words been uttered by a frustrated warehouseman or production manager, "Why can't you get your predictions right?"

The fact is that Turnover, or Sales relative to Production and Supply, predictions are the best probabilities available at the time they are given, but they are tied into a Time Lock Factor which is affected by situations and happenings that are outside of the control of anyone. To overcome this problem the only answer I have ever come across is to have everybody aware of the numbers almost as soon as they happen, so that minor difficulties do not become major problems at a later date.

SALES—Enter in this box the number of Sales made in the period being entered. In the small box next to it enter the plus or minus figure relative to the predicted sales for this period.

TARGET—In this box enter the overall target figure being aimed for, and in the small box next to it enter the plus or minus figure gained by subtracting the 'Actual Sales Made' from the 'Overall Target' number set.

This information will be of unbelievable help to everyone involved in Sales, Marketing, Production and Supply, therefore it should be circulated as soon as it is available.

STOCK CONTROL				DISCOUNT ANALYSIS				
Despatch	Forward Order	Available Stock	W/house Stock	Trade	7½%	15%	25%	

STOCK CONTROL

If Salespeople knew the 'Supply Situation' they could work far more effectively by concentrating on what is available, rather than on what will become available.

It takes little effort for the Distribution arm of the firm to pass on numbers it already has to the Marketing Administrator, but by this simple act the Distribution management of the firm will become far easier and perform more effectively.

DISPATCH—Enter in this box what will be dispatched during the period (week) being entered.

FORWARD ORDER—In this box show what is being held against already submitted orders for dispatch or for back orders that are waiting to be filled by production or manufacturing.

WAREHOUSE STOCK—In this box enter the actual stock held in the Warehouse after subtracting those items to be shipped during this period.

AVAILABLE STOCK—This entry is the result of subtracting orders on 'Forward Order' from 'Warehouse Stock.' This is what is actually available for the salesperson to sell!

(In the case of services, the 'Available Stock' number will relate to 'Free Production Hours Available.')

DISCOUNT ANALYSIS

More companies lose money by giving away discounts than anyone would ever believe. Why discount 20% when 18% might be accepted? On a product with a 50 percent markup, the 'discount figure' saved can be doubled as related to income, and may affect 'actual net profit' increase by as much as 100% with some products or services.

Also, why allow Salespeople the right to decide on the spot a discount amount? The Salesperson, like any human being, will take the path of least resistance, and in the case of price this can relate directly to the fact that the easiest way to get someone to take something is to give it away for nothing. Someone should at least be monitoring this dilution of the company's Net Profits and Earning Capacity.

TRADE—In this box enter the number of items/man-hours sold or delivered this week at a negotiated contract price which cannot be altered.

7.5%—In this box enter the number of products/man-hours sold at a discount below this figure.

15%—In this box enter the number of products/man-hours sold at a discount below this figure.

25%—In this box enter the number of products/man-hours sold at a discount below this figure.

In the last box add up the total number of products/man-hours sold in this period, and you will have a good understanding of every Salesperson's, Manager's, and Product's performance relative to Net Profit during this period.

DELIVERY

Most companies have two methods of delivering goods to their paying customers; the first is the Normal Method, upon which most Delivery Cost Budgets are worked out from at the beginning of the year, and the second is the 'Special Arrangements Method' which is used to justify the difference between 'Predicted Delivery Costs' and 'Actual Delivery Costs' at the end of the year.

DELIVERY		AREA SALES ANALYSIS			
Agent	Direct	1	2	3	4

AGENT—Enter in this box the number of products which were shipped by Normal Method during the period we are examining.

DIRECT—Enter in this Box the number of products shipped by 'Special Arrangement Methods' during this period.

If ever the Agent's numbers are less than 10 to 1 compared to Direct numbers, you have a problem somewhere and when you get the norm down to 1 in 10, change the objective and aim to get it down to 1 in 100, etc., etc.

AREA SALES ANALYSIS

On the form shown only four Sales Areas are provided, whereas this number can be increased to include every Client on a Salesperson's Account Book if necessary, or it can be used to show four salespersons' efforts in a particular area. However you decide to use and enter your information, this factor is essential, for it allows you to isolate 'Receptive' as opposed to 'Negative' areas, good salespeople compared to ineffective salespeople, and so on.

To do this all you have to do is identify every entry relative to the AREA SALES ANALYSIS FACTORS. For example, is Joe selling everything at 25% discount whereas Josephina is managing to sell everything at below 15% discount, etc.? Or is Joe selling 10 products in Sales Area 2 compared to only one product in Sales Area 4, while spending the same amount of time in both.

Obviously you will be able to adapt these numbers to answer just about any question you care to raise; for example, does Product Number 5 on the Sheet consistently outsell Product Number 9 with the same amount of income or does Product Number 3 always demand a discount of 25% whereas Product Number 5 never needs more than a 5% discount to get the sale? I think you will see immediately that not only does this system give you immediate access to effective Marketing Management, but it can also assist every other part of the Company from Research and Development to Cash Flow Management, from Production Quotas to improving Distribution and Warehousing Management on an on-going basis.

At the bottom of the sheet shown there are a series of boxes which allow the most important factor in a company's life to be analyzed, that of Growth Performance.

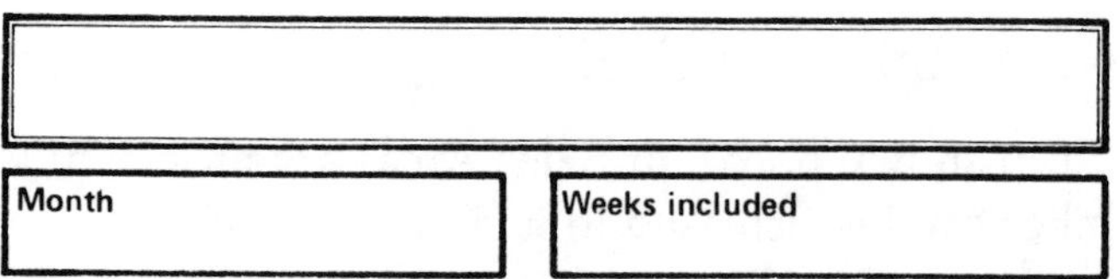

In the long double-lined box enter the Salesperson or Territory being analyzed. Underneath in the two boxes provided enter the Calendar Period covered, and the actual week numbers involved.

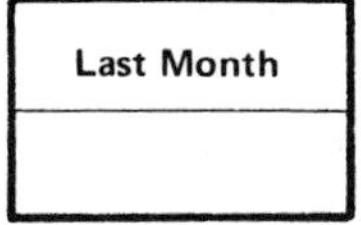

£		£	
£		£	
Sales (Cash)		Difference (Cash)	

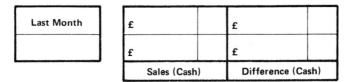

LAST MONTH—Enter in this box the total number of products covered on the sheet which were sold in the period being noted.

SALES (CASH)—In the Top Box enter the last Period's Cash received from Sales number, and the plus or minus figure that was the DIFFERENCE from the previous period.

In the Lower Box enter this Period's Cash received from Sales number and give the DIFFERENCE from the previous period.

In the small boxes to the right of each entry put in the percentage above or below the Targeted Cash Sales Figure or Difference (Increase or Decrease) over the previous period.

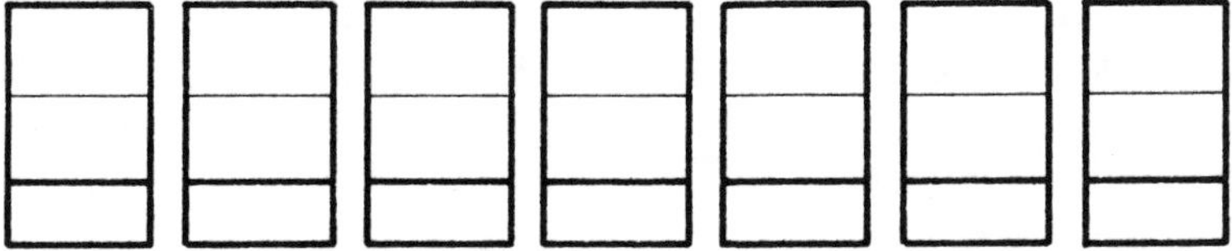

To the right of the Sales (Cash) entries are 16 small boxes with three separate divisions.

In the upper box write the Product or Service Code of what is being entered.

In the middle box enter the number of Products/Hours sold the previous period.

In the lower box enter the number of Products/Hours sold in this period.

OR

In the upper box write the Product or Service Code of what is being entered.

In the middle box enter the number of Products/Hours sold above or below 'average discount' during the previous period.

In the lower box enter the number of Products/Hours sold above or below 'average discount' in this period.

OR

In the upper box write the Product or Service Code of what is being entered.

In the middle box enter the number of Products/Hours shipped by the 'Normal Method' in the previous period.

In the lower box enter the number of Products/Hours shipped by 'Special Arrangement Method' in this period.

OR

In the upper box write the Product or Service Code of what is being entered.

In the middle box enter the TARGET SET for number of Products/ Hours sold during this period.

In the lower box enter the ACTUAL SALES number of Products/ Hours sold in this period.

OR

In the upper box write the Product or Service Code of what is being entered.

In the middle box enter the number of Products/Hours held in AVAILABLE STOCK at the end of the previous period.

In the lower box enter the number of Products/Hours held in AVAILABLE STOCK at the end of this period.

OR

In the upper box write the Product or Service Code of what is being entered.

In the middle box enter the number of Products/Hours sold as a percentage of total sales the previous period.

In the lower box enter the number of Products/Hours sold as a percentage of total sales in this period.

OR

In the upper box write the Product or Service Code of what is being entered.

In the middle box enter the number of Forward Orders held at the end of the previous period.

In the lower box enter the number of Forward Orders held at the close of this period.

OR

In the upper box write the Product or Service Code of what is being entered.

In the middle box enter the average of Products/Hours sold at the end of the previous period.

In the lower box enter the average of Products/Hours sold at the end of this period.

The options available for instant information by just keeping information like this can realistically be expected to save a great amount of time, and an even greater amount of money for any firm. For as the man said, 'There is no substitute for the right information at the right time,' and none of us know when the right time will suddenly appear.

Turnover through Agents	£	
Turnover by Sales Staff	£	

Area 1	
Area 2	
Area 3	
Area 4	

SALES STAFF vs. AGENTS ANALYSIS

A box is provided so that actual cash generated through sales by Agents (persons not employed by the company) can be compared to the sales brought in by on-staff salespeople. The small box to the right of the entry allows a comparison by percentage of the Total Sales to be shown.

The last box on the Spread Sheet is provided to keep a running total of the Cash received from Sales for all the Sales Areas involved in this Analysis.

CHAPTER SEVENTEEN

CHECKLISTS FOR TACTICAL MARKETING AND MANAGEMENT MEETINGS

Introduction: Gathering, analyzing and using information is of paramount importance to any business undertaking. Yet there are many executives, officers and owners who find it hard to prevent a fact-finding and policy-making meeting from turning into a 'general conversation' or 'show and tell' event. Perhaps our culture does not normally allow for hard and fast investigation and interaction of people outside of the accepted social gathering without rules and organization, or perhaps they fail to achieve everything they could because most in-house meetings are between people who have daily contact and ongoing relationships. Whatever the cause, it is not unusual for company meetings to become more social than investigative, and to develop into individual speeches and presentations made by everyone in order of their importance within the hierarchy of the firm. The fact is that investigative and policy-making meetings **must** be organized, minuted, and totally interactive to have any value at all.

To make meetings more productive, I suggest you bear in mind the following points when organizing or holding such a gathering of executive talent:

1. Do not allow personal 'fear of retribution' or 'in-house loyalties' to detract from the gathering and policy-making needs for such a meeting.

2. Prepare and circulate an Agenda as far in advance as possible.

3. Do not allow a meeting called for one purpose to be used as a platform for any other purpose. People tend to think that once a meeting is called they will have the opportunity to bring up their personal requests for information or agreement. Insist that only the subject matter at hand is to be discussed at the meeting.

4. Prior to the meeting, explain that it will not end until all the points on the Agenda have been covered. Then dictate the amount of time you wish to spend on each item, and run the meeting so that no 'out-of-context' conversation or sidetracking reduces your time allowed for a particular subject.

5. Arrange all 'concentration' factors before the meeting starts. Agree that no telephone calls will be accepted, no interruptions will be allowed, and no one will be excused until the meeting ends. Refreshments, pads and pencils, etc., should all be arranged in advance.

6. Many meetings fail because everyone takes their own notes. Meetings are called to 'record' information and opinion, therefore have someone take minutes and, if possible, record the whole meeting on tape for future reference.

Perhaps the most common destructive factor to information-gathering and policy-making meetings is the 'fear of being put on the spot' that some of the people present may carry into the meeting with them. Next in line to make the whole process worthless, is the ego of the person in authority. (I have watched many competent executives ignore, and refrain from commenting on, a subject which they know a lot about and could prevent costly mistakes being made, simply because they know it is a 'pet theory' of the person in charge. They will nod, smile and agree as everyone allows the senior person present to set off on a course to destruction. Obviously, I will not advise anyone to destroy their career prospects by standing up to a self-willed egocentric boss, so all I can do is pass on the advice I was once given to the person who runs the meeting. A true leader gathers a team of professionals to advise him or her, and when all the advice is in makes the final decision. If the leader has to defend a position against the advice of his or her experts, then there is serious trouble somewhere down the line.

I have found that there is only one really productive way to hold an investigative or policy-making meeting, and that is to write down all of the 'important questions' to be answered, then arrange them in logical order and present them as 'titles for discussion.' I would even suggest that they are circulated along with the Agenda of the meeting; this will allow everyone to gather the information they will need to answer them fully and with authority. The following 'Lists of Questions' are ones that I have used successfully over the years, and I trust that they will assist you in discovering the true 'potential' and 'possibilities' available to your organization to allow it to grow and prosper in the future.

CHECKLIST NUMBER ONE

ADAPTABILITY TO CHANGE

All firms or individuals have to learn today to adapt to change much faster than was once necessary. The following checklist can help evaluate values, talent availability in the firm, flexibility of application and new opportunities.

1.01 From which type of client did we draw the best/most profitable business each year, over the last five/ten years?

1.02 Have we kept up with the requirements of our traditional clients, or are we finding competitors are getting harder to beat?

1.03 Has our relationship with our traditional clients changed over the past five/ten years, and how?

1.04 Have we stopped doing any particular type of work, or lost our position of respect with it?

1.05 How has our service changed in the last five/ten years?

1.06 Have our clients dictated solutions, or have we developed new answers, or are we doing what we always did?

1.07 Are our senior staff keeping up with all the developments in their respective fields?

1.08 How many seminars, conferences, training courses, exhibitions, etc., do our staff attend each year?

1.09 Are we benefiting fully from the input of younger staff members?

1.10 What are the main constraints to our growth?

1.11 What research material (amount and type) relevant to our field do we receive?

1.12 Is there information we need but are not getting?

1.13 What new approaches to management systems or renumeration might assist our development?

1.14 With what level or type of client are our client contact/sales personnel most likely to be successful?

1.15 How do our ongoing education/training schemes compare to that of our competitors?

1.16 Compared to one/five/ten years ago, do we have more/about the same/less client satisfaction, delay of payment, referrals, staff turnover, large projects or small projects?

1.17 Can we be satisfied with our growth to date?

1.18 Can we be satisfied with the competence of our staff?

1.19 Have our profits relative to inflation and our growth stayed the same, increased or dropped?

1.20 Have our clients themselves changed in a way which affects us, compared to one/five/ten years ago?

1.21 What are our goals for one/five/ten years from now, and what do we need to change to achieve them?

CHECKLIST NUMBER TWO

BENEFITS AND PROBLEMS OF MEMBERSHIP

There are of course many political, professional and economic reasons for being, or not being, involved in institutes or associations. The following checklist can help develop a decision.

2.01 Which trade or professional associations and institutes do individual members of our staff or our firm belong to already?

2.02 Do these bodies have listings, educational benefits, seminars or meetings which could provide us with new business opportunities?

2.03 Which trade or professional bodies could possibly benefit us if we were involved, and give us opportunities for new business?

2.04 What are the costs (both time and money) of our staff or firm belonging to such organizations, and would the expenditure be worthwhile?

2.05 What magazines or journals are read by our clients or competitors, and would we (or do we) benefit from using them as tools to get new business?

2.06 Which research or government lobbying bodies do we belong to, or are represented on (or should be), and does it affect our sales ability or professional status?

2.07 Are we represented (as a firm or by individual staff members) in any professional, business, social or political sense which assists our business activity?

2.08 Where should we be represented, and at what cost would our representation be justified?

2.09 Do we have a system for gathering information regarding seminars, conferences or meetings where our interests are discussed?

2.10 What is the basis of decision on which seminars, conferences, meetings, exhibitions, etc., shall be attended by a representative of our firm?

2.11 Where and under what situation do we meet our competitors, and can we use these meetings (or suggest new ways) to develop new business or information?

2.12 Have we any involvement as speakers or delegates at the seminars, meetings, conferences, etc., which our potential clients attend?

2.13 Would we gain new business contacts by giving staff time to develop positions within any trade or professional organization?

2.14 How would our competitors be able to answer the foregoing questions differently than we have?

CHECKLIST NUMBER THREE

CONSIDERATION OF NEW SERVICES

Growth can come in many ways; size of firm, profits or geographical spread, but one of the most common ways these days is the addition of new services or capabilities. Analyzing where, how and when to adopt new services to be able to offer one's clients is very important, and the following checklist can help discussion.

3.01 What services could we offer in addition to those we presently provide without employing more staff?

3.02 Considering our present service, what would be the next logical development to add to our capabilities?

3.03 Is there a demand that we could supply which we are not now exploiting due to lack of inhouse experience?

3.04 Is there a service we are asked for more often than others which we do not provide?

3.05 What would it cost, and when could we be ready to offer such a new service?

3.06 Would diversification affect our present image, client acceptance or profits?

3.07 What would we need to provide or sacrifice to introduce a new service?

3.08 If we do not diversify, how could it affect us five/ten years from now?

3.09 If we do diversify, what five- or ten-year projection of costs, profits and growth would we predict?

3.10 Do we have the relevant knowledge or advice to evaluate the long-term effects of diversification and/or continuing to offer what we do now?

3.11 What possible diversification or change to our present services could be dictated to us by manufacturers, clients, regulations, or other developments over the next five years?

3.12 Is there an obvious gap in our present services which our competitors have filled?

3.13 Who evaluates changes in supply and demand market situations for us, and is the present system adequate?

3.14 Historically, who are the leaders in our field, and what are they doing that we are not?

3.15 If we wanted to expand or diversify would our staff and systems be able to handle it?

3.16 Do we want to expand or diverisfy? why, and what goals would it accomplish for us?

3.17 Do our clients see us as *specialists*?

3.18 Does our staff believe we *specialize*?

3.19 Would it profit us to conduct an inquiry program to discover if our clients or staff have a different understanding of the extent of our reputation, or ability for specialization?

3.20 Is there any part of our business which we might lose if we tried to escape a *specialist* reputation?

3.21 What business do we lose due to a *specialist* reputation?

CHECKLIST NUMBER FOUR

SALES POLICY AND PERFORMANCE

Before embarking upon the development of a new Marketing Program, it is wise to take stock of the existing tools, image and people you will be expecting to make it successful. Quite often in the excitement of innovation everyone forgets that a new program can only be as efficient as those employed to promote it, and the tools they will be expected to use. Using an analogy, one would always check out the family car very carefully before setting out to drive across country, and new Marketing Programs can be compared to this very closely. Any major change must be preceded by a thorough investigation of what has been accepted as "usual" in the past, and suitable steps taken to prevent old bad habits ruining the chances of success for the new directions.

4.01 Have any of our staff ever voiced the opinion that we have a *monopoly,* and if so in what, and how could the statement be defended?

4.02 Do any of our competitors use a monopoly claim as part of their sales techniques, and how could we benefit by referring to it?

4.03 Have any of our services, systems or equipment fallen *behind accepted efficiency levels*?

4.04 How would our clients answer the same question?

4.05 How would the sales executives of our firm answer the same question?

4.06 How many of the purchases made in the last year could actually be seen as unrelated to our efficiency?

4.07 With the benefit of hindsight, what purchases would not have been agreed if the same request arose today?

4.08 Do we have a realistic evaluation system to check requests for equipment, business aids, incentives, etc.?

4.09 What parts of our business make no real contribution to our overall goals?

4.10 Are any of our staff underemployed, and how best could we reorganize their duties?

4.11 What would be the consensus of opinion amongst our staff of the professional relationship we have with our clients?

(1) a) We advise and the client accepts.
b) An equal participation development of ideas.
c) The client lists requirements and we arrange the details.

(2) a) We try to keep up with developments in our field.
b) We are innovators and leaders in our field.
c) We are some way behind the innovators and leaders.

(3) a) Most projects are landmarks in our profession.
b) Occasionally we do a top-rate project.
c) We are really just a production shop.

(4) a) We make a worthwhile contribution to our profession.
b) We are well above average in achievement.
c) We are average, or even slightly below, in our work.

4.12 What business activities no longer serve a profitable contribution to our firm or have not fulfilled the original expectations?

4.13 Which of our departments, services or equipment needs to be updated?

4.14 What percentage of our clients could be seen as belonging to any particular group?

4.15 Are we effectively losing business because of our existing client list?

4.16 What steps can we take to spread our potential client list?

4.17 Do we have a problem in the area of *one-for-one sales*?

4.18 Do we have a problem in the area of *Bought Influence Sales?*

4.19 Have we ever been represented as being willing to *underbid* on a project?

4.20 How do we prevent any misrepresentation?

4.21 How many potential clients have we approached by *blanket canvassing*?

4.22 Do we have a long-term problem from the results of blanket canvassing?

4.23 What decision is necessary in regards to ''independent'' action by our staff in the *blanket canvassing* area?

4.24 Do we hold ''copies'' of contacts made by our staff?

4.25 What problems should we list in relation to our sales management, sales techniques, etc., for further consideration, investigation or action?

CHECKLIST NUMBER FIVE

COMPETITORS

There are many oversimplified reasons and sayings for and about competition, but however you care to look at it, competitors cannot be ignored. Many individuals, and most firms, work much harder than they need to because they do not bother to investigate what their competitors are doing to the extent that they might. The following checklist of questions may be uncomfortable for some, and the answers may be a shock to many, but at least they will help establish the true state of affairs.

5.01 Have we a complete listing of all our competitors, their capabilities, and services?

5.02 Do we know which firms or individuals *claim* to be able to supply the services we do?

5.03 Is there any way we are able to discover or judge the amount of business gained by our competitors—and compare their success to our own?

5.04 Which of our competitors do we lose business to—how much—and why?

5.05 What advantages in real capability do our major competitors have over us?

5.06 Do any of our competitors have greater client loyalty than we do—and why?

5.07 What sales tools do our major competitors use that we do not?

5.08 How does our literature compare to that of our competitors?

5.09 Do we know how their terms of agreement or contracts differ from ours?

5.10 What do we possess that our competitors lack—is it enough—and do we promote it?

5.11 Taking our main competitors, do we in comparison have better/about the same/worse:

a) Leadership at all levels
b) Morale
c) Staff turnover
d) Technical ability
e) Experience
f) Levels of client referral
g) Standards of quality
h) Ability to meet deadlines
i) Ability to meet completion dates
j) Level of fees/profits
k) Ability to win awards
l) Value for money service
m) Management systems
n) Marketing systems
o) Production systems
p) Quality of offices
q) Contact network
r) Contract terms
s) Level of overall service
t) Training programs

5.12 What one factor can we credit to each of our major competitors that we lack or are low on?

CHECKLIST NUMBER SIX

CONSULTING SERVICES POTENTIAL

6.01 What expertise or knowledge do we possess that our clients would consider worth hiring on an *open contract* consultancy basis?

6.02 How many of our clients would have benefited if they had hired our advice or knowledge on an ongoing basis?

6.03 What firms similar to ours offer *open contract* consultancy services?

6.04 In what ways could we prove the cost effectiveness of being retained consultants to our existing clients?

6.05 How could we present *open contract* consultancy services in a way which our clients would accept?

6.06 Outside of our present client sector, where could our services be valuable on an ongoing retained consultancy basis?

6.07 Would we benefit from offering *open contract* consultancy services relative to our:
1) Costs?
2) Profits?
3) Image?
4) Time involved?

6.08 Who could head such a program for us?

CHECKLIST NUMBER SEVEN

LINKED BENEFIT POTENTIAL

7.01 What services offered by our competitors, which we do not possess, could we include by becoming *Linked Benefit Partners* ourselves?

7.02 What commission/introduction fee could we consider to give a *Linked Benefit Partner,* considering the savings on normal sales costs?

7.03 Can we ethically offer a payment for introductions?

7.04 What would we have to invest extra to what we pay out now to introduce *Linked Benefit Marketing*?

7.05 Who sells to, or is retained by our potential clients whom we are not in direct competition with?

7.06 What services/products can logically be *linked* to ours without being competitive?

7.07 Who would we like to recommend us to their clients?

7.08 What access do we have to the potential *Linked Benefit Partners* we have isolated?

CHECKLIST NUMBER EIGHT

IMAGE MARKETING (1)

The following checklist will help you isolate the subject which might afford you a way to **fame.**

8.01 In your field and experience, which subjects or areas lack immediately recognizable *experts?*

8.02 If you can discover an area without recognized experts, what do you know which might help others?

8.03 What obvious points or data are you not conversant with in your chosen subject?

8.04 Who or what could help you increase your knowledge?

8.05 Is there sufficient interest in the subject you have chosen to *afford* your effort?

8.06 Who wants or needs to know about the subject you have chosen?

8.07 How long will it take you to become an *''expert,''* and be able to provide real advice to others?

8.08 Will the effort be worth the reward, and can being an expert in your chosen subject bring you real and profitable business growth?

CHECKLIST NUMBER NINE

IMAGE MARKETING (2)

Any company can develop more business if they present the right image to their potential clients. The problem is many firms promote an image geared to their opinion, rather than the understanding and philosophy of their clients. It is wise therefore, to explain to the client from time to time how your existing clients see you, and to determine how other firms are seen by the market place as a whole.

9.01 What is the general public's *image* of our trade or profession, and how do we compare to it?

9.02 What *image* of us do our suppliers have?

9.03 What *image* does our staff have of our firm?

9.04 How do our competitors see us?

9.05 How often do we review the matter of our *image*?

9.06 What *image* do our advisors have of us? (Our bankers, relatives, accountants, consultants, etc.).

9.07 What *image* would we like to promote?

9.08 Should we spend more or less time on developing an *image*?

9.09 Do we need a definite *image policy*?

9.10 What changes in *image* could benefit us, and how?

CHECKLIST NUMBER TEN

IMAGE MARKETING (3)

Clients and potential clients are really evaluating intangibles such as taste, opinion, style and to some extent fashion, and they are dealing with trust, presentation and individual reaction as the main components of the agreement. Therefore, it is imperative that you develop your presentation to give you the opportunity to prove your ability. In other words, you must *sell* to prove you can perform, and so the reasons why you or your firms were **not chosen** are important to discover and remedy. The followinwg checklist (from which you must formulate questions to ask the lost client or yourself) can identify mistakes and give you the input to overcome them.

10.01 Who was present when the order was lost?

10.02 Is it possible that personalities were overplayed or mismatched with the client, and how so?

10.03 Was the lost project of a type we usually lose or gain?

10.04 Did we lose to a competitor we regularly lost to/beat, and what were the reasons?

10.05 Was our presentation too detailed/average/or not detailed enough?

10.06 What advantages did the competitors have, and can we reverse the situation in the future?

10.07 Did we do enough research into the client's background and needs before making our proposal?

10.08 How many of our staff met the client compared to the numbers put forward by our competitors?

10.09 Do we know the point where we lost the contract, and how will we overcome that weakness in the future?

10.10 What tools, people, research or other input might have won the contract for us?

10.11 What was the client's main motive for buying, and did we present enough proof of our ability to satisfy it?

10.12 What benefits or service did our competitors offer which we did not?

10.13 Was our presentation more/equal/less professional than that of our competitors?

10.14 Knowing what we know after the fact, could we have presented our case in another way and won?

10.15 Do we need to change our presentation?

10.16 Do we need to change our research methods?

10.17 Do we need to polish our communication skills?

10.18 What is the most important lesson we have learned by losing this client?

CHECKLIST NUMBER ELEVEN

PRICING POLICY

Possibly one of the most common areas of debate in business is the method of pricing and cash flow. The following checklist of questions to be asked can assist in arriving at agreeable solutions for the client and supplier alike.

11.01 How do we evaluate our prices, charges and fees?

11.02 Relative to our main competitors, how does our pricing policy differ?

11.03 If we use varying methods of pricing, what part of our total income does each generate?

11.04 Why was our present pricing structure decided upon, and when? Are the reasons why we adopted the present method of pricing still relative to the market place?

11.05 How often are our profit predictions met?

11.06 Do we regularly earn less profit, or more, than we predicted at the contract signing stage—and why?

11.07 Who has the authority to change or modify our regular pricing policy?

11.08 Is our pricing policy, and presentation of it, significant to our image and position in our field of business?

11.09 How has our income to overhead costs changed in balance over the last year, or five years?

11.10 What reasons can slow the payment of our invoices, and what immediate steps or management changes could prevent slow payment?

11.11 Is there any way we could speed up our invoicing of clients, without harming our relationship?

11.12 What do we offer that our competitors do not, and are we gaining income from this extra service relative to its cost?

11.13 When did we last compare our prices, fees or charges to those of our competitors?

11.14 Have our prices or fees moved behind/with/ahead of inflation and costs?

11.15 Is it possible that closely controlled stage invoicing of special services could increase our profit or cash flow?

11.16 Does our pricing policy affect anyone besides the client —(competitors, suppliers, associated trades and professions)?

11.17 How have the prices or fees of our business arena changed in the last five years, compared to our own?

11.18 What price or fee increases or extras would be accepted as justifiable by our clients and potential clients?

11.19 How could we reorganize our system or service to justify price or fee reductions/increases/continuation at the present level?

11.20 Is the way we calculate and present our prices or fees acceptable and understandable to our clients?

CHECKLIST NUMBER TWELVE

NETWORK OF CONTACTS

A network of contacts able and willing to refer new business to an individual or a firm, is one of the most beneficial advantages available. Developing and increasing these contacts is something which should be reviewed at regular intervals. The following checklist may help.

12.01 How many of the projects *that* we have gained in the last year/two/three/five years were referred to us?

12.02 What percentage of our invoiceable work was made up of referred business in the last year?

12.03 Is referred business more/equal/less profitable than our sales developed business?

12.04 Which four or five contacts provided us with the best referrals leading to new business?

12.05 What percentage of our total business did our best five contacts each provide of our total workload last year?

12.06 Compared to each other, which of our five best contacts provided the most profitable new business?

12.07 Are there any of our contacts who used to provide us with a lot of new business leads, but have not recently done so? If so, why did they stop helping us?

12.08 What is the best source of new contacts for us, social clubs, business organizations, relatives, past clients, etc.?

12.09 Do we have good contacts who do not provide us with

any/the number of leads which we would expect them to, and why?

12.10 Do we spend enough time cultivating or keeping up-to-date the contacts we have?

12.11 How often do we meet/talk to our contacts relative to referrals from them?

12.12 Do we need a program of open-house, exhibitions, parties, etc., to retain our contacts?

12.13 What ethical incentive would be acceptable by our contacts which might increase our business?

12.14 Are we making more/the same/less new contacts than we were a year ago, and why?

12.15 Which manufacturers give us business leads, and why?

12.16 How do we improve our amount of referral business?

CHECKLIST NUMBER THIRTEEN

RELATED GROWTH MARKETING

Related Growth Marketing is dependent entirely upon gathering facts, and then by logical progression being able to predict probable conclusions. Input from sales personnel and senior experienced executives is vital to establish any *change* taking place. The following checklist can help ascertain such developments:

13.01 Have we found an increase in awareness, inquiries or acceptance (or reduction in the same) by any particular category of client which is greater than could have been expected?

13.02 Are there any obvious reasons for this change?

13.03 Is the change *geographic* in being confined to a particular area?

13.04 Are we able to establish if our competitors are experiencing the same increase of interest from this category of client, or area, without alerting them to our interest?

13.05 Is the increased interest going to be short- or long-term?

13.06 What effects will concentration on this sector or specialization have on our overall operations—short- and long-term?

13.07 Are we able to service this potential increase should it be established—with staff capabilities, financing, production, etc.?

13.08 What steps do we have to take to verify our opinions?

13.09 Who should head the investigation, and how long will

it take to establish a conclusion?

13.10 Is the variety of projects we are presently working on less/about the same/greater than the variety a year ago?

13.11 Are we specializing to a lesser/about the same/greater extent than we were a year ago? Five years ago?

13.12 Have our capabilities narrowed/stayed the same/become more versatile than they were a year ago? Five years ago? in relation to:
a) finance?
b) promotion?
c) staff qualifications?
d) management ability?

13.13 Are our systems of Market Research adequate?

13.14 Are we able to take advantage of market changes should they occur?

13.15 Do we know enough about our clients to predict how their actions could affect others?

13.16 What steps must be taken to place us in a position to be able to:
a) identify market changes?
b) organize to take advantage of them?

13.17 Which of our present clients have the greatest effect on the overall economy of their area or business?

13.18 Do they have competitors, or are there similar potential clients which we could offer our services to?

13.19 Which companies, areas or individuals will be most affected by the work we are presently doing?

13.20 Have we systems or methods to identify these potential clients?

13.21 Is there any recent or past comparison with our present experience which might help us judge its overall effects on the market?

13.22 What local events are taking place which might affect our potential clients that could promote them to use our services?

13.23 What proposed legislation, technology or other potential change could affect our market?

13.24 How could we benefit or protect ourselves from it?

13.25 Are we spending enough time considering the future?

13.26 What tools, systems or input would help us predict our future markets?

13.27 Which products/services produced or supplied by others have a direct effect upon our growth and success? (Reliance Factor)

13.28 If we compare the growth/success ratio of these products/services to our own progress on a yearly basis over the past five years, how do we show?

13.29 What major changes are predictable to the products/services constituting our "Reliance Factor" in the next year/five years?

13.30 How could we benefit/suffer from these changes?

13.31 What do we need to do to take full benefit of these "potential" changes?

CHECKLIST NUMBER FOURTEEN

ASSOCIATION MARKETING

14.01 Which of our past projects should we attempt to have plaques bearing our name installed in?

14.02 Of our present or recent clients, where have we met the most gratitude, satisfaction or helpfulness?

14.03 Of these *satisfied* clients, which have the best reputation to recommend us?

14.04 How can we enlist their help in gaining new clients?

14.05 Which areas of business would we most like to get into?

14.06 Of our existing and past clients, which of them have contacts or interests in the areas of business we wish to exploit?

14.07 Of the areas of business we are not presently in, which of our recent or existing work could be seen as associated or applicable to that area's needs?

14.08 What systems, methods or tools do we most need to have to fully exploit the "contacts" our present clients could introduce us to?

CHECKLIST NUMBER FIFTEEN

RESPONSIBILITY AND AUTHORITY IN SALES

The following checklist can assist in identifying authority and responsibility requirements for those involved in gaining new business for an organization.

15.01 What is the progression of responsibility for acquiring new business within our organization?

15.02 Which members of our staff (not included in the responsibility list answer for Question 01) are allowed or invited to pass judgment or advise on the policy, performance or development of our new business-gaining activity?

15.03 Are these *non-accountable and non-participant* executives or others contributing to improvements in our performance profits or morale?

15.04 Who is not allowed, nor invited to comment on our new business-gaining methods, efficiency or policies?

15.05 Are the answers to Questions 03 and 04 logical, and do we need to make any changes to improve our efficiency?

15.06 Who is consulted to evaluate the possibility of change, addition to, or curtailment of our new business-gaining activities or performance?

15.07 Do we invest enough time in considering our efficiency in gaining new business, and if not, why not?

15.08 Who is most often the first member (or members) of our company that a client meets?

15.09 Who is most often the last member (or members) of our company that a client meets?

15.10 Who spends the most time with, or is in communication with our clients?

15.11 Who actually obtains the contracts, orders or commissions for our company from the client?

15.12 Are we devoting enough time to training our staff to understand and employ these facts to our overall long-term benefit and image?

15.13 Who prepares, is responsible for developing, or has the authority to change our proposals to clients?

15.14 Are we gaining, or utilizing, the fullest input from our staff in sales performance or marketing methods?

15.15 Who is authorized to *accept* an order for our company?

15.16 Who is authorized to *turn down* an order from a client or potential client?

15.17 Who is responsible for instructing or checking letters, proposals, bids or terms to potential clients?

15.18 Who has access to our sales records and orders, and why?

15.19 Who has the authority to hire, fire or discipline any member of our business development or sales team, and does this answer correspond to the answers 01 — 02 — 04 — 05 — 06 — 13 — 15 — 16 — 17?

15.20 How would our competitors answer these questions differently to us?

DATE DUE

APR 25 '97			